Separation-Individuation

THE SELECTED PAPERS OF

MARGARET S. MAHLER, M.D.

Volume II

Separation-Individuation

New York ● JASON ARONSON ● London

MT

Copyright © 1979 by Margaret S. Mahler

ISBN: 0-87668-371-5

Library of Congress Catalog Number: 79-51915

Manufactured in the United States of America

12/20/05

CONTENTS

PART ONE
Seminal Papers on Separation-Individuation

PART TWO

The Clinical Application of the Theory of
Separation-Individuation to Infantile Neuroses
and Borderline Conditions

Part One

SEMINAL PAPERS ON

SEPARATION-INDIVIDUATION

Chapter 1

THOUGHTS ABOUT DEVELOPMENT AND INDIVIDUATION

[1963]

At an advanced stage in their lifework, some psychoanalysts seek to come closer to the actual fountainhead of their reconstructive efforts. Some, like myself, seek verbal and preverbal observational data—*statu nascendi*—such as will confirm, refute, modify, or elaborate psychoanalytic hypotheses. Through a study of normal infants and their mothers, I have been trying, not only to complement my psychoanalytic work with neurotic adults and children, but also to gain additional perspective and to validate previous studies in the area of infantile psychosis.

I have maintained a rather personal interest in one specific aspect of the rich heritage that Freud bestowed upon us, namely, his emphasis on the fact that a lifelong, albeit diminishing, emotional dependence on the mother is a universal truth of human existence. The biological unpreparedness of the human infant to maintain his life separately conditions that species-specific prolonged phase which has been designated "the mother-infant symbiosis." I believe it is from the symbiotic phase of the mother-infant dual unity that those experiential precursors of individual beginnings are derived

The Abraham A. Brill Memorial Lecture, November 1962.

which, together with inborn constitutional factors, determine every human individual's unique somatic and psychological make-up.

But translation of the observable phenomena of the symbiotic phase into psychological terms is exceedingly difficult. Extrapolations drawn from preverbal behavioral data are even more precarious than the use of hypotheses deduced from observational data of later phases of childhood. To understand preverbal phenomena, we are compelled to seek out their connotations through their continuance into later stages, or through appraisal of regressive manifestations (Bonnard 1958). Thus, the understanding and conceptualization of symbiotic phenomena seemed to me to require following them into a later phase of the mother-infant relationship, namely, the "separation-individuation" phase (Mahler, Furer, and Settlage 1959). In order to study the symbiotic phase, I organized a research project, and we are still struggling with its methodology, designed to investigate the phenomena of the infant's emergence from the symbiotic relationship.

Our research into the separation-individuation phase consists of a systematic study of average mothers with their normal babies from five months through the second and third year of life. Numerous papers dealing with the sequelae of separation from the mother have greatly enhanced our knowledge of the traumatic effect of the child's physical separation from the mother, and its pathogenic influence on personality development. In contradistinction to those studies, the design of our research project emphasizes the normal individuation-separation process of the infant in the actual presence of his mother. Although in our setting, the individuation process also confronts the child with those minimal threats of object loss which the maturationally predetermined ascendance of autonomous functioning by necessity entails; nevertheless, because of the libidinal presence of the mother, the developmental process is characterized by the predominance of the child's pleasure in independent functioning. During this phase, the infant develops into a toddler, and his hitherto symbiotic relationship at the level of need satisfaction is gradually transformed into object relationship. I repeat, this is normal individuation-separation, in contrast to situations of traumatic separation, and it takes place in the presence of the mother.

In this separation-individuation study the mothers with their babies may avail themselves of our indoor, playgroundlike setting for two and a half hours, four mornings a week. I shall not in this paper embark on a discussion of our complex methodology, which has been described in a separate paper by Pine and Furer (1963). But since the present study is derived from my previous work, I shall briefly summarize two of my cardinal hypotheses which formed the backbone of this research.

1. In the symbiotic psychotic child the maturation of ego apparatuses, which is biologically predetermined, takes place alongside of a lag in development toward emotional separation-individuation and is therefore experienced as a catastrophic threat. The panic reactions which ensue when such a child is confronted with the possibility and the necessity of separate functioning trigger the psychotic defense mechanisms and create restitutive pictures described in the literature.

2. The second hypothesis, developed in several of my papers from 1957 on, stated that normal separation-individuation is the first crucial prerequisite for the development and maintenance of the "sense of identity." My concern with the problem of identity arose from observation of the puzzling clinical phenomenon that the psychotic child never attains a feeling of wholeness, of individual entity, let alone "a sense of human identity." I had discussed (*SPI*:9) autistic and symbiotic infantile psychosis as the two extreme disturbances of "identity." I could not help noting that something had gone basically astray at the root of these extreme disturbances, that is, in the very earliest interreactions within the mother-infant unit. Briefly, one could summarize my hypothesis as follows: whereas in primary autism there is a deanimated frozen wall between the subject and the human object, in symbiotic psychosis, on the other hand, there is fusion, melting, and lack of differentiation between the self and the nonself.

I have suggested that the feeling of identity may be defined as the cohesive cathexis of our securely individuated and differentiated self-image, and that its beginnings may be traced back to the first two years of life, at which time the child gradually emerges, that is to say, "hatches," from the symbiotic common membrane. I likened this subphase of individuation to a second birth experience.

In conceptualizing the genesis of the eventual "sense of identity," I tend to regard demarcation of the body image from the image of the object, the mother, as the core of the process. Greenacre (1958) and Jacobson (1961) have stressed the fact that the sense of identity, or awareness of identity, is maintained by comparison and contrast. The matrix of the first experiences of comparison and contrast is in the realm of sensorimotor sensations during the symbiotic phase. We know that for the formation of structure, predictable rhythmic alternations of gratification-frustration experiences are necessary. The predictability of this rhythm associated with the availability of the love object lays the foundation for the development of object constancy in Hartmann's sense (1952, 1953).

Striking a balance between mothering without undue frustration on the one hand, and without intrusion or stifling of the infant's individual, inborn rhythm of needs on the other hand, is a task not easily achieved by the average mother in our culture. The perplexities, anxieties, and conflicts, the unconscious fantasies of mothers, have been the subject of scrutiny in the psychoanalytic situation. We have all had the opportunity to analyze maternal behavior, which ranges from normal, through neurotic patterns of conflict, to severely narcissistic reactions; from a more or less easy adaptation to motherhood, to severe reactive and defensive struggles. In the present separation-individuation study, we do not have material gained through psychoanalysis. Nonetheless, we believe that from the wealth of samples of behavior obtained from our bifocal, multiobservational and interview material, in the course of our long acquaintance with the mother-baby pairs, the mother's unconscious conflicts may be deduced with fair accuracy. The leitmotifs of their maternal vicissitudes are reflected in their children's individuation. For professional reasons, I shall refer to the maternal role in the individuation process only to the extent that it is absolutely relevant to an understanding of those aspects of the individuation process which I wish to discuss.

We believe that our study bears out the assumption that the optimal evolution of the infant's partial ego functions—whose maturation follows a timetable, and which we, along with Hartmann (1939), attribute to the conflict-free sphere of the ego—is either facilitated or hindered by the conscious and, more particularly, the unconscious attitudes of the mother.

We begin by studying elements of the genesis and dynamics of the highly unique and distinctive patterns of interaction of the baby-mother pairs at the height of the symbiotic phase at six to eight months of age. We study changes in the variables of each pair's interaction, as well as in certain variables of the child's individuation patterns over time. We compare clusters of data culled from participant and nonparticipant observations, from weekly interviews with the mother, and from other more formal procedures: such as tests, and controlled ratings of independent variables in certain areas. Certain variables were found to be particularly pertinent for the assessment of the individuation process.

Since we have had the repeated opportunity to observe younger siblings of previously studied toddlers, we seem to be able to determine the very first signs of individuation by the end of the third, or the beginning of the fourth month. We have tried to devise methods by which certain changes and differences in postural behavior, molding or its opposite, stiffening of the body, can be determined, the mother holding the infant as compared with somebody else holding him. We have observed changes in the same infant, and differences among the infants with regard to visual focusing, visual following, scanning, and smiling (Spitz 1946, 1950, 1957).

Certain action and ministration schemes of the mother, which are evident in the symbiotic phase, seem to be assimilated by the infant. This is an imitation without mental content, a complex individual patterning acquired within the symbiotic community. These patterns are too complex to be regarded as inborn, yet ·they seem to be irreversibly established at an age at which they could not have been the outcome of ego identifications.

In the second half of the first year, certain sensorimotor patterns and autonomous developmental profiles unfold rapidly and in rich variation. They seem to reflect the basic general and leading individual themes of the mother's fantasies, unconscious and conscious expectations, predilections, anxieties, and idiosyncrasies. These seem to have acted upon the infant's equipmental endowments, and they influence both its inborn and its symbiotically acquired reaction patterns.

Marjie and Mathew, born just one week apart, are set on the mattress in the baby corner of our nursery; they are six months old. Both are delightfully alert, each in individually quite characteristic and different ways. Marjie, plump, rosy-cheeked, and a tiny bit flabby, with a frequent and easy smile, takes in the world with her big dark eyes. If something or somebody is in her proximity, she uses her hands to explore; and only once in a great while is she seen to put the object of exploration to her mouth. Mathew, wiry and a bit pale, seldom remains in a sedentary, prone, or supine position; instead he explores large segments of reality with his whole body, his mouth wide open, using a rapid crawling motion. He mouths everything within his reach.

Marjie is a little girl, to be sure, and Mathew a typically motor-minded baby boy. Yet, from our long acquaintance with Mathew's mother, Mrs. A.—Mathew is the third of Mrs. A.'s children to be in our research—we know that all her children preferred motor and oral modalities of exploration and contact. Her only daughter, Genie, who was in the first group in our study, was the most conspicuously motor-minded of Mrs. A.'s children. This motor-mindedness had multiple determinations. There was undoubtedly an inborn motor proclivity, or a very early hypercathexis of the motor apparatus, but to this constitutional basis was added a powerful secondary impetus: the mother's predilection for her children's independence, her insistence that they learn to "shift for themselves" as soon as possible. In Genie's case, the preference for locomotion, her incessant climbing, balancing herself on the seesaw, and other kinesthetic and muscular activities seemed, first of all, to serve a pleasurable autonomous pursuit. Secondly, these skills were exercised persistently in spite of bumps and falls, because she sensed her mother's approval. Thirdly, however, her agility and hyperactivity served a defensive purpose as well: it seemed to make up for the unfulfilled need that ensued from her mother's tendency to ward off physical closeness and cuddling. Danny, Mrs. A.'s middle child, had also used motility and mouthing quite extensively when he was an infant. In other words, what we saw in Mathew, as early as at six months, had been characteristic of Mrs. A.'s daughter as well as of both her sons. It was not primarily determined by the male child's greater motor-mindedness.

When we observed Mrs. A. with Genie, the mother's peculiar defensive attitude concerning bodily closeness and cuddling was very conspicuous; she even protested against any of the observers picking Genie up. Reconstruction of the motives underlying Mrs. A.'s unconscious conflict, from which this attitude derived, became possible by our bifocal, multiobservational and interview method, during our observation of Genie and of her two later infants.

So much for the "A. family."

To return to the little girl Marjie: her older sibling, Tommy, has also been a member of our separation-individuation study. By contrast with Mrs. A.'s children, both of Mrs. B.'s children—Tommy and Marjie—seemed to reflect *their* mother's predilection for quiet passivity. When Mrs. B. joined our project, Tommy was one year old. Tommy's most conspicuous feature was then, and has been ever since, his soulful, often melancholy brown eyes, with what Ernst Kris has described as the "searching look." He appeared solemn, passive, and somewhat suspicious.

Tommy's individuation process reflected the vicissitudes of his mother's conflict about maternity and her perplexities in child rearing which acted upon this oversensitive infant's inborn endowment and influenced his early experiential patterning. That Tommy must have felt his mother's tension can be deduced from the fact that, from a very early age on, he had been particularly fretful at wakening, which in turn had distressed his mother. Reconstructive data about Tommy's earliest somatopsychic patterning in the symbiotic phase led us to conclude that Tommy's sleeping-waking pattern was evidence of ego precocity since, at so very early an age, the transition from sleep to wakefulness had become difficult for him. Furthermore, intolerance of any change in routine as well as stranger anxiety manifested itself particularly early. From four to five months on, it was impossible to leave Tommy with any substitute for his mother. At four months, he is said to have become terrified when he saw his mother with a shower cap on. He seemed to have developed a premature perceptual awareness, a capacity for Gestalt perceptions such as is not commonly encountered at the age of four months. Tommy's symbiotic history is slightly reminiscent of that of the oversensitive infants described by Bergman and Escalona (1949).

We may assume that, because Tommy's rudimentary ego was far advanced in its sensori-perceptive faculties, the balance between his sensori-perceptive intake (which was added to the enteroceptive-proprioceptive stimuli), and his motor discharge, seemed to be out of kilter. This imposed a heavier than ordinary organizational task upon his primitive ego (Escalona and Heider 1959).

Tommy's mother, Mrs. B., was undoubtedly confronted with a very difficult task in her efforts to be "a good-enough mothering partner," in Winnicott's sense (1957), to her oversensitive infant. But now that we have the opportunity to observe Mrs. B. with her smiling and placid second infant, Marjie, we recognize that her difficulties with that task did not arise only from Tommy's oversensitivity as an infant.[1] Mrs. B. is particularly happy and comfortable with Marjie, a fact which she herself explains in this way: "Marjie does not express anger when I go out, and is always happy and joyous to see me come back; but Tommy, ever since I can remember, was angry and desperate whenever I left him, and never showed any joy upon my return." Yet, even with Marjie, Mrs. B. is clearly unable to respond specifically enough to the infant's specific cues.[2]

The average toddler, whose symbiotic phase is more satisfactory than Tommy's was, seems from the end of the first year on to become so preoccupied with practicing the emerging autonomous functions of the ego, that he does not seem to mind his mother's casual short departures from the familiar playroom.[3] Some infants behave as though they were drunk with their newly discovered ability to toddle in space and to widen their acquaintance with large segments of reality. The average infant, following the inception of toddling, does not clamor for his mother's attention and bodily closeness during this practicing period. He toddles up to his mother once in a while,

1. The differences in innate factors have been variously conceptualized as "congenital activity type" (Fries and Woolf 1953), "variations in drive endowment" (Alpert, Neubauer, and Weil 1956), "differences in sensory thresholds" (Bergman and Escalona 1949), etc.

2. Compare a similar case reported by M. Kris (1957), where observation of the mother with her second child helped to elucidate her conflict with her first child.

3. Compare Mahler (1963b) and the film presented at the workshop on "Ongoing Research" at the Annual Meeting of the American Psychoanalytic Association, St. Louis, 1963.

for what Dr. Furer aptly calls "libidinal refueling," but his behavior seems to indicate that for the most part he takes his mother's emotional presence for granted.

However, as soon as free locomotion is mastered, the normal toddler seems to need to return to the mother to seek proximal communication with her in a quite directed way. The phenomenology of this behavior leaves no doubt that the representations of his self and that of the love object are now well on their way to differentiation. After an interlude of greatly varying length, ranging from a few weeks to a period of months, and with various degrees of insistence and impetuousness, the toddler's active approach behavior toward his mother gains prominence. It is interesting to note how, in general, by the time the toddler has mastered the ability to move from and to the mother, the balance dramatically shifts within the bipolar mother-toddler interaction from activity on the part of the mother to activity on the part of the child. Once the toddler has mastered locomotion and begins to learn manipulation, these important partial functions and every new skill become elements of a language weighted with a steady accretion of secondary and largely unconscious meaning—a wordless appeal for love and praise from the mother, an expression of longing, a search for meanings, a wish for sharing and for expansion. The mother, as the catalyst of the individuation process, must be able to read the toddler's primary-process language. Modulated vocalizations, which vary widely among infants, appear at first as mere accompaniments of the toddler's ventures. Gradually the infant begins to express, and thus to communicate, a wide range of affects: fear, pleasure, annoyance, affection, jubilation, distress, astonishment, and the rest. This expressive jargon is the essential raw material out of which his representational symbolic language develops.

With the average mother-toddler pair, the hatching from the symbiotic orbit takes place smoothly. But in a number of presumably normal mother-toddler relationships, rapprochement occurs with conspicuous drama and may even constitute a crisis in the mother-toddler relationship.

As soon as Tommy started to walk, his separation anxiety manifested itself with even greater urgency: he followed his mother relentlessly, like a shadow. He was one of those toddlers in whom locomotion had already brought about an awareness of the self as separate from the mother, before he was emotionally ready to cope with this awareness of individuation. The danger signals in such cases are ever so often temper tantrums lasting not, as in normal cases, a few minutes but much longer.

The period of growing awareness of separateness is ushered in by a behavior which we observe rather frequently in our setting and which I would like to call "shadowing the mother." In Tommy's case, the outstanding feature of his individuation process was this phenomenon of "shadowing": his refusal to let his mother out of his sight. He would follow her every move from out of the corner of his eye. He would dash in her direction as soon as she walked toward the door. His widely ranging vocal communications were directed exclusively to his mother and gradually developed into predominantly petulant and not clearly enunciated verbal communications to her.

The mother too has to adjust to the anticipated crucial event of that inescapable separation which the maturation of apparatuses dictates. She must face the fact that her formerly completely dependent lap-baby can and does actively move to and from her. We know from the psychoanalysis of mothers that, in their unconscious, the infant's body during the presymbiotic and symbiotic phase is part of the representation of her "self." In the same way, through psychoanalysis of mothers, we have learned that the phallic meaning of the baby's body is often, if not always, discernible.

In our study we have also gathered evidence that her infant generally represents a part of the mother's body, and we sometimes see, in the way some of the mothers talk about the baby's body, how they hold and handle it, that the infant has the meaning of an illusory phallus for the mother (SPII:2). Furthermore, as is also to be expected, each individual child has a certain specific meaning for the mother, according to the general and the specific fantasy connected with each child by that mother. This leitmotif with its elaborations changes with the maturation of the infant, and is dependent in turn upon the development and adaptation of the mother to the emotional and actual task of motherhood (Coleman, Kris, and Provence 1953, Bibring et al. 1961). We have seen veritable mourning reactions to the anticipated event of active locomotor separation. We have also seen a rationalized unconcern about the event. Frequently we hear a mother saying about her child who has just taken his first unaided steps into the world, "Now he is grown up." Depending on her own adjustment, the mother may react, in the period of rapprochement following the child's mastery of locomotion, either by continued emotional availability and playful participation or by a gamut of less desirable attitudes. From the data we have accumulated so far, we would hypothesize that the mother's emotional availability is essential if the child's autonomous ego is to attain optimal functional capacity. If the mother is "quietly available" with a ready supply of object libido, if she shares the toddling adventurer's exploits, playfully reciprocates and thus helps his attempts at imitation and identification, the relationship between mother and toddler progresses to the point where verbal communication takes over, even though vivid gestural behavior, that is, affectomotility, still predominates. The predictable emotional participation of the mother seems to facilitate the rich unfolding of the toddler's thought processes, reality testing and coping by the end of the second or the beginning of the third year. The toddler's "shadowing" at fifteen to twenty months of age seems obligatory to an extent, except in the cases of those mothers who, by their protracted doting and intrusiveness due to their own symbiotic-parasitic needs, become themselves the "shadowers" of the child. In normal cases, a slight shadowing by the toddler after the hatching process gives way to object constancy toward the end of the third year. However, the less emotionally available the mother has become at the time of the above described rapprochement, the more insistently and even desperately does the toddler attempt to woo her. In some cases, this process drains so much of the available developmental energy that, as a result, not enough neutralized energy may be left for the evolution of the many ascending functions of the ego.

In Peter's case his mother's second pregnancy as well as his weaning occurred at the height of the symbiotic phase. His mother, Mrs. C., joined our project when Peter was a little over nine months old. He crawled to his mother frequently and clamored to be taken on her lap; he seemed to need contact and steady "refueling" by his mother. This occurred before he began gracefully practicing the preliminaries of upright locomotion, short of walking, a period in which he, like the other infant toddlers, seemed completely happy and self-sufficient. Peter's earlier approach behavior, occurring prematurely before the upright locomotor practicing period, had been due to his mother's conspicuous emotional aloofness. At eleven to thirteen months, Peter was carrying out motor feats which surpassed those of the other children in his age group and which were admired by everyone, but were only taken for granted by his mother. After he had finally mastered active locomotion, his mother did not respond to his renewed active wooing. Thereupon Peter proceeded to adopt more and more exaggerated voiceless devices to appeal to her. Even during the hot summer months, he would perspiringly carry heavy toys in both arms up to his mother as quasi "offerings," but to no avail. The exaggerated character and the repetitiveness of this approach over a period of weeks was obviously symptomatic and overdetermined. In it were incorporated elements of the mother's practice from the very beginning of substituting toys instead of herself. It contained somatopsychic elements of identification with the mother's far-advanced gravidity as Mrs. C. smilingly interpreted herself. Peter's symptomatic behavior also contained elements of compliance with his mother's conscious and unconscious wish that her son be big and strong (he was rather puny). Finally, it also contained elements of primitive defense.

If an appeal for comfort or reaching out for contact goes unheeded, the child seeks substitutions. In our study, we observed that the substitution used most frequently was eating, rather than autoerotic sucking activities. In the home setting, the bottle retains a similar emotional meaning. But, of course, oral gratification is not an adequate substitute for emotional supplies. Wherever there is a greater than average conflict, the normal phenomenon of active wooing of the mother and pleasure in sharing with her turns into repetitive, coercive, aggressive patterns of wooing. Shadowing of the mother becomes a desperate appeal to, and pursual of, her. The toddler aggressively excludes any other goal-directed activity, or substitute comforting by any person other than the mother. In such cases, the social adaptive functions of the ego, particularly the modulated and object-related language development and synthesis of partial functions, may show a developmental lag, a disharmony or an unevenness. Somewhat stereotyped behavior such as throwing things, hitting, etc., soon follows. If this unpatterned, diffuse and aggressive behavior is not counteracted by object love, it may lead at a very early age to the toddler's turning his aggression against his own body. Under such libido-economic conditions, socially adaptive as well as autonomous ego development is less than optimal. This may mean that the child's primarily autonomous functions have become enmeshed in intrapsychic conflict.

As one would expect of a research team made up of psycho-analysts and other psychoanalytically trained workers, we are trying to understand the phenomena of the autonomous unfolding of the ego in the context of psychosexual development. In progressing from symbiosis to separate functioning, the toddler seems to show a bipolar mode of self-orientation: his own body and its functions, along with the erogenic zones, representing the landmarks of one pole; the mother representing the other pole. We have seen how the oral phase enters into the process of separation-individuation. But we get only glimpses of the anal phase, even though we know that it must contribute substantially to individuation in terms of the distinctions between inside and outside, animate and inanimate, I and non-I. In some children we are able to reconstruct with impressive accuracy the details of their very early discovery of the anatomical sexual difference.

The overlapping of oral, anal, and phallic strivings and conflicts, as well as the steps of her separation-individuation process, could be reconstructed with particular clarity in Cathy's case, because she was so eminently verbal.

On one occasion, while waiting for her mother to come for her, Cathy, then aged twenty-six months, caught sight of one of our workers seated on a low stool. In response to Cathy's question, "Why don't you go home?" the worker playfully replied that she was about to, and left the room. A few minutes later, after playfully searching for the worker, and inquiring as to her whereabouts, Cathy went toward the bathroom, saying, "Oh, she is sitting on the potty." The fact that this reasoning had its roots in the matrix of bodily functions can be inferred from the merging of the idea of the worker's disappearance with the disappearance of the cyballum; and further, from her playful transformation of a previous dramatic acting out of the idea of castration. At Cathy's age, the belief in the magic power of words and wishes is paramount. It is implied in the sequence of first her provocative question: "Why don't you go home?" and then the worker's disappearance which her words had brought about and which she now playfully wished to undo.

Very early in her life Cathy and her mother had to cope with separation when her father left for the armed services at the beginning of Cathy's second year of life.

In Cathy's utterances and behavior we observed a striking succession of stages as she attempted to cope with the separation-individuation problem. When she was only a little more than one year old, Cathy would woo every adult who happened to enter the nursery. This was a pattern of behavior which, we now feel in retrospect, may have served her well to prevent the development of prolonged and too exclusive symbiosis with her mother, during the absence of her father. The earlier indiscriminate, and seemingly quite shallow, object relationship took on a deeper and more modulated character, and became more specific toward the mother, and toward Cathy's father, upon his return when she was just two years old. At the Center, Cathy graduated at this time to the room in which the mothers of the two-year-olds took turns going out of the room and, later, out of the building. In this period, when Cathy arrived at the Center, she would invariably cling to her mother, although she did not fail at the same time to smile back at whoever happened to look at her. When Mrs. D. announced for the first time that she was going to leave the building, Cathy looked momentarily distressed, but then quickly took to reassuring herself by repeating her mother's parting words, while she started to play. During this same period, she would playfully admonish her mother, at home, that she may go into the next room at the Center, but may not leave the building to go shopping. Only a short time later, Cathy dealt with her mother's temporary absences from the Center in a more actively playful fashion, hugging her and making a kind of exchange of snacks with her as she made ready to leave and, upon her return, greeting her with "Hi, mommy!" and smiling coyly at her (see Bowlby et al. 1952).

In a still later stage of Cathy's coping with the separation problem, the picture with regard to the mother's return became somewhat reminiscent of a reaction which we have come to know so well as a first behavioral sequelae in such a traumatic experience as, for example, a young child's temporary hospitalization. In such situations, as we know, when the mother comes to take the child back home, the child will often refuse even to acknowledge her presence as a way of punishing her for the previous act of separation. In Cathy's case, on this occasion, she rather pointedly asked, upon her arrival, about a toddler-mate who had not yet arrived; when he did, Cathy busied herself with him and did not respond to her mother's parting words. After her mother left, Cathy immediately made an aggressive attempt to wrest their jointly used toy from her toddler-mate. As this was unsuccessful, she withdrew to help herself to a large amount of pretzels and raisins, eating them all by herself. When her mother returned, Cathy paid no attention to her greeting, even though it was repeated, pretending to be too engrossed with a playmate even to hear it. It was only after several such unanswered greetings by her mother that Cathy gave up looking at her out of the corner of her eye and turned to smile squarely at her.

In contrast to Cathy, Tommy underwent great and prolonged separation anxiety. Imperceptibly but gradually, and along with a spurt in speech development, he came to accept his mother's leaving the room for increasingly extended periods and played contentedly. On such an occasion, Tommy spontaneously set up a kind of talking session with a baby group leader whom he, by then, accepted as a substitute. He earnestly related the story of "the event," for him undoubtedly symbolic of all separations: "Mommy, go away—Mommy come back—Marjie come back," and, with a sort of pride, "Tommy not cry, mommy come back."

It is amazing to observe to how great an extent, and with what resiliency, the child's autonomy unfolds from within his own ego, if only he feels a fair degree of emotional acceptance and a fair degree of what I, for brevity's sake, would call *communicative matching* on his mother's part (see Pine and Furer 1963). One can recognize in the toddler's increasingly concentrated, less motor-minded, and less diffuse play, in which manipulation and fantasy have become an integral part, the consolidation and organization of what shortly before were unintegrated islands of ego.

Though we have observed seeming contamination of the conflict-free sphere of the ego in Peter's case as early as in the second half of the second year, and though it was observed that this hindered the optimal unfolding of his communicative language, his capacity for substitute satisfactions, and play, it was nevertheless amazing how readily he could cope with structured situations when the mother held him quietly on her lap. We believe that a fairly satisfactory period of symbiosis saved Peter from irreversible damage, in spite of the described traumata during individuation.

In conclusion, a few words of explanation for my having chosen to share with you thoughts which are derived in part from observations made and impressions gained in a still ongoing study. I felt that we psychoanalysts are so very much habituated to seeing the results and reconstructing the genesis of pathological conflict solutions that these examples of the powerful and rich adaptive faculties of the human infant, of those which are innate as well as of those acquired symbiotically, would be interesting to contemplate.

I feel that our study has already proven clinically, clearly enough, that the libidinal availability of the mother, because of the emotional dependence of the child, facilitates the optimal unfolding of innate potentialities. I have tried to demonstrate by specific instances how this factor contributes to, or subtracts from, harmonious synthesis of the autonomous functions in the service of the ego, the neutralization of drives, and sublimation, by activating or temporarily hindering the flux of developmental energy, a process, which Ernst Kris (1955) has so beautifully described. The rich abundance of developmental energy at the period of individuation accounts for the demonstrated regeneration of developmental potentialities to an extent never seen in any other period of life, except perhaps in adolescence. It illustrates the sturdiness and potential adaptive capacity of the human species and demonstrates the importance of the catalyzing influence of the love object. I hope I have succeeded in conveying what I wished to indicate in particular: the extent to which the normal infant-toddler is intent upon, and usually is also able to extract contact supplies and participation from the mother, sometimes against considerable odds; how he tries to incorporate every bit of these supplies into libidinal channels for progressive personality organization. On the other hand, I also want to point out in what predicament mothers in our culture find themselves: in spite of their own unconscious conflicts about their maternal role, and while struggling with their fantasies about the growing infant, they must nevertheless respond to the rapidly changing primary-process-dominated cues of their infant's hatching from the symbiotic membrane to become an individuated toddler.

Chapter 2

CERTAIN ASPECTS OF THE SEPARATION-INDIVIDUATION PHASE

[1963]

Study of the normal development in the separation-individuation phase (from the end of the first year through the second and third years of life)[1] was suggested by the cardinal hypothesis concerning symbiotic child psychosis derived from Mahler's studies. This hypothesis states that in symbiotic child psychosis the biologically predetermined maturation of ego apparatuses, together with a concomitant lag in development toward emotional separation-individuation, is experienced as a catastrophic threat by the child in the symbiotic phase of development. There is a cessation of further ego development, and fragmentation of the ego seems to ensue from the panic which the potentially psychotic child experiences when confronted with the task of separation-individuation.

1. Early during the pilot study our observations of the one-year-olds led us to realize that separation-individuation was already far advanced. As our observations continued, the peak of the symbiotic phase and the beginning of the separation-individuation process were placed earlier and earlier. We finally designated the fifth month as the peak of the symbiotic phase and I discovered that the subphase of differentiation overlaps the symbiotic phase in the very first months of life.

In collaboration with Manuel Furer, M.D.

Our study of normal infants, ranging in age from six to ten months to three years, has as its focus the elucidation of various aspects of the separation-individuation process. Most studies to date, based on reconstruction and direct observation, have emphasized the child's passive experience of being physically separated from the mother, and have correctly indicated the traumatic effect of this passive experience and its disturbing effect on personality development. From our experience, however, it would appear that the separation process of the child from the mother is the prerequisite for normal individuation. Normal separation-individuation makes possible the child's achievement of separate functioning in the presence of the mother while continually confronting the child with minimal threats of object loss. However, in contrast to situations of traumatic separation, normal individuation-separation takes place in the setting of a developmental readiness for, and pleasure in, independent functioning. The predominance of pleasure in separate functioning in the atmosphere of libidinal availability of the mother enables the child to overcome that measure of separation anxiety that seems to obtain with each new step of separate functioning. This is illustrated with particular clarity in the development of motor skills since these allow for active experimentation with separation and return.

Several aspects of the separation-individuation process have especially impressed us. First, in the symbiotic phase which precedes separation-individuation there does not appear to be a clear awareness of the body-self boundaries as separate from the mother. Toward the end of the first year there occurs tentative experimentation at separation-individuation, such as self-feeding, feeding of mother, and, later, peek-a-boo games. After many intermediate steps, toward the end of the third year this process culminates in a relatively stable differentiation of self-nonself, self-object, inside-outside, animate-inanimate. Second, the separation-individuation process parallels the maturation and integration of such autonomous functions of the ego as motility and language. Characteristic individual patterns of integrated functioning emerge from the circular interaction between the child's innate patterns involving these primary autonomous functions in such areas as signaling of needs and the mother's selective perception of and response to these needs.

METHODOLOGY

Our aim in setting up this study of normal infants was to obtain material comparable to that already acquired from a therapeutic action research program of preschool-aged symbiotic psychotic children. We set up procedures in which each psychoanalytically trained worker, who also participates in the therapy project, observes the mother-infant interaction and interviews the mother. This procedure elicits valuable material even from these normal mothers who are not motivated by a need for treatment. Evaluation of the material from these interviews in our research conferences has enabled us to focus our investigation on those areas that are most comparable to the material from the treatment group.

In addition to these interviews, the infants and their mothers are seen in a specially designed large playroom divided into the mothers' and the children's sections only by a waist-high partition. The mother's presence and interplay with her infant allows an optimal position for observing the normal separation-individuation process as it·evolves. The infants and their mothers attend the group for several hours four mornings a week. Each week the mother is interviewed alone and also with her child present. The interviews with the mother alone permit us to assess her personality; the interviews with her infant present make it possible to evaluate various aspects of the mother-child relationship. Further, each research associate observes the particular mother and child he interviews as they participate in the group. Two participant observers collect clinical material of a general nature and also focus on specific behavior in the mother and child that the interview data has shown us to be particularly relevant to the separation-individuation at that time.

As our study progressed, we found that from the middle of the first year into the second year of life there was some evidence of an increased differentiation of the body-self in general and striking individual differences in the timing, quality, and hierarchy of the constellation of emerging ego functions in the infants. Among the many elements of the mother-child relationship in the early period of infancy we were especially impressed with the "selection of cues" which appears to be important in the genesis and later development of the differentiated body image and of individual characteristics. As illustrated in the clinical material which follows, we observed that infants present a large variety of cues to indicate needs, tension, and pleasure, and that, in a complex manner, the mother selectively responds to only certain of these cues. The infant gradually alters his behavior in relation to this selective response in a characteristic way—the result of his innate endowment and the mother-child relationship. From this circular interaction, patterns of behavior, functioning, and certain overall qualities of the personality of the child emerge. We seem to see here the beginning of the child as an individual, separate from his mother.

I

Sara, a particularly outgoing, well-endowed baby, and her mother, Mrs. Y., entered the group when the infant was in the second half of her first year. When tested at eleven months, Sara performed two months beyond her chronological age level in "personal-social" development on the Gesell scales. Her communications[2] and signals were easily understood and similarly interpreted by all observers. The mother, however, although particularly devoted and closely attending, showed a peculiar inability to understand and respond in a natural and simple way to the baby's signals and to meet Sara's needs as her individuation progressed. If the child asked for something that the mother had not anticipated, Mrs. Y. became confused. For example, one of the first things the mother recognized as a communication from the child was Sara's "honking": Sara honked once and the mother swept her into her arms, explaining that she wanted to be picked up; when Sara repeated the same sound the mother explained that she wanted a cracker and gave her one; when Sara honked a third time, the mother appeared perplexed and asked an observer what Sara could want now.

2. We are grateful to Sally Provence, M.D., of the Child Development Center at Yale University for testing these children.

A reaching gesture interpreted by the mother, according to her own state of mind, as a wish on Sara's part to be picked up one day, on the next day would be explained by the mother as Sara's wish to hold her hand as she learned to walk. The mother's interpretation of signals was modified depending on whether the child impressed her as a continuation of herself or as a separate individual. This mother, we predict, will continue to resist separation and yet maintain it as highly valuable, turning intermittently and suddenly to Sara for the direction of the baby's own care, always expecting Sara to function at a distance and yet as an extension of herself.

II

Danny, just under thirteen months, had developed considerable ability to function independently, particularly in the motor sphere. This quality appeared to be fostered by the mother's striving for her children's independence,[3] her defense against impulses to hold and cuddle him, and her preference for communication through distance receptors—hearing and sight. During the weeks preceding the events to be described, however, Danny's expressed need for his mother had occurred more frequently and vociferously. He crawled scramblingly in the direction in which she disappeared, refused substitute gratifications in her absence, and bellowed in grief-stricken fashion on her return from brief absences. The mother continued to strive to have the little boy function independently despite his increasing frustration. She often refused contact, holding her hands above her head as he pulled at her skirt.

At age thirteen months, it was noted that Danny seemed more "grown-up" and more boylike in that his relations to adults other than his mother, and to children, changed abruptly from transient, rather blank, eye engagements to long smiles of pleasure and seeming recognition. When this was brought to the mother's attention, she expressed no surprise but stated that he was "grown-up now" as he had walked for the first time two days before. Subsequently, Danny showed much less separation anxiety.

3. We had the older sister of this child in our group for two years.

In this case apparently the demand for separate functioning had exceeded Danny's capacity to function separately in the mother's presence—that is to say, exceeded his capacity to control his degree of separateness by his own motor efforts. Learning to walk, therefore, brought a marked relief from separation anxiety; he was able to gratify a chronically frustrated wish toward the mother—to initiate physical contact—and the external and perhaps internal wish to comply with the mother's high values. Concomitantly the quality of Danny's relatedness seemed to imply that a new level of individuation had been achieved.

III

Cathie, eighteen months of age, and her mother, Mrs. A., entered the group when the child was a year old. The mother's narcissistic pride in her child was of such a nature that she seemed to regard the little girl as an extension of her own self and, at the same time, as a wonderful semianimate doll. Within the limits of this type of relationship, Cathie was capable of a great deal of precocious, seemingly independent activity which, however, appeared to be somewhat skewed in the direction of achievement and performance rather than in pleasure in her activity. To an unusual degree this child was ready to approach any adult and elicit a strong, admiring response which seemed to serve the mother's narcissistic need. It was our impression that the precocious development of Cathie's ego functioning was perhaps enhanced and promoted by the mother's too exclusive preoccupation with her child (the father was serving in the United States Army abroad). We wonder about many aspects of Cathie's development, which we predict will continue to show precocity for a relatively long period: will the more mature object-related aspects of her ego functioning (the capacity for empathy and for reciprocity, for giving as well as receiving) catch up with this child's advanced autonomy or will it lag as a result of the relative exclusiveness of the mother-child interaction? We feel, on the other hand, that in this unusually well-endowed child, other aspects of her personality may develop and the mother's narcissistic pride may change its form. The result could be a shift in the balance toward object-relatedness and a particularly rich personality development in Cathie.

IV

Carl and his mother, Mrs. H., were first seen by us when the baby was four months old. Mrs. H. is a vigorous, masculine woman, with a gruff, pal-like manner. As a child her physical activity had to be restrained because she was in the care of an elderly woman. She emphasized the fact that her husband is an athletically built man who has a great deal of enthusiasm. They were both very pleased that their first child was a boy although the mother recalled that for a few days she was concerned because the boy had inherited her own weak chin.

When Carl first entered the group at four months of age he had just been weaned. Whenever he was near his mother he tried to suck at any part of her body or clothing that he could reach. She grimly ignored these signals and did not remember his behavior a week later when it had ceased. However, when his sucking seemed to become very intense, his need was responded to by the mother moving him in a vertical position up and down on her lap. She told the interviewer that this activity always made Carl feel better. Four months later at eight months, when Carl was able to stand by himself, we saw him repeat the same up-and-down movements of his body at times when he appeared to be fatigued or was frustrated and, particularly whenever he became aware that his mother had left the room. He thereby actively repeated alone the behavior which had been initiated by his mother with him to lessen his tension. When his mother returned to him after an absence, she repeated these movements with him in her arms although she was not consciously aware of her actions. When this bodily activity of Carl's was brought to her attention, she pointed to the fact that this was how he showed his pleasure, especially when he became excited on his father's homecoming in the evening.

Starting at about five or six months of age his parents played their particular form of the peek-a-boo game with Carl by covering his face with his blanket, removing it, and saying, "There he is." Later the child himself occasionally repeated the game with the blanket, but the mother stated that an ecstatic peek-a-boo activity began at about eleven months of age when he was able to run behind the couch. He hid and then stood up expecting his parents to say, "There he is," again actively using his body. At fourteen months of age he greeted newcomers to the house with this same game, insisting by grunts and groans that they do as his parents had done. This behavior illustrates Carl's effort to master the anxiety of separate functioning by repeating himself the highly libidinally cathected activity that had taken place between him and his mother. The selection of a motor activity from among many other kinds is consistent with his general motor orientation that probably has an innate predisposition but also reflects both parents' preferred modality of interplay with Carl. He integrated into his own rendition of the peek-a-boo game the earlier, passively experienced, and then actively used, behavior of moving his body up and down. We believe that doing this for himself, as his mother had done for him at four months, was his first pattern and preferred form of mastering anxiety in her absence.

At fourteen months Carl displayed certain overall qualities in his behavior and personality that are very similar to those of his mother. This development seems to have come partly as a result of their interrelationship and by complex means that we have yet to define. However, it appears that it is in large measure based on the particular form of the sending and responding to cues between mother and child. For instance, at four months, as described above, the mother grimly denied Carl's reaction to weaning and his insistent demand to continue sucking at her body, determinedly substituting another form of tension reduction.

At about six months of age, when Carl appeared to be distressed he made various noises, all of which appeared to the observers to indicate this distress. However, the mother chose to interpret one of the noises as his wish to be picked up and he gradually limited his expression to this sound. When questioned about this Mrs. H. said she always knew when Carl wanted her.

In many other areas of her interaction with Carl, this mother's character traits of determined persistence and directedness were expressed. When Carl started to walk he made a very striking contrast to some of the other children. The latter seemed to wander about happily pleased with their newly found ability of independent locomotion. Carl, on the other hand, always seemed to be going after something, and if it was hard to get, he kept after it again and again. It was very impressive to see him return repeatedly to an object that he had not been able to reach a few weeks before because his balance had not been good enough, until he finally was able to get at it. Mrs. H. has often remarked that Carl will have to become stubborn if he wants to deal with her.

Carl's experimentation with differentiating his own body from his mother's probably started as early as the fourth month, but was much reinforced at the time of that further step in reality testing in differentiating the image of his mother from that of strangers.

When he was four months of age we observed very little exploration of his mother's body by Carl. The mother said that he occasionally seemed to look in her mouth at that age but it was at about six to seven months of age that he became very interested in exploring the inside of her mouth and nostrils with his finger. He also began to pat her on the face sometimes rather forcefully. At this age we frequently observed his offering a cracker from his mouth to his mother. It was at about seven to eight months of age when he showed the onset of anxiety with strange adults.

V

A mother-child pair in which the mother and baby appeared to be diametrically different in temperament were Mrs. B. and Heather, forty-one weeks old when first seen. The mother was efficient, abrupt, impatient, impulsive, and loudly articulate. Though cultured and intelligent, she was rough in her behavior and almost crudely so with Heather, her small, puny baby. She gave little consistent, predictable, or tender mothering to the infant, and set goals and "deadlines" for her baby's developmental achievements;

from the beginning she imposed her own rhythm and needs on the child.

At fourteen months, Heather did not show any of her mother's vigor and abruptness. The mother's seemingly unmotivated bursts of attentiveness, unpredictable overstimulation, and rough, if playful, handling, alternating with long periods of inattentiveness, did not seem to be incorporated in the form of the separation-individuation pattern of this child.

As early as the second interview with Mrs. B., it was noticed that a constant, uneven struggle was going on between this mother and her barely ten-month-old "lap baby." The mother was most eager to "discuss" her observations and "opinions." Heather seemed to be regarded as a kind of accessory by the mother. Mrs. B. never failed to gather a few toys and bring them along with Heather to the interviewing office, clearly as a substitute for her own attention. She would place the baby on the floor near her chair, take the child on her lap for a few minutes when she began to fret, and then "plop" her down again. On one occasion, in her impatient, abrupt, and ridding gesture, the mother jammed the chair leg on the baby's foot, bruising it. There were many other evidences of Mrs. B.'s efforts to extricate herself and offer transitional objects to Heather in place of tender mothering.

When the child was eleven months of age, Mrs. B. was so intent on Heather's learning to walk that, holding her by one hand, she walked with the baby at her pace, not the child's, so that Heather was dragged along. The mother was disappointed at the child's "late" walking. But long before she walked, Heather exercised and practiced in a patient, persistent, and competent way all kinds of preliminary well coordinated motor patterns. At nine months she would propel herself to her goal with a belly crawl; later, when she could pull herself up, she would climb from chair to table, keeping perfect balance, and then examine the mirror surface of the observation booth. By eleven months, she seemed to fret less frequently to be taken on the lap but instead would pull herself up at her mother's feet and stand there. Even before she learned to walk she showed amazing innate resourcefulness and unusual endowment for manipulating toys and occupying herself with her own body skills. If she were in danger of losing her balance, she would slide into a safe sitting position.

By age one year, Heather had accepted separate functioning, or individuation, on the level demanded by her mother. It seemed that she complied emotionally even before her autonomous ego was mature enough in the locomotor area to function on the level of the walking toddler. In this way she complied with and complemented, rather than imitated or identified with, the mother. A few weeks later, she could occupy herself contentedly for a half hour with various toys, looking at her mother occasionally but not crawling to her. All this was done with hardly a sound and only rare appeals to her mother or other adults.

This placid, patient little girl was amazingly resourceful and self-sufficient, and showed remarkable readiness to accept substitute satisfactions as well as substitute objects, in marked contrast to her mother.

It is interesting to note, however, that in some of her behavior during separation-individuation, Heather did take over patterns of the mother. For instance, in her self-comforting devices she seemed to play mother to herself with patterns in many ways reminiscent of the mother's handling of her in the symbiotic phase. In her solitary occupation at the beginning of the separation-individuation phase one could see in her self-comforting peek-a-boo pattern, the derivatives of earlier peek-a-boo games with the mother. Also, Heather showed increasing interest in gathering, holding, and manipulating toys, acting out what her mother had done for her.

When she began to walk she turned to transitional inanimate objects and appealed less and less to her mother. Instead of toddling to her mother—usually engrossed in conversation with other mothers in the group, often with her back turned to Heather—she would quietly toddle to a rocking boat and rock herself as vigorously as possible, in a way reminiscent of the mother's handling of her. Heather also used the same vigor when riding the hobby horse or when working the seesaw. Elements in her active individuation patterns were obviously those of the rough handling she had passively experienced and visibly enjoyed in her first year of life with mother.

CONCLUSIONS

Certain postulations are possible from the material thus far available from our study of separation-individuation in normal children.

One generally assumes that a normal mother reacts to cues sent out by her child depending upon the needs of the child for her. We do not know whether these changes in behavior and expressions of the infant, apprehended as cues by the mother, are only discharge phenomena or whether they are also active communications. In general, however, we have observed a shift from discharge to signaling, as well as the mother's accurate, selective, or distorted responses to these cues which indicate the child's need for her. It is also apparent that mothers vary in their interpretation of the degree of independence or new developmental gain indicated by certain cues and respond in accordance with their own interpretations. Although many cues are misinterpreted, or even read into the child by the mother, normal infants have an amazing capacity to adapt to the needs, emotions, and demands of the mother.

In addition to the separation-individuation process in the infant, it appears that there is a concomitant and similar process of separation in every mother from her child. This can be observed in the mother's various misreadings of cues, especially in terms of whether a need is indicated and of what type. It is believed that the change of the infant from a "babe in arms" to a toddler who can physically separate from his mother also marks a developmental step in motherhood, one that produces many conflicts in the mother. In our investigation it became increasingly evident that the normal mother anticipates the separation-individuation of her baby and that this anticipation is one of the determinants of her behavior toward her "babe in arms" long before the infant is ready for separation-individuation.

The clinical material describes many instances in which the mother reads cues correctly, others in which they are misread, and still others where cues are selectively neglected. The mother's selections often indicate conflicts in her and are not simply errors of perception of the child's needs. However, the result in the child's pattern of individuation in our experience has proven to be determined in large part by the mother's attempts to adapt to the maturation of her child, as well as the child's own active efforts to adapt to his mother's conscious and unconscious fantasies.

There appears to be a wide range of response in normal mothers in dealing with the anticipated separation from their children. In some cases we have seen reactions that appear close to mourning; in others an attempt is made to precipitate actively the independent functioning of the child; in other instances subtle combinations of or alternations between ridding herself of and clinging to the infant are evinced.

During the process of separation-individuation we suspect that there are particular developments of the unconscious meaning that her infant has for the mother. Very likely the infant has certain fixed meanings for the mother, but it also seems to be true that these meanings change with the maturation of the infant, and that the mother changes her behavior accordingly. For example, it appears that the infant, with varying degrees of intensity of cathexis, represents a body part for the mother, usually her illusory phallus. The mother's behavior toward her infant is molded by this fantasy but is modified by the infant's innate equipment and maturation. For instance, when the child develops the capacity for separate locomotor functioning, the mother will project her fantasy into different patterns of expected behavior from the child.

Beyond the mother's specific reactions to cues which indicate the child's maturation and consequent readiness to function separately, the mother's general character is a major determinant in her reactions to the child, and the child must adapt to her reactions in some way. The clinical material illustrates some of the child's adaptations to characteristics of the mother as was seen in the directedness that developed in Carl which paralleled a similar directedness in his mother; and the self-sufficiency and patient independent functioning and placidity of Heather was an effort to comply with and complement her mother's attitudes. The alternation between symbiotic needs and ridding reactions found in Mrs. Y. generated an ambitendency on the part of Sara which resulted in a constant back-and-forth movement between them.

In general, as the child grows older and his personality unfolds and shows increasing complexity, we continue to find as its central core, and pervading it throughout, the residue of the earliest infant-mother relationship.

Chapter 3

MOTHER-CHILD INTERACTION DURING
SEPARATION-INDIVIDUATION

[1965]

THEORETICAL DISCUSSION

The first weeks of extrauterine life of the infant were designated as the stage of normal autism by Mahler. This normal autistic phase,[1] from birth until about the second month of life, corresponds to the "undifferentiated phase" of Hartmann, Kris, and Loewenstein (1946). During this phase there is no discernible distinction for the infant between inner and outer reality, nor does there seem to be any distinction for him between himself and his inanimate surroundings.

As the infant gradually passes into the symbiotic phase, he seems to become dimly aware that what relieves his instinctual tensions

1. Many objections have been raised to this term, which Bleuler reserved for a severe pathological state. In the present context it conveys the meaning that there is no polarity between the self and any object. Although the autistic phase is characterized by relative absence of cathexis of external stimuli, this does not mean that there is *no* responsiveness to external stimuli. In fact, it is this fleeting responsivity to external stimuli that makes for the continuity between the normal autistic and later phases.

In collaboration with Kitty La Perriere

(hunger and other needs) comes from the outside world, whereas painful accumulation of tension is generated within himself. For this dim recognition to exist there must be, during the symbiotic phase, some rudimentary differentiation of the ego. In the intrapsychic organization of the infant, the boundaries of self and mother are still more or less confluent and fused. They are distinct for him when he is, for a short time, in a state of affect hunger (Levy 1938), and they disappear again when he experiences gratification and satisfaction.

At the peak of the symbiotic stage at around five months, we can note the beginning of *separation-individuation.* Preliminary studies (*SPII:1, SPII:2*) have led to tentative descriptions of four characteristic subphases of separation-individuation, which we hypothesize occur in all normal infants (*SPII:4*).[2]

1. The first subphase of the individuation process, *differentiation,* begins at the age of five or six months, and lasts for the next four or five months. It is characterized by decrease in bodily dependence on the mother, which has hitherto been total. This subphase coincides with the maturational growth of locomotor partial functions, such as creeping, climbing, and standing up. The child now also begins to look beyond his immediate visual field (scanning) and makes progress in coordination of hand, mouth, and eye; he begins to express active pleasure in the use of his entire body, shows interest in objects and in pursuit of goals, and turns actively to the outside world for pleasure and stimulation. Primitive sensory-motor investigation of his mother's face, hair, and mouth are characteristic of this period, as are the peek-a-boo games initiated by his mother

2. My discovery of the subphases of separation-individuation came gradually. Each year new facets of the clustering of the observational data became capable of more precise organization. In 1955 I had already begun to speak of the separation-individuation process (*SPI:6*). However, it was not until my two 1965 papers that the first descriptions of the subphases of separation-individuation appeared in print. Thus, the reader will find that these descriptions are repeated in *SPII:3* and *SPII:4*. These 1965 descriptions of the subphases, although not entirely precise, have been left in for historical reasons—to demonstrate aspects of the evolution of the discovery of the subphases. The descriptions in *SPII:3* and *SPII:4* should therefore be compared with my final formulations (1972) in *SPII:8* and *SPII:9*.

and then taken over by the infant. These emerging functions are expressed in close proximity to the mother, and the child seems chiefly interested in his own bodily movements and in his mother. This is particularly clearly shown by the fact that the young baby, up to ten months, prefers to play around his mother's feet, a preference made manifest by his much better functioning and consistency of mood when he is near his mother.

2. The second subphase of separation-individuation is the *practicing period*. It overlaps the previous subphase, beginning at any time after the tenth month and lasting until about the fifteenth month. The child now steadily increases his practicing of motor skills and exploration of his expanding environment, both human and inanimate. This is true whether the infant has started to toddle or is in the process of becoming proficient in ordinary crawling, righting himself, or paddling around rapidly, using his entire body in a belly crawl. The main characteristic of this subphase is the great narcissistic investment of the child in his own functions and his own body, as well as in the objects and objectives of his expanding investigation of reality. He is relatively untroubled by knocks and falls and other frustrations, such as having a toy grabbed away by another child. Familiar adults are usually accepted as substitutes for his mother, in surroundings to which he is accustomed. (By contrast, he will change greatly in this respect during the next subphase of separation-individuation.)

With maturation of his locomotor apparatus, the child begins to venture further from his mother's feet, and is often so absorbed in his own activity that he seems oblivious to her for long periods of time. However, he returns to her periodically, seeming to need "emotional refueling" (*SPII*:2) by physical contact with her. In this second subphase he crawls to his mother, rights himself on her leg, and touches her, or merely stands leaning against her leg. His striving to explore and, as Greenacre (1960) puts it, his "love affair with the world," lasts for only short periods of time; they wane as soon as he becomes tired, and he then again needs to "refuel" by being near his mother.

3. The third subphase, *rapprochement*, begins as the child becomes able to walk, and lasts from about fourteen to about twenty-two months. As he masters locomotion, the infant becomes aware

that he is now able and destined to move away from his mother. This creates in him both pleasure of mastery (differing in degree in different children) and separation anxiety. Early in our study it was recognized that small amounts of separation anxiety promote the process of individuation.[3]

By the middle of the second year, when the infant has become a toddler, he grows more and more aware of his physical separateness. With this awareness, he begins to lose his previous imperviousness to frustration and his relative obliviousness of his mother's presence. We hypothesize that the great narcissistic investment demanded by the practicing period is no longer required once mastery is achieved, and libido can therefore be redistributed and directed toward objects. A little fear of object loss can be observed—just enough for the toddler to seem suddenly quite surprised by his separateness. We see this, for instance, when he hurts himself and discovers, to his perplexity, that his mother is not automatically at hand.

During the whole period of separation-individuation, but especially during the subphases of practicing and rapprochement, maturation of the mental apparatus, particularly of the motor apparatus and of cognition, makes the ego of the infant and toddler aware of separateness. He is therefore faced by the necessity of emotional separation from his mother just at the time when he must cope with an expanded outside reality. And all this occurs in the midst of the psychosexual conflict. Relative obliviousness to his mother's presence, which is characteristic of the second subphase, the practicing period, is replaced by active approaches to her. A seemingly constant concern with mother's whereabouts characterizes the third subphase. As he becomes aware of his ability to move away from mother, the toddler seems to have increased need and desire for his mother to share with him every new acquisition of skill and experience. For this reason we call the third subphase the period of rapprochement.

Incompatibilities and misunderstandings between mother and

3. The beginning of the well-known negativistic phase (of which rudiments can be detected as early as the middle of the symbiotic phase [cf. B. Spock 1963]) is also relevant to the child's tendency to disengage himself from his symbiotic tie with his mother. This tendency culminates in the second year of life in the somewhat stereotyped gestures and expressions of "No!" (Spitz 1957).

child can be observed even in the average mother and her normal toddler. In the subphase of rapprochement, the toddler's renewed active wooing and demand for his mother's constant participation seems to her contradictory. While he is now not as dependent and helpless as he was six months ago and seems eager to become even more independent, he nevertheless insistently expects the mother to share every aspect of his life. During this subphase some mothers cannot accept the child's demandingness; others are troubled by the fact that the child is becoming increasingly independent and separate.

This third subphase demonstrates with particular clarity that the process of separation-individuation has two complementary parts: one, individuation, the other, separation. Individuation proceeds very rapidly, and the child exercises it to the limit. Yet as the child becomes aware of his separateness, we observe how he tries to cope with it by experimenting with actively moving away from and moving toward his mother. The quality and amount of this experimentation is one of the best clues for assessment of the normality or deviation from normality in the separation-individuation process. One significant characteristic of the third subphase is the great emotional importance for the child of sharing with his mother, so that the degree of his pleasure in independent functioning and in ventures into his expanding environment seem to be proportionate to, and dependent on, the degree to which he succeeds in eliciting his mother's interest and participation. Whether the wooing behavior of the toddler may be considered normal depends on the history of the previous subphases, as well as on the mother's reaction to the rapidly individuating toddler and her communication with him during this period of rapprochement.

The first signs of directed aggression during this subphase coincide with the anal phase; so do growing possessiveness toward the mother and impulsive acquisitiveness. It is at this period that the toddler's need is specifically for his mother; substitutes are not easily accepted, particularly for physical contact. Another important characteristic of this subphase is the beginning replacement of vocalization and preverbal gestural language with verbal communication. The words "me" and "mine" have great affective significance.

Signals of potential danger are several: unusually great separation anxiety or "shadowing" of the mother, or the opposite, a continual impulse-driven darting away from her with the aim of provoking her pursuit, and excessive disturbances of sleep.[4] Because the separation-individuation struggle is at its peak in the third subphase, falling asleep is like a regression and is an experience of separation; hence, disturbances in falling asleep are indicators of the child's progressive individuation and of his defense against the threat of symbiotic fusion represented by sleep (Lewin 1950).

4. The fourth subphase is characterized by unfolding of complex cognitive functions: verbal communication, fantasy, and reality testing. During this period of rapid ego differentiation, from about twenty or twenty-two months to thirty or thirty-six months, individuation develops so greatly that even a cursory description of it exceeds the scope of this paper. Suffice to say that establishment of mental representations of the self as distinctly separate from representations of the object paves the way to object constancy (SPI:6, SPII:4). The actual continual presence of the mother is no longer so imperative.

CLINICAL ILLUSTRATIONS

Although our study[5] is focused on children five to about thirty months old, we prefer to begin to observe mother and child as early as possible—at an age somewhere between four weeks and two months. Understanding the early interactions and adaptive patterns of the normal autistic and symbiotic periods helps in assessment of the progress and vicissitudes of the ensuing phases of separation-individuation.

Charlie, a full-term but in many ways an immature infant, was brought to the Center by his mother when he was approximately four weeks old. At seven weeks, his neurological status was estimated as

4. Transient disturbances of sleep are characteristic of the second year of life (SPII:2, Friend 1956).

5. For a description of the setting and methodology of the research from which these observations are derived, see Pine and Furer (1963).

more than two weeks less mature than expected at his chronological age, but his potential endowment appeared to be well above average.

His mother had participated in our research with her first child, a pretty, precocious, and eminently verbal little girl who gave her mother much narcissistic satisfaction and whom the mother treated as a cherished and "better-than-I" part of herself. With her infant son, on the contrary, we found this mother anxious, awkward, listless, markedly depressed, and perplexed in her attempts to understand his cues.

Charlie's immaturity was observed in the slow differentiation of waking and sleeping, in his inconsistent rhythm of hunger and satiation, and in his undirected, vague, and diffuse patterns of discharge. These characteristics of the normal autistic phase persisted in Charlie well into the symbiotic phase, not only because of his immaturity at birth but also because of his mother's inability to become predictable in her ministrations to him. We know that the infant learns to discriminate the object world and the difference between inside and outside through the observation that when inner tension mounts, only limited relief can be provided by discharge from within; that to be really satisfactory, relief must come from an outside source.

Charlie's mother was unable to respond to many of his cues; if she responded at all it was to interpret a wide variety of cues, such as crying, squirming, or whining, as "Charlie wants to be fed." Every so often, because of her own anxieties, she would push the bottle into the mouth of the sleeping infant, thereby contributing to the child's difficulties in establishing a more distinct pattern of sleep and wakefulness. The infant nursed from the bottle for long periods without reaching satisfaction, at times without even being permitted to drop off to sleep, as his mother would thrust the bottle vigorously into his mouth and move it rhythmically in and out. She was incapable of using her body to comfort him; for instance, she was never observed cradling him. As the result of all this, Charlie could not be easily calmed; even when he advanced in age to the peak of the symbiotic phase, he seemed to continue, well into his fifth month, to respond mainly to enteroceptive-proprioceptive stimuli.

Interviews with this mother disclosed her fear that the sleeping infant might have died, which caused her to wake him frequently and to keep him awake by means of feedings. An excessively small nipple hole, through which very little milk could be obtained, was deliberately used to prolong the feedings, which were made to last one or two hours. The child's mother openly complained of the burden of caring for this small, inadequate infant, and she expressed her concern over his immaturity, which she contrasted with the very satisfactory babyhood of her older daughter. (Since we did not observe the sister before the peak of her second subphase, we do not know whether the mother retrospectively distorted the history of her daughter's earliest months.)

The relationship between Charlie and his mother improved dramatically when the infant was about four months old. At that time, a maturational spurt seemed to provide Charlie with internal mechanisms for reduction of tension, so that he no longer depended solely on comforting by his mother. Her depression lifted as her anxiety about her son grew less. By the age of five months, Charlie had developed an adaptive pattern of holding himself rigidly straight, not molding himself against anyone who held him. His motor development was accelerated. The closeness of the tie between mother and infant was apparent during the entire symbiotic phase in their parallel shifts in mood, appearance, and functioning. Charlie's motor and perceptual alertness on any particular day reflected his mother's affective state. For example, when he was six months old, at the peak of the normal symbiotic phase, his mother's depression recurred. Once again the baby's development suffered a setback, as reflected in his increased signs of discomfort and psychosomatic manifestations, such as skin rash and upper respiratory afflictions.

Charlie and his mother are an illustration of the circular nature of the interaction between mother and child, which—as we predicted and subsequently have observed—fall within the broad range of average, normal relations of mother and infant.

Consideration of two mothers and their infants illustrates the first subphase of separation-individuation, *differentiation.*

Bernie had had a blissful early relationship with his mother who seemed to find great fulfillment in breast-feeding her infant. For reasons related to her guilt feelings toward her first son (which cannot be elaborated here), she abruptly and impulsively weaned Bernie to the bottle. The weaning brought about a marked change in the mood of the symbiotic relationship. At first the infant insistently and fretfully rooted about for the lost breast, while the mother desperately denied the obvious reaction to the weaning trauma suffered by the infant. The radiance and contentment that his mother had exhibited during the breast-feeding gave way to listlessness and apathy, while the infant in turn became fretful, listless, and apathetic. The happy, smiling, well-molding infant at the breast became a passive, nonmolding, sacklike baby. It is interesting to note that in the arms of the participant observers this infant felt quite different from Charlie with his rigid postures and Stuart who, as we shall see, adapted and molded so well.

The generally difficult interaction of Bernie and his mother was favorably affected by each maturational spurt of the infant's autonomy. Bernie showed great interest in locomotion: he practiced such activity as crawling or pulling up with great pleasure and persistence. As he became able to engage others with his eyes and to give signs of differential recognition of his mother, and as he gained gratification from his own developing partial motor functions, his scope of exploration expanded to include the entire playroom area (and the entire apartment at home). His mother, relieved by the lessening of her son's symbiotic demands, was able to provide appropriate encouragement and protection for him (an achievement, by the way, that she had not been able to attain with her older son, who had also been in our project).

A strikingly different transition from the symbiotic to the separation-individuation phase was observed in Stuart, who enjoyed a close and prolonged symbiotic relationship with his mother. Both Stuart's parents had symbiotic-parasitic needs, overvalued their child, and kept him in continued symbiotic dependency. This clearly slowed down Stuart's libidinal investment in his motor functions, in which perhaps he was also constitutionally weakly endowed. Whereas Bernie entered the separation-individuation phase with a preferred modality of motor exploration, Stuart's preferred modality was that of the tactile and visual sense organs. This preference seemed to be the outcome of several factors. Both parents insisted that he be brought relief of tension as soon as he manifested it, so that he did not need to exert himself in the least to get what he wanted. His mother displayed to us, and communicated in a nonverbal way to the child, her preference that he remain sedentary and accede to being handled.

It is possible that Stuart, by endowment, was a child slow to mature in motor functions. His musculature was flabbier, his large body movements more cautious and less energetic than the other children in our study of the same age. A notable exception was his vigorous kicking of his legs whenever he was excited. Confined to a small area by his lack of locomotor capacity, Stuart made the most extensive use of his visibly emerging perceptive, cognitive, and prehensile faculties to occupy and amuse himself for long periods of time with "making interesting experiments last" (Piaget 1936). At the same time, he remained extremely visually alert to happenings around him; he willingly engaged others and accepted their comforting.

We have the impression that Stuart's mother, who had intensely enjoyed the symbiotic relationship with her breastfed baby, belongs among that group of mothers who cannot endure the gradual disengagement of the infant at the beginning of the separation-individuation phase. They attach the infant to themselves and discourage his groping for independent functioning; instead of allowing and promoting gradual separation, they push their infant toddlers precipitously into "autonomy."

It was interesting to observe that Stuart showed definite signs of wanting to remove himself from the symbiotic-parasitic closeness imposed on him by his mother's holding of him. He had shown a slight but definite stemming of his hands and forearms against his mother's chest as early as his fifth month, and by the end of his eighth month this gesture had developed into a consistent bending backward with a rigid body posture, minimally yet clearly reminiscent of the opisthotonus of some symbiotic psychotic children who are seeking to extricate themselves from their symbiotic-parasitic fusion with mother (Friend 1956).

Bernie and Stuart have shown us two different ways of entering the first subphase of separation-individuation, differentiation. It may be worth noting that they are equally matched in overall performance on developmental tests.

Three mothers and their children will serve as examples of the interaction of mother and child in the second subphase of separation-individuation (the *practicing period*).

Marjie and Mathew had gone smoothly through the symbiotic as well as the first subphase (differentiation). Both children were enabled to "confidently expect" their mothers to relieve their instinctual tensions, to be emotionally available. At ten months of age, both infants were observed entering the practicing period with great investment of interest in their emerging partial motor functions and other autonomous functions of the ego. We were able to observe in them Greenacre's "love affair with the world." For long periods of time, they happily occupied themselves with exploring the physical environment on their own, showing what Hendrick (1951) has described as pleasure of mastery *(Funktionslust)*. They returned to their mothers from time to time for "emotional refueling." Both mothers accepted the gradual disengagement of their infant toddlers and fostered their interest in practicing. They were always emotionally available, according to the child's needs, and provided the kind of maternal sustenance necessary for optimal unfolding of the autonomous functions of the ego.

In contrast to these mothers, Anna's mother, a highly narcissistic woman, exhibited a much less than optimal availability so that her child's capacity for "confident expectation" was severely taxed. The maturational sequence of Anna's emerging ego functions took place exactly on time. But so hard was her struggle to get the attention she needed from her mother that she had not enough libidinal energy left to cathect adequately her autonomous ego functions or to devote to pleasurable explorations and mastery of her expanding reality. The child was seen during the first subphase (differentiation) sitting at her mother's feet, imploring and beseeching her unresponsive mother with her eyes. This subphase seemed to last much longer in Anna than in Marjie and Mathew.

Anna's second subphase was also atypical. It was characterized by brief, tentative forays on her own, in which she absented herself from her mother's feet only for short periods. The practicing period—the time when toddlers invest so much libido in their own autonomous functions and in their expanding reality testing—was quite transient and abbreviated in Anna's case.

Usually after locomotion is mastered, large quantities of libido are freed and become available for reinvestment in the love object. The child actively seeks out his mother to share with her his every new acquisition, whether it be a skill or a possession. This period, the third subphase of separation-individuation, we call *rapprochement*.

During the period of rapprochement Barney behaved with particular poignancy. He went through a typical, although somewhat precocious, "love affair with the world" in which he would often fall and hurt himself and always react with great imperviousness. Gradually he became perplexed to find that his mother was not on hand to rescue him, and he then began to cry when he fell. As he became aware of his separateness from his mother, his calm acceptance of knocks and falls disappeared.

Early maturation of Barney's locomotor function confronted him with the fact of physical separateness from his mother before he was sufficiently "individuated." For this reason he displayed during his period of rapprochement the opposite of "shadowing" (Hartmann 1939). In order to undo or to deny his physical separateness from his mother, he would challenge her by darting away from her, confidently—and correctly—expecting her to run after him and sweep him into her arms. Her increasingly frantic response made him intensify and prolong this behavior; at the same time his mother could not cope with his recklessness. This behavior was the result of the precocious maturation of the child's locomotor functions and the relative lag in maturation of his emotional and intellectual functions, which did not permit him to evaluate properly the potential dangers of his locomotor feats (cf. Frankl 1963). His mother would alternately restrict him and, from sheer exhaustion, relinquish her usual alertness to his needs and attunement to his cues. She would either rush to him in any situation, whether or not his need was real, or she would keep away from him when she was really needed; in other words, her immediate availability became completely unpredictable. The disturbance of their relation during this period was not total, however. Barney over and over again brought everything within reach to his mother, filling her lap, and would sometimes sit quietly and do a jigsaw puzzle with her.

The relationship between Barney and his mother again became mutually satisfactory with the advent of the fourth subphase, when he became a patient, well-functioning, and normally sedentary child.

The imbalance observed in the second and third subphases appears to have set a pattern of accident-proneness in this child which was overdetermined. Further, Barney's reckless behavior no doubt also derived impetus from identification with his father, a sportsman whose children were permitted to watch and admire, and, at times participate in, his highly risky adventures.

A different manifestation of the third subphase (rapprochement) was observed in Anna. Her mother's marked emotional unavailability made Anna's practicing and exploratory period brief and subdued. Never certain of her mother's libidinal availability, she found it difficult to invest libido in her surroundings and in her own functioning. After a brief spurt of practicing, she would return to her mother with greater intensity, trying to engage her by all possible means. From such relatively direct expressions of the need for her mother as bringing her a book to read to her, or hitting at her mother's ever-present book, she turned to more desperate measures, such as falling or spilling cookies on the floor and stamping on them, always with an eye to gaining her mother's participation.

At the same time Anna's language developed rapidly; the usual period of baby talk was almost entirely omitted. This quickness at talking may have occurred because her mother could communicate with her better by verbal then by other means; she addressed and "consulted" her daughter as if the child were her equal in age.

Anna also showed what we have come to regard as a danger signal in the third subphase. She had an oversensitive awareness of her mother's whereabouts at all times and tended to shadow her whenever her mother moved about the room or left it. She displayed marked separation anxiety and could not be easily comforted in her mother's absence. The relationship was at that early stage beset by many precursors of serious neurotic conflicts. However, Anna showed to an unusual degree the usual characteristics of the subphase.

A markedly harmonious interaction was observed during the third subphase between Mathew and his mother. She was adept at encouraging independence and autonomy in her child, while at the same time remaining fully libidinally available to him; in other words, she gauged her responses to him with great intuitive understanding of his changing needs. His mother's ability to do this ensured Mathew's smooth progression into the subphase of rapprochement. Despite her pregnancy and the arrival of a new sibling when Mathew was eighteen months old—when the toddler's renewed need for the mother increases in intensity—the child remained self-sufficient. He was able to use other adults as mother substitutes and seemed to have achieved some identification with his mother, as shown by his interest in other babies and in his little brother, in which the aggressive element was relatively well controlled. He was able, in sum, to sustain a prolonged "love affair with the world" while at the same time sharing whatever his mother was ready to share with him.

CONCLUSION

The average mother makes the gross adaptation needed to meet her infant's biological needs. Yet it seems to be the infant who takes on the task of more subtle adaptation to the patterns and rhythms of his mother's personality. We observed the relation of mother and child throughout the subphases of the separation-individuation process and were impressed by the fact that their patterns of interaction showed marked fluctuations related to the specific characteristics of each developmental subphase. Time and again we found that a poor relation between mother and child in one subphase does not necessarily or usually preclude impressive changes for the better in the next subphase.

It seems that difficulties in the relation of mother and child come when the child is unable to make the proper adaptation. Nevertheless, it should be added that the normally endowed child has remarkable resiliency and finds many ways in which to adapt to his mother's unconscious fantasies, needs, and expectations.

Chapter 4

ON THE SIGNIFICANCE OF THE NORMAL SEPARATION-INDIVIDUATION PHASE WITH REFERENCE TO RESEARCH IN SYMBIOTIC CHILD PSYCHOSIS

[1965]

There is a growing tendency to complement psychoanalytic theory and practice with psychoanalytically oriented developmental observation and clinical research. The overall program which has been in progress at the Masters Children's Center in New York City is one such effort.

We have been studying two groups of child-mother pairs:

In the first group are symbiotic-psychotic children of about three to five years of age. They have been treated with their mothers' active participation in the process.

The second group consists of normal infants of average mothers, who are observed as they develop from the age of four-five to thirty-six months, that is to say, at the time when they presumably emerge from the symbiotic phase and are going through the normal process of *separation-individuation*. Like the sick children, these infants are also studied in the continuous attendance of their mothers.

According to our hypothesis, the core deficiency in infantile psychoses is the infant's and toddlers inability to utilize the symbiotic (need-satisfying) object, "the external ego" (of the mother) as an outside organizer, to serve his rudimentary ego in the process of orienting and adapting himself to reality.

If during the symbiotic phase defenses have already been built up against apperception and recognition of the living maternal object world, because it has not been experienced as symbiotic, that is, need-satisfying, but somehow as unpredictable and painfully frustrating, then retreat into secondary autism dominates the clinical picture. If, on the other hand, disturbances of the symbiotic phase go unrecognized, then the psychotic picture emerges at the chronological age when separation-individuation should begin and proceed. In this case we see the predominance of delusional symbiotic, restitutive mechanisms—separation panic, dread of dissolution of the self, and dread of loss of identity.

As a result of either of these disturbances the complex task of organizing the stimuli that impinge upon the locomoting toddler, a task arising out of the preordained maturational sequence, seems to become so perplexing to these vulnerable infants that the steps of separation-individuation are experienced as a catastrophic threat. This arrests further differentiation and integration of and by the ego. According to our hypothesis, therefore, the psychotic small child is only half an individual, one whose condition can be optimally studied only through as complete as possible a restoration of the original mother-child unit. We must be able to learn continually about both partners of the primal mother-child dual unit by studying the interaction of the psychotic child and his mother. Only in this way do we have the optimum opportunity to reconstruct and attempt to reconstitute—that is to say, correct—the earlier mother-infant symbiotic relationship and to determine to what extent the missed or distorted symbiosis can be replaced; that is to say, whether and to what extent such a child can be helped to individuate.

Maturation of the mental apparatuses, especially that of the motor apparatus, confronts the ego of the infant and the toddler in the separation-individuation phase with an awareness of separateness, which increases the challenge of the necessity of emotional separation from the mother, and the need for more individuated coping with an expanding outside reality—all this in the midst of the phase-specific psychosexual conflict. The designation of early psychotic pictures as the *symbiotic-psychotic syndrome* derives from and rests upon these hypotheses.

In the course of our studies of psychotic children and their mothers, we were able to learn about the natural history of this disease. However, we had to recognize that we reached a dead end as soon as we sought to understand the etiology and genesis of the disturbance. This was partly due to the woeful lack of available data on the process of the normal toddler's separation from the mother, in the second year of life on the *normal* steps toward individuation.

We know very little about the continuous mother-child interaction during this phase as a progressive and rather rapidly changing, mutually adaptive developmental process. Most research studies of infants beyond six months of age deal with the child's development alone or record sample interactions between mother and infant.

Our research methodology is a rather informal, naturalistic one, in which the continuous bifocal and multifaceted data collection about the mother-child interaction is designed to substitute for more strictly controlled quasi-experimental samplings of fewer, even though controlled, variables.

One of the cardinal hypotheses at the base of our research is that such (autonomous) ego functions as memory, reality testing, loco-motor integration, cognition, etc., which, according to Hartmann (1939, 1952), are essential for the development of ego autonomy and belong to the conflict-free sphere of the ego, need the libidinal availability of the mother for their optimal unfolding and synthesis. The mother receives the child's cues as to his needs. Soon—the age is still to be determined—a circular process is established, and the infant's response reflects the mother's own emotional needs and predilections. These seem to reinforce or modify the baby's inborn life rhythms.

Even within the normal symbiotic phase discrepancies between the mother's temperament and the infant's inborn rhythms may be discernible. In contrast to our severely disturbed group, however, such discrepancies are not too pronounced. In the normal separation-individuation phase, from five months onward, there may also be misreadings of cues, but they never seem to be of the same magnitude as we reconstruct from the history of the psychotic group. Marked mismatching and miscueing between mother and infant are always evidence of disturbance in either, or both partners, of the mother-child unit. They may reinforce dispositional or constitutional proclivities to psychotic, neurotic, or psychosomatic disturbances.

What impressed us already in the pilot study of the separation-individuation project was the great extent to which it is the normal infant who actively takes on the task of adaptation in the mother-infant interaction! Of course, the average nursing mother readily meets the major biological needs of her infant.

It is in the area of the more subtle differences in the infant's need rhythms that the mother's own largely unconsciously motivated fantasies blur optimal empathy and interfere with the infant's in-born gratification-frustration needs. In our initial study we could observe that the toddler must occasionally adapt to the mother's sometimes diametrically different temperament. Now, however, when we are observing second and third babies of the same mother, we note that even the very young baby may have to strain his innate equipment to elicit "good enough" mothering, in Winnicott's sense (1960), from his mother.

During our preliminary studies, and as a result of them, I have tentatively described four characteristic subphases of individuation:

The *first subphase* of the individuation process begins at the peak of the symbiotic phase, at the age of five or six months, and lasts for the next four to five months. It is the phase of *differentiation* in which we see a decrease of the hitherto complete bodily dependence. It coincides with the maturational growth of locomotor partial functions, that is, creeping, climbing, standing up, etc. It also includes looking beyond the immediate visual field (scanning), along with progress in hand, mouth, and eye coordination, expression of active pleasure in the use of the entire body, interest in objects and going after goals, active turning to the outside world for pleasure and stimulation. Primitive sensorimotor investigations of the mother's face, hair, and mouth are characteristic of this period, as are the peek-a-boo games initiated by the mother and then taken over by the infant. All these functions emerge and are expressed in close proximity to the mother, and the infant's interest in his own body movements as well as in the mother seems definitely to take precedence over all activities. This can be clearly seen in the fact that the young baby, up to ten months, prefers playing around the mother's feet.

The *second subphase* of separation-individuation (ten to fifteen months) is the *practicing* period. This period overlaps with the previous subphase and may begin at any time after the tenth month. During this subphase, there is steadily increasing investment in practicing motor skills and exploring the expanding environment, both human and inanimate. This is true whether the baby has started toddling by then, or is in the process of developing a proficiency in crawling, righting himself, or paddling around rapidly with a belly crawl of his entire body. The main characteristic of this subphase is the great narcissistic investment of the child in his own functions, his own body, as well as in the objects and objectives of his expanding reality testing. We see a relatively great imperviousness to knocks and falls and other frustrations, such as a toy being grabbed away by another child. Substitute familiar adults in the familiar set-up of our nursery are easily accepted (by contrast with what occurs during the next subphase of separation-individuation).

As the child, through the maturation of his locomotor apparatus, begins to venture further from the mother's feet, he is often so absorbed in his own activity that he seems oblivious to the mother for long periods of time. However, he returns to the mother periodically, seeming to need her physical proximity. We see ten-month-olds frequently crawling to the mother, righting themselves on her leg, or touching her in other ways, or just standing, leaning at her leg. This phenomenon was termed *emotional refueling* by M. Furer.[1] In this second phase of the individuation period, the striving for exploration and the "love affair with the world" (Greenacre 1960) diminish quite rapidly, however, and wane as soon as the child becomes tired. Then the need for refueling through the mother's proximity supervenes.

The practicing of locomotion culminates around the twelfth or thirteenth or fourteenth month in free toddling, ambling, walking.

1. Personal communication.

The *third subphase* of separation-individuation is characterized by mastery of upright locomotion (fourteen to twenty-two months); it is ushered in by the appearance of the gesture, of vocal affective expressions, of "no" (Spitz 1957).

By the middle of the second year of life, the infant has become a toddler. He now becomes more and more aware of his physical separateness. Along with this awareness, his previous imperviousness to frustration and his relative obliviousness of the mother's presence wane. Minimal fears of object loss can be observed—just enough for the toddler to appear suddenly quite conspicuously surprised by his separateness. This can be seen, for instance, when he hurts himself and discovers, to his perplexity, that his mother is not automatically at hand. The relative obliviousness to the mother's presence, characteristic of the previous subphase of "practicing," is replaced by *active approach behavior* and the seemingly constant concern with the mother's presence. As he realizes his power and ability physically to move away from his mother, the toddler now seems to have an increased need and a wish for his mother to share with him every new acquisition of skill and experience. We may call this subphase of separation-individuation, therefore, the period of *rapprochement.*

Incompatibilities and misunderstandings between mother and child can be observed even in the case of the normal mother and her normal toddler. In this subphase of renewed active wooing, the toddler's demand for his mother's constant participation seems contradictory to the mother in that, while he is now not as dependent and helpless as he was half a year before, and seems eager to become less and less so, nevertheless, he even more insistently expects the mother to share every aspect of his life. During this subphase some mothers cannot accept the child's demandingness; others cannot face the fact that the child is becoming increasingly independent and separate.

This third subphase of separation-individuation demonstrates with particular clarity that the separation-individuation process has two complementary parts; one of these is individuation, the other separation. In this subphase individuation proceeds, on the one hand, very rapidly, and the child exercises it to the limit; on the other hand, as the child becomes aware of his separateness, he resists separation from the mother by all kinds of mechanisms. It has been observed and demonstrated in films[2] how in some children pre-cocious maturation of upright locomotion at nine or ten months of age hinders their ego's mastery of their impulsivity and delays optimal integration of their personality. In other words, maturation of one autonomous function may run literally far ahead of the rest of their personality.

As I mentioned before, one significant characteristic of the third subphase is the great emotional investment in sharing with the mother, so that the degree of pleasure in independent functioning and in the ventures into expanding reality seems to be proportionate to, and dependent on, the degree to which the child succeeds in eliciting the mother's interest and participation. The quality and measure of the wooing behavior of the toddler during this subphase provide important clues to the assessment of the normality of the individuation process. This depends on the history of the previous subphases, as well as on the mother's reaction to and intercom-munication with the rapidly individuating toddler during this per-iod of "rapprochement."

The first signs of directed aggression during this subphase coincide with the anal phase, as do growing possessiveness toward the mother and impulsive acquisitiveness. During this period the specificity of the mother-toddler relationship is very marked, par-ticularly in that physical contact with substitutes is not easily accepted. Another important characteristic of this subphase is the beginning of the replacement of vocalization and other preverbal, gestural language with verbal communication. The words "me" and "mine" gain great affective significance.

Potential danger signals are as follows: a greater than average separation anxiety, a more than average shadowing of the mother, or its opposite: continual impulse-driven "darting away" from the mother, with the aim of provoking the mother to run after him; finally, excessive sleep disturbances (transient sleep disturbances are characteristic of the second year of life).

2. The presentation of all versions of this paper was accompanied by the film entitled "The Normal Separation-Individuation Phase: The Subphases."

The *fourth subphase* of separation-individuation is the period during which an increasing degree of object constancy (in Hartmann's sense) is attained (twenty-five to thirty-six months). At the beginning of this subphase, the child still remains in the original playroom setting, with the mother readily available in the mothers' sitting section. We have found that, as this phase proceeds, the child is able gradually to accept once again separation from the mother (as he did in the "practicing" period); in fact, he seems to prefer staying in the familiar playroom without the mother, to going out of this room with her. We regard this as a sign of the achievement of beginning object constancy. We transfer the child to another nursery room on the same floor. In this setting in the room of the senior toddlers the mothers do not remain continuously with them. This allows for natural, built-in, experimental separations between mother and child, such as are appropriate to this stage of development, and gives us a unique chance to observe the gradually increasing ability of the toddler in the fourth subphase to separate from the mother.

As the child learns to express himself verbally during this period, we can trace some of the vicissitudes of the intrapsychic separation process from the mother, and the conflicts around it, through the verbal material that we get from him, along with the phenomenology of his behavior. Verbal communication, which began during the third subphase, develops rapidly during this period, and slowly replaces other modes of communication, although gesture language of the whole body and affectomotility still remain very much in evidence. Play becomes more purposeful and constructive. There is a beginning of fantasy play, of role playing, and make-believe. Observations about the real world become detailed and are clearly included in play, and there is an increasing interest in adults other than the mother and in the child's playmates.

A sense of time begins to develop and, with it, an increased capacity to tolerate the delay of gratification and to endure separation. Such concepts as "later" or "tomorrow" are not only understood but used by the child of this age: they are experimented with, polarized by his mother's comings and goings.

We see a lot of active resistance to the demands of adults, a great need and a wish often still unrealistic for autonomy (for independence). The child is still to a great extent in the phase of primary-process thinking. Recurrent mild or moderate negativism, which seems so essential for the development of a sense of identity, is also characteristic of this fourth subphase.

Like the previous subphase, this one also harbors potential crises. The extent of the characteristic potential crises of this phase depends upon the extent to which the mother understands and accepts the normal negativistic behavior, as well as the primary-process communications and actions of the child. Not all mothers are able to help the child to bridge the communicative gap between his and the adult's world. This requires the deciphering of his primary-process language and actions, playing along with them, and gradually offering him secondary-process expressions and solutions.

Our study has clearly established that because of the emotional dependence of the child, the libidinal availability of the mother is necessary for the optimal unfolding of the child's innate potentialities. It has given us an inkling of the sturdiness and potential adaptive capacity of the infant-toddler, and of the importance of the catalyzing influence of the love object.

It is quite impressive to observe the extent to which the normal infant-toddler is intent upon extracting, and is usually able to extract, contact supplies and participation from the mother, sometimes against considerable odds; how he tries to incorporate every bit of these supplies into libidinal channels for progressive personality organization.

Chapter 5

NOTES ON THE DEVELOPMENT OF BASIC MOODS: THE DEPRESSIVE AFFECT

[1966]

One of the significant trends that has been inspired by Heinz Hartmann's classic work, *Ego Psychology and the Problem of Adaptation* (1939), has been the interest awakened in psychoanalytically oriented observational research into early psychic development.

Hartmann proposed that we adopt the term "conflict-free ego sphere" for "that ensemble of functions which at any given time exert their effects outside the region of mental conflicts" (pp. 8-9). He then went on to say: "If we take seriously the claim of psychoanalysis to be a general theory of mental development, we must study this area of psychology too, from our points of view and with our methods, *both by analysis and by direct observation of infant development*" (pp. 10-11; my italics).

Hartmann drew attention to the many aspects of human psychology that involve or are based upon nonconflictual adaptive processes in development, emphasizing that the description and definition of mental phenomena must include its reality oriented and adaptation facilitating characteristics and regulations: "Adaptation . . . involves both processes connected with conflict situations, and processes which pertain to the conflict-free sphere" (p. 10).

The most fruitful approach to the exploration of the conflict-free sphere would be direct and indirect observation of *undisturbed development* rather than the study of disturbed function.

"The degree of adaptiveness can only be determined with reference to environmental situations (average expectable—i.e., typical—situations, or on the average not expectable—i.e., atypical—situations)" (Hartmann 1939, p. 23).

Adaptation is in general a reciprocal relationship between the organism and its environment. One dimension of the latter that observational research into normal development might consider is "the average expectable environment." The infant's environment consists at first of the mother-infant dual unit, which coincides with Hoffer's (1955) "internal milieu,"[1] and which I believe has its "autistic" beginning before the "symbiotic phase." Adaptation may be regarded as beginning with the infant's fitting into his symbiotic environment. This adaptation is synonymous with his success in drawing his mother into his "internal milieu," that is, with finding "good enough mothering" (Winnicott 1962a). As soon as this occurs, the infant passes from a brief "normal autistic phase" into the symbiotic phase, in which the mother functions both as the infant's (external) auxiliary executive ego (Spitz 1951) and also as his "protective living shield," thereby complementing and replacing the "protective barrier or shield against stimuli" and rescuing him "with care" from potentially overwhelming, inundating inner tensions and outer excitations (Freud 1926, Kris 1956a, Winnicott 1956b, Khan 1964).

It is in the "dual-unity" sphere of preverbal intercommunication and interaction that cumulative (or, as I would rather say, with Kris, "strain") traumata may occur within the "average expectable environment."

The complexity and difficulty of mother-infant psychological development is compounded by the fact that "good enough" mothering necessarily falls far short of optimally adaptive mothering in our culture, a fact which should be emphasized.

Ernst Kris and his coworkers (Coleman et al. 1953) as well as

---

1. Claude Bernard: *milieu intérieur*.

Therese Benedek (1959) have drawn our attention to the fact that mothering is a developmental variable, with a succession of phases marked by varied and complex adaptive tasks that average mothers cannot be expected to meet with even gradations of success.

As workers in the field map out important landmarks of early psychic maturation and development, it is an important and interesting task to study the circular mother-child interaction as a developmental process which shapes the personality of the young, but also shapes the personality of the adult maternal partner (Benedek 1959). Hartmann (1939) says that "the task of man to adapt to man is present from the very beginning of life" (p. 31).

The task of man to adapt to man, as it has to do with the very beginning of individual life, is the topic of my present study of the "normal separation-individuation" process.

I came to the study of the normal separation-individuation phase from a study of symbiotic child psychosis, which had strongly suggested that childhood schizophrenia could be traced back to vicissitudes of personality development during the second part of the first year and particularly to the second year of life. During that period, the maternal partner of the dual unit for some reason could not be used by the infant-toddler either as auxiliary ego or as a "protective shield against stimuli," nor could she be used as "the beacon of orientation in the world of reality" (*SPI*:6). Minute study of the separation-individuation phase—about which we know comparatively little, especially in so far as the ego's developmental tasks are concerned—would therefore help to understand better the genesis and the still entirely puzzling nature of schizophrenia.

It is my hypothesis that, in certain toddlers, the maturational spurt of locomotor and other autonomous ego functions, if it takes place concomitantly with a lag in their emotional readiness to function separately from the mother, produces organismic panic, the mental content of which is not readily discernible, because the child (still in the preverbal stage) cannot communicate. Acute or insidious "organismic distress," with concomitant inability to utilize the mother as external organizer or auxiliary ego, arrests structuralization of the ego. The very fact that maturation proceeds while development does not, renders the rudimentary ego extremely brittle.

Fragmentation may result, and the well-known clinical picture of infantile psychosis then ensues (*SPI:7*).

The maturational spurt I referred to above presumably occurs within the age span after the infant "hatches" (if he hatches at all) from the symbiotic dual-unity stage with his mother.

As early as 1955, Gosliner and I suggested that there is a *normal* developmental phase of separation-individuation, which confronts *every* child with certain developmental tasks and is beset with potential crises. The normal separation-individuation process requires developmental readiness on the part of the infant-toddler to differentiate from the mother within the framework of the usual emotional availability of the mother (*SPI:15, SPII:2*), the most important factor of "the average expectable environment" (Hartmann 1939, 1950a).

Within the pilot phase of the separation-individuation research project (an observational study), we were able to distinguish the outline—the contour, as it were—of the main steps of the separation-individuation process. We conceptualized these in terms of four subphases (*SPII:3, SPII:4*).

THE FIRST EIGHTEEN MONTHS OF LIFE

The first step, or "subphase," is *differentiation*, which begins with the hatching process, and which is conceptualized as the emergence of the infant's self-representation from within the imaginary "symbiotic membrane" of the mother-child dual unity. In some infants a veritable hatching process may be seen, which has observable phenomenological characteristics. With this hatching process is ushered in the period of differentiation, which extends approximately into the ninth and tenth months.

The second step, or subphase, can be designated as the *practicing period par excellence*. It extends from about the ninth or tenth month to about the sixteenth to eighteenth month. This period, which coincides with what Phyllis Greenacre (1957) has termed the child's "love affair with the world," results in the "mastery" of certain locomotor skills, cognitive capacities, and other partial autonomous ego functions. These functions, during the practicing period, attract so much libido that the junior toddler is emotionally relatively independent of the love object and absorbed in his own narcissistic pleasures. Upon the attainment of mastery of some autonomous ego functions, however, he becomes increasingly aware of his separateness and *pari passu* very much aware of his need for his mother's acceptance and renewed participation.

The subphase in which renewed approach behavior can be observed usually extends from about the sixteenth or eighteenth month well into the third year of life. This period of *rapprochement* is very important for laying down the foundation of later mental health or psychopathology.

This very crucial period of development gradually goes over to the fourth subphase of separation-individuation in which a certain degree of *object constancy* will be attained: that is, mental representations of the mother become intrapsychically available (Hartmann 1952). The memory traces of the love object enable the child to remain away from the mother for some length of time and still function with emotional poise, provided he is in a fairly familiar environment. Presumably this is so because inner representations of the mother are available to him.

In our studies we came across unmistakable evidence for the belief that a basic mood is established during the separation-individuation process. This basic mood or individually characteristic affective responsiveness is not due solely to innate factors but seems, at least to some extent, to be accentuated experientially and to counteract the constitutional characteristics of the individual child. This characteristic "base line" of the child's emotional responsiveness seems to derive from the preponderance and perpetuation of one or the other general emotional colorings that we found to be characteristic of one or the other of the subphases of the separation-individuation process (the practicing period or the period of rapprochement).

The psychoanalytic literature has recently been filled with observations and discussions about separation anxiety, object loss, and depression. These concepts are intertwined both clinically and dynamically. It is not always clear in the literature, however, that what is referred to as object loss is, more often than not, not real object loss, but *intrapsychic* "loss" of an object. Thus, the questions of a predisposition to depressive moods and separation anxiety, as well as of the relationship of the latter to object loss, are badly in need of further clarification.

Real object loss—that is, loss of a love object in reality—does not occur frequently enough to account for the widespread proclivity, especially on the part of women, toward depressive moods or depressive illness. It must be a loss in fantasy—that is to say, *intrapsychic conflict* of a particular type or constellation (more frequent than real object loss, if not perhaps actually ubiquitous)—which is the genetic cause for the occurrence of depression as an affect, as a proclivity toward a basic mood. It might therefore be profitable to examine the nature of the *intrapsychic process* which seems to result in this *sense* or *feeling of loss*, and which seems to set in motion the affective reactions of helplessness, sadness, grief, and depression (Bibring 1953, Mahler *SPI*:15).

In our separation-individuation study, we could see the earliest behavioral, mimetic, vocal, and verbal manifestations of affective reactions in our subjects—in small children who were never actually separated, for any length of time, from their primary love object or objects. We observed depressive reactions as well as their opposites— moods of exhilaration—in our children. This "mood predisposition" seems as a rule to be related to the intrapsychic vicissitudes of their separation-individuation process, which seems to activate characteristically either relatively positive or relatively negative mood dispositions (Jacobson 1957b).

From the point of view of my main hypothesis, what we see in the toddlers' behavior is a reflection of their intrapsychic working through of that unavoidable, predetermined growing away from the previous state of "oneness" with the mother, which is entailed by maturational differentiation and individuation. This loss—the necessity for a more or less gradual relinquishing of claims upon the need-satisfying, symbiotic object—implies the gradual giving up of the more or less delusional fantasy of symbiotic omnipotence, although this is to some extent compensated for by increased secondary autonomy (Hartmann 1952) and sound secondary narcissism.

The subphase of differentiation represents the first step of the individuation process. It begins at the peak of the symbiotic phase.

By the fifth or sixth month, the infant seems to recognize his mother as the object through which his gratifications are provided and his discomfort relieved. One can readily observe that, when his mother's face is near him, the five- to six-month-old will take the initiative to seek contact, even to force the mother to respond (Brody and Axelrad 1966). This first subphase of the individuation process develops parallel with the maturational growth of locomotor partial functions, such as creeping, paddling along, climbing, standing up, etc. It also includes looking beyond the immediate visual field (scanning), as well as progress in hand, mouth, and eye coordination, the expression of active pleasure in the use of the entire body, a much more active interest in inanimate objects, active turning to the outside world for pleasure and stimulation, and much more successful efforts at self-stimulation. It is a period in which peek-a-boo games, initiated by the mother, are taken over by the infant.

These functions are continually stimulated by close proximity to the mother, as can be seen in the greater vivacity and the longer-sustained activity of the infant when he is in the mother's proximity compared with his lower-keyed activity when he is at a distance from her.

What we learn from our observations about this first subphase of differentiation—and this is true of affective development in general—is that the momentum of libidinal responsiveness is greatly augmented by visual, tactile, and auditory contact and intercommunication—by the "dialogue" with the mother (Spitz 1963).

With the infant's spurt in autonomous functions, especially upright locomotion, begins his "love affair with the world," as Phyllis Greenacre has characterized it. During those precious six to eight months, from the tenth or twelfth to the sixteenth or eighteenth month, the world seems to be the junior toddler's "oyster." Libidinal cathexis seems to shift so substantially into the service of the rapidly growing autonomous ego and its functions that, during this so-called practicing period, some children appear to be intoxicated with their own faculties and with the greatness of "their own world." At any time after the tenth month, which marks the onset of the reality-testing period *par excellence,* there begins a steadily increasing libidinal investment in practicing motor skills and in exploring the expanding environment, both human and inanimate. This is true whether the child has already started toddling by then, or is still in the process of developing a proficiency in crawling, righting himself, or paddling around rapidly with a "belly crawl" of his entire body.

Elation seems to be the phase-specific characteristic or basic mood during the second subphase of individuation (the "practicing period").

The chief characteristic of this practicing period is the child's great narcissistic investment in his own functions, as well as in the "objects and objectives" of his expanding reality. Along with this, we see a relatively great imperviousness to knocks and falls and other frustrations (*SPII:1, SPII:3, SPII:4*).

As the child, through the maturation of his locomotor apparatus, begins to venture further away from the mother's feet, he is often so absorbed in his own activities that for long periods of time he appears to be oblivious to the mother's presence.[2] However, he returns periodically to the mother, seeming to need her physical presence from time to time. We see ten-month-olds crawling to the mother, righting themselves on her leg or touching her in other ways, or just standing and leaning against her for "emotional refueling." It is easy to observe and to interpret how the wilting, fatigued infant "perks up" in the shortest time upon such contact.

The practicing of locomotion culminates in the toddler becoming more sure-footed; and the freely walking infant is at the height of his mood of elation. For some, this is an intermittent mood; for others, an almost continual one.

During the second eighteen months of life, however, very important libido-economic shifts and changes take place. The little child who is practicing his skills, perceiving and coping with expanding segments of reality, appears to be largely preoccupied with his narcissistic pleasures. He seems, at least intermittently, to be delighted and impressed by his own rapidly developing new skills and his

2. This apparent obliviousness seems to be in direct proportion to the mother's emotional availability during that subphase.

growing perceptual and cognitive capacities (which are presumably expanding with equal rapidity).

Just around the time of mastery (of important partial ego functions), he reaches the high point of his mood of elation, which is buttressed by his sense of *his own magic omnipotence*. This great pervasive secondary narcissism had as its precursor the delusion in the symbiotic phase of the symbiotic omnipotence of the mother-infant dual unit.

THE SECOND EIGHTEEN MONTHS OF LIFE

The period during which the junior toddler of ten to eighteen months grows into the senior toddler of eighteen to twenty-four months and beyond represents a most important turning point. Now the toddler experiences, more or less gradually and more or less keenly, the obstacles to his "conquest of the world."

The period of rapprochement demonstrates with particular clarity that the intrapsychic separation-individuation process consists of two distinct, yet intertwined and complementary tracks of development: one of these is "individuation"; the other, "separation." During the practicing period, and during the period of mastery, which continues well into the second half of the second year, individuation proceeds very rapidly, on the one hand, so that the child exercises independence "to the limit." On the other hand, along with the acquisition of primitive skills and perceptual cognitive faculties, there is a clearer and clearer differentiation of the intrapsychic representations of the love object and of the self. Along with the child's awareness of his separateness comes his realization of the very large number of obstacles that stand in the way of his own magic omnipotent wishes and fantasies. At the very height of mastery, toward the end of the practicing period, it dawns on the junior toddler that the world is not his "oyster," that he has to cope with it on his own, every so often as a relatively helpless, small, and lonesomely separate individual. No matter how insistently the toddler tries to coerce his mother, she and he no longer function effectively as a dual unit—that is to say, he cannot partake, either, in the delusion he still maintains of parental omnipotence. Verbal communication and secondary-process thinking thus become more and more necessary; gestural coercion on the part of the toddler or mutual preverbal empathy between mother and child will no longer suffice to bring him to his goal of satisfaction, of "narcissistic 'well-being'" (Sandler and Joffe 1965).

In addition to this growing awareness of individual separateness, the junior toddler gradually comes to realize that his love objects (his parents) are also separate individuals; they seem to act on diversified interests, the focal points of which are less and less identical with his own. This realization is arrived at, however, at a time when the toddler's delusion about his parents' unlimited power still persists. As for his inability to recreate the "omnipotent unity" of his earlier life, no matter how insistently he coerces his mother, at this point he can only regard it as her *withholding* from him an omnipotence which she possesses, but which *he* is no longer permitted to share. It remains for him to recognize—much later, in the postoedipal period—that he is not the only one who is not omnipotent, but that his parents are by no means omnipotent either. Hence, they cannot either share with him or deny to him an omnipotence that they themselves do not have (Jacobson 1947b).

There are mother-child pairs in whom the child has already had to exert himself quite a bit during the practicing period in order to obtain from the love object the libidinal supplies—the refueling—that were necessary for him to maintain a basically contented emotional affective state. Such a deficit of emotional supplies, which may have gone unrecognized at the time, may later become compounded and manifest itself (after the child's relatively brief and low-keyed "love affair with the world") during the course of the rapprochement subphase.

It is the mother's love and acceptance of the toddler and even of his ambivalence which enable the toddler's ego to cathect his self-representation with "neutralized energy."

If there is a significant lack of acceptance and "emotional understanding" by the mother during the rapprochement subphase (which is also the beginning of verbal communication); or, at any rate, if there is an absence of a higher level of "dialogue" (Spitz 1963), this circumstance compounds the stress trauma that may have existed during the preverbal mother-infant interaction. This deficit in mothering has tended to result in a diminution of the child's self-esteem and a consequent narcissistic vulnerability. Ambivalence in behavior (which I would call "ambitendency"), and especially aggressive repetitive coercion of the mother and sometimes the father as well, seem to be age-adequate phenomenological signs, along with the normal negativism of this phase of "separation," which characterizes the anal phase. But prolonged and increasing ambivalence is a sign of skewed emotional development, an indication of increase of unneutralized aggression and of disturbance of the child's progress toward object constancy.

Our reconstructive and observational data suggest that, in those small children who show the "basic depressive mood," not enough sound secondary narcissistic libido has remained available, beyond the period of mastery, to be vested in the "objects and objectives" of his expanding world, and particularly not enough to cathect his own self-representations. Too great a portion of his unneutralized aggression (Hartmann, Kris, and Loewenstein 1949) is being taken up by the mechanisms of splitting and projection—a potentially pathological combination of defense, which serves to ward off the child's hostility (aggression) and his fear of annihilating the love object by his aggressive ambivalent fantasies while he struggles to restore the state of oneness with the love object.

The mother's renewed acceptance and active support during the rapprochement phase is thus a necessary prerequisite for the toddler's gradual realization and acceptance of the unreality of his "omnipotence"—a realization which will allow the secondary narcissistic investment in his own autonomy to take place gradually, thereby protecting him against acute deflation of his "omnipotence" and preventing serious injury to his self-esteem.

The phenomenological, behavioral signs of unusual conflict become evident in some cases in the form of an increased coercion and perhaps an increased "shadowing" of the mother. Less often, we have been able to observe (or receive reports of) an exaggerated form of the game of darting away from the mother in order to provoke her into pursuing him and scooping him up. This means to the child a passive physical reunion with the mother, a symbolic and repeated undoing, as it were, of the "separation."

The quality and measure of the toddler's wooing behavior during the rapprochement subphase provide an important clue for the assessment of the normality of the child's individuation process. Some of our children have stubbornly refused to accept substitute adults; even though they had seemed to be continuously dissatisfied in their mothers' absence, they nevertheless displayed a constant whining and demanding as soon as their mothers reappeared. There have also been severe and protracted separation reactions to everyday routine separations, with a surplus of unneutralized aggression expressing itself in temper tantrums.

From the data collected thus far, I believe that the collapse of the child's belief in his own omnipotence, with his uncertainty about the emotional availability of the parents, creates the so-called "hostile dependency" upon and ambivalence toward the parents. This ambivalence seems to call for the early pathological defense mechanisms of splitting the good and bad mother images and of turning aggression against the self; these result in a feeling of helplessness, which, as Bibring (1953) has emphasized, creates the basic depressive affect. These libido-economic circumstances may become the basis for responding habitually with negative mood swings.

The two pillars of early infantile well-being and self-esteem are the child's belief in his own omnipotence and his belief in the parents' omnipotence, of which he partakes; these beliefs can be replaced only gradually by a realistic recognition of, belief in, and enjoyment of his individual autonomy, and by the development of object constancy (Hartmann 1952).

We could frequently observe that the "confident expectation" (Benedek 1938) of those toddlers who were already, whether for extrinsic or intrinsic reasons, carrying over a deficit of emotional supplies from the previous subphases was more readily depleted during the second eighteen months of life. They succumbed more easily than others to an increasingly angry mood, which was interpreted by Bowlby (1960) as "continual protest." In some instances, they seemed periodically to fall prey to a desperate feeling of helpless loss (from which, however, a child usually recovers intermittently, and with relative rapidity). The intrapsychic experience of loss is compounded by the affect-laden symbolic significance of toilet training, and by the advent of the castration anxiety of the phallic phase of psychosexual development. I believe—contrary to Weinberger (1964) —that, in those cases in which the birth of a sibling has coincided with these intrapsychic conflicts, the significance of that event, even though it was great, nevertheless lay primarily in the fact that it accentuated, dramatized, and compounded the basically negative mood predisposition of the child. It was not the original cardinal conflict, and it did not generate per se the depressive affective mood or the proclivity to depressive illness.

The negative affective responsiveness, the "depressive mood," may be represented predominantly by separation and grief reactions—perhaps following a dramatic struggle with the love object— marked by temper tantrums, continual attempts to woo or coerce the mother, and then giving up in despair for a while; or it may be revealed in impotent resignation and surrender (in some cases with marked masochistic coloring). On the other hand, discontentment and anger may persist after a shorter period of grief and sadness— which, I believe, had constituted or represented an abbreviated period of mourning for the "good," need-satisfying, symbiotic mother (SPI:15). In all cases, there is an increased clinging to the mother (not necessarily physically), and a focusing of highly ambivalent cathexis on her. This, in turn, stands in the way of the development of object constancy.

It is by no means the rule—indeed, it seems to be the exception— that the autonomous functioning of the ego is impaired. If anything, children who are prone to affect-laden behavior in their immediate interaction with the mother may function beautifully in other, more neutral situations. As far as we can tell from the limited data of a still ongoing project and our limited follow-up impressions, in the average toddler this negative-depressive affective responsiveness or mood either persists or gives way to a premature earnestness, a kind of unchildlike concern which may possibly indicate a precocity of superego structuralization. Even though in this paper I cannot elaborate on this problem, I must emphasize the importance of the double trauma of toilet training and of the discovery (at a much earlier age than we have thought) of the anatomical sexual difference as contributory factors in the genesis of the propensity of girls to depressive moods.

Sadness with psychic content, that is, sadness which has an ideational as well as an affective component, must be distinguished from earlier physiological reactions (somatopsychic, at best) of unpleasure and pain—such as transient reactions to weaning, or longer-lasting bodily distress, which the later depressive response may or may not compound.

We have seen at least one male child who was continually fretful, fitful, and unhappy up to the ninth month of age. Until then he suffered from an undetected inguinal hernia and recurrent severe bronchitis. His mother was quite inept at making her young babies comfortable and at reading and responding to their cues. Following the discovery of the inguinal hernia and its repair, however, there was a most favorable change in the libido-economic balance in the mother-child interaction as well as (and even more importantly) in the child's intrapsychic economy. The mutual cueing of mother and child, which till then had been perplexing to the partners as well as to the observers, became quite satisfactory, and the little boy resumed the process of separation-individuation at an emotionally higher level. His "love affair with the world" now proceeded in high gear at the beginning of and during the practicing period.

Among two scores of infants and toddlers whom we have studied intensively so far during the separation-individuation period, the depressive response—with or without a generally angry mood—has been observed in girls definitely more often than in boys. Their anger toward and disappointment with mother for not having given them the penis could be traced convincingly in several cases. In two girls, in both of whom we have observed the separation-individuation process from the tenth month onward, signs of conflict and manifestations of depressive reaction increased after the period of the normal psychological elation of autonomous mastery.

Let me cite one case in whom the elements of a basic depressive mood, or negative emotional responsiveness, could be observed to become patterned during the vicissitudes of the separation-

individuation phase. Ann showed intensification of approach behavior as early as during her ninth and tenth months; this was the
result of her mother's relative emotional unavailability and aloofness. This deficit of emotional availability of the "love object," the
mother (even though she was physically present), blunted the "zest of
life" that is generally so characteristic of the practicing period.

Gradual depletion of "confident expectation" produced great
ambivalence and the deflation, without sufficient substitution, of
Ann's waning "sense of magic omnipotence." This went parallel
with a decrease in self-esteem. The usual abandon at the beginning of
the practicing period was almost completely canceled out in Ann's
case by her increased need for "refueling." She was seen beseeching
her mother constantly with her eyes, wordlessly appealing for emotional supplies. The "love affair with the world," which clearly took
place during Ann's fourteenth and fifteenth months, was observable,
nevertheless, but it was of short duration and rather subdued.

For a while, the mother's apprently increased interest, which was
in fact based on the desire for the child to become toilet-trained,
seemed to have offered, when Ann was twenty to twenty-two months
old, a common ground for *rapprochement* between mother and
daughter. However, the toilet training, which was initially successful in this respect, also became enmeshed in conflict. Concomitantly
with the mother's narcissistic withdrawal because of her third pregnancy, it too became a battlefield between mother and child.

When sister Susie was born, Ann expressed her ambivalence, and
her pregnancy and birth fantasies, in pernicious withholding of
feces. The "baby-stool" equation seemed to be unequivocal in her
behavior and in her verbal material. At the same time, material about
penis envy (she had an older brother), and an intense coveting of
gifts, particularly from her father, came to the fore. We heard Ann tell
her mother, during a painful defecation, that her daddy had "a little
piggy—no, not a piggy, a baby horse in his stomach." She verbalized
in primary-process fashion many other fantasies, anxieties, and
wishes.

I would like to describe one routine separation situation which
showed with particular clarity the splitting of the mother image as a
result of Ann's great ambivalence and her need to preserve the good

object against her own rage and destructiveness. From about thirty months on, Ann was left, once in a while and routinely, at our Center with her familiar and usually most cherished "play teacher," along with two other playmates (both within one week of her exact age). Whereas the two other children parted easily from their mothers, Ann (even though she herself had difficulty parting from the Center) displayed all the signs of anxious-angry-ambivalent separation problems. She delayed her mother's leaving by pretending to have to go to the toilet and by many other subterfuges. After her mother left, she cried and stamped her feet and then clung to the play teacher, at the same time scolding the very adult to whom she was clinging bodily and saying, "You are bad, you are bad." Anybody who came in by the door of the nursery she ordered *out* with angry determination. I decided to verbalize to Ann that I could see that she did not want anybody but her mother to come into the room. After repeating this a few times, I then left the room and observed from the booth for a while. When I came back and unobtrusively sat down at a far corner of the large playroom, Ann glanced at me out of the corner of her eye, then gently and petulantly muttered, "I want my mommy, I want my mommy." She laid her head on her teacher's shoulder and cried softly. In other words, as a consequence of the interpretation, a longing, libidinal mood had gained the upper hand, enabling Ann to give up for a time the splitting of the good and bad mother images. For quite a while, my entrance or the entrance of any other less familiar female adult became the trigger for Ann's longing for her mother. It was quite instructive to observe, however, that the actual reunion with the mother, which Ann seemed to desire so much, was never an unambivalent, joyous affair. For both partners, it was a visible disappointment; in Ann's case, the disappointment was also freely verbalized.

Our observational data support Bibring's contention (1953) that the depressive response is "a basic affective reaction, very much as anxiety is." In some children during the course of the individuation process, the increased intensity and duration, the habitual and continual character of the depressive response seem to represent this habitual negative affective reaction, which eventually may create a proclivity to depression. I believe that the depletion of "confident expectation" and diminution of self-esteem, with concomitant deficit in neutralized aggression, create the libido-economic basis for the depressive mood. It is a relatively great and sudden sense of helplessness, as Bibring (1953) emphasized in his analysis of the causation of depression, which results from depletion of "basic trust" (Erikson 1950) and from the collapse of the child's belief in his own and, after the oedipal period, in his parents' omnipotence (*SPI*:14, Jacobson 1947b). On the basis of identification with the "aggressor," the mother (A. Freud 1936), we then observe a turning of aggression against the self (as the victim of the "aggressor")—all this, even before superego precursors are consolidated into a superego structure.

While the primary autonomous functions of the ego do not seem to be adversely affected during the time span that we have studied so far (four to thirty-six months, and some follow-up to the fourth and fifth year), the amount of neutralized libido and deaggressivized aggression necessary for sound secondary narcissistic cathexis of the self, and for maintenance of structural harmony between the ego and the ego ideal, does not seem to be as readily available to these children as to those who have not suffered acute loss of self-esteem and depletion of trust in the love objects, during the second eighteen months of life. Disturbance in interstructural harmony and interference with the achievement of object constancy are signaled by severe separation anxiety, along with the other signs of increased ambivalence; or else what occurs is a masochistic surrender of the child's own individuality, precocious overidentification, pseudo self-sufficiency, and flattened affective reactivity.[3]

3. The girl's fantasy of being castrated and its influence on the ensuing ambivalence toward the mother seem to account for the greater frequency of the early and later depressive responsiveness in the female.

Chapter 6

ON HUMAN SYMBIOSIS AND THE VICISSITUDES OF INDIVIDUATION

[1967]

The term *symbiosis* is borrowed from biology, where it is used to refer to a close functional association of two organisms to their mutual advantage.

In the weeks preceding the evolution to symbiosis, the newborn and very young infant's sleeplike states far outweigh in proportion the states of arousal. They are reminiscent of that primal state of libido distribution that prevailed in intrauterine life, which resembles the model of a closed monadic system, self-sufficient in its hallucinatory wish fulfillment.

Freud's (1911) use of the bird's egg as a model of a closed psychological system comes to mind. He said: "A neat example of a psychical system shut off from the stimuli of the external world, and able to satisfy even its nutritional requirements *autistically* . . . is afforded by a bird's egg with its food supply enclosed in its shell; for it, the care provided by its mother is limited to the provision of warmth" (p. 220n., my italics).

In a quasi-symbolic way along this same line, conceptualizing the state of the sensorium, I have applied to the first weeks of life the term *normal autism;* for in it, the infant seems to be in a state of primitive hallucinatory disorientation, in which need satisfaction belongs to his own omnipotent, *autistic* orbit.

The newborn's waking life centers around his continuous at-tempts to achieve homeostasis. The effect of his mother's ministra-tions in reducing the pangs of need-hunger cannot be isolated, nor can it be differentiated by the young infant from tension-reducing attempts of his own, such as urinating, defecating, coughing, sneez-ing, spitting, regurgitating, vomiting, all the ways by which the infant tries to rid himself of unpleasurable tension. The effect of these expulsive phenomena as well as the gratification gained by his mother's ministrations help the infant, in time, to differentiate between a "pleasurable" and "good" quality and a "painful" and "bad" quality of experiences (SPI:6).

Through the inborn and autonomous perceptive faculty of the primitive ego (Hartmann 1939) deposits of memory traces of the two primordial qualities of stimuli occur. We may further hypothesize that these are cathected with primordial undifferentiated drive ener-gy (SPI:6).

From the second month on, dim awareness of the need-satisfying object marks the beginning of the phase of normal symbiosis, in which the infant behaves and functions as though he and his mother were an omnipotent system—a dual unity within one common boundary.

My concept of the symbiotic phase of normal development dovetails, from the infant's standpoint, with the concept of the symbiotic phase of the mother-child dual unity, which Therese Benedek (1949, 1959, 1960) has described in several classical papers from the standpoint of both partners of the primary unit.

It is obvious that, whereas, during the symbiotic phase, the infant is *absolutely* dependent on the symbiotic partner, symbiosis has a quite different meaning for the adult partner of the dual unity. The infant's need for the mother is absolute, while the mother's for the infant is relative (Benedek 1959).

The term *symbiosis* in this context is a metaphor. It does not describe, as the biological concept of symbiosis does, what actually happens between two separate individuals (Angel 1967). It was chosen to describe that state of undifferentiation, of fusion with mother, in which the "I" is not yet differentiated from the "not-I," and in which inside and outside are only gradually coming to be

sensed as different. Any unpleasurable perception, external or internal, is projected beyond the common boundary of the symbiotic
milieu intérieur (cf. Freud's concept of the "purified pleasure ego"),
which includes the mothering partner's Gestalt during ministrations. Only transiently—in the state of the sensorium that is termed
alert inactivity—does the young infant take in stimuli from beyond
the symbiotic milieu. The primordial energy reservoir that is vested
in the undifferentiated "ego-id" still contains an undifferentiated
mixture of libido and aggression. As several authors have pointed
out, the libidinal cathexis vested in symbiosis, by reinforcing the
inborn instinctual stimulus barrier, protects the rudimentary ego
from premature phase-unspecific strain—from stress traumata.

The essential feature of symbiosis is hallucinatory or delusional,
somatopsychic, omnipotent fusion with the representation of the
mother and, in particular, delusion of common boundary of the two
actually and physically separate individuals. This is the mechanism
to which the ego regresses in cases of the most severe disturbance of
individuation and psychotic disorganization, which I have described
as "symbiotic child psychosis" (*SPI*:6, *SPI*:7).

In the human species, the function of, and the equipment for,
self-preservation is atrophied. The rudimentary ego in the newborn
baby and the young infant has to be complemented by the emotional
rapport of the mother's nursing care, a kind of social symbiosis. It is
within this matrix of physiological and sociobiological dependency
on the mother that there takes place the structural differentiation
that leads to the individual's organization for adaptation: the ego.

Ribble (1943) has pointed out that it is by way of mothering that
the young infant is gradually brought out of an inborn tendency
toward vegetative, splanchnic regression and into increased sensory
awareness of, and contact with, the environment. In terms of energy
or libidinal cathexis, this means that a progressive displacement of
libido has to take place, from the inside of the body (particularly
from the abdominal organs), toward the periphery of the body
(*SPI*:7, Greenacre 1945a).

In this sense, I would propose to distinguish, within the phase of
primary *narcissism*—a Freudian concept to which I find it most
useful to adhere—two subphases: during the first few weeks of

extrauterine life, a stage of *absolute* primary narcissism, which is marked by the infant's lack of awareness of a mothering agent. This stage I have termed "normal autism," as discussed above. In the other, the symbiotic stage proper (beginning around the third month) although primary narcissism still prevails, it is not such an absolute primary narcissism, inasmuch as the infant begins dimly to perceive need satisfaction as coming from a need-satisfying part object—albeit still from within the orbit of his omnipotent symbiotic dual unity with a mothering agency, toward which he turns libidinally (Schur 1966).

Pari passu, and in accordance with the pleasure-pain sequences, demarcation of representations of the body ego within the symbiotic matrix takes place. These representations are deposited as the "body image" (Schilder 1935).

From now on, representations of the body that are contained in the rudimentary ego mediate between inner and outer perceptions. The ego is molded under the impact of reality, on the one hand, and the instinctual drives, on the other. The body ego contains two kinds of self-representations: there is an inner core of the body image, with a boundary that is turned toward the inside of the body and divides it from ego; and an outer layer of sensoriperceptive engrams, which contributes to the boundaries of the "body self."

From the standpoint of the "body image": the shift of predominantly proprioceptive-enteroceptive cathexis toward sensoriperceptive cathexis of the periphery is a major step in development. We did not realize its importance prior to psychoanalytic studies of early infantile psychosis. We know now that this major shift of cathexis is an essential prerequisite of body ego formation. Another parallel step is the ejection, by projection, of destructive unneutralized aggressive energy beyond the body-self boundaries.

The infant's inner sensations form the *core* of the self. They seem to remain the central, the crystallization point of the "feeling of self," around which a "sense of identity" will become established (Greenacre 1958, Mahler 1958b, Rose 1964, 1966). The sensoriperceptive organ—the "peripheral rind of the ego," as Freud called it—contributes mainly to the self's demarcation from the object world. The two kinds of intrapsychic structures *together* form the framework for self-orientation (Spiegel 1959).

The two partners of the symbiotic dyad, on the other hand, may be regarded as polarizing the organizational and structuring processes. The structures that derive from the double frame of reference of the symbiotic unit represent a framework to which all experiences have to be related, before there are clear and whole representations in the ego of the self and the object world! Spitz (1965) calls the mother the auxiliary ego of the infant. In the same line, I believe the mothering partner's "holding behavior," her "primary maternal preoccupation," to be the symbiotic organizer (Winnicott 1956a).

Hitherto, I have described, in a number of papers, extreme failures of these structuralization processes. In those papers I referred to and extrapolated from the most severe disturbances and disorganization of those structuralization principles in infantile psychosis. In this paper, I wish to draw heavily upon observations of normal development as well.

Greenacre (1958) has remarked how "extremely difficult [it is] to say exactly at what time the human organism develops from a biological to a *psychobiological* organization." Schur (1966) puts the time at the point when the "wish" replaces the purely "physiological need."

The implications of new sleep-physiological studies about REM activity in very young infants are most interesting and challenging indeed (Roffwarg, Muzio, and Dement 1966, Fischer 1965).

Experimental psychologists tell us that, in the first two months of life, learning takes place through conditioning. Toward the third month, however, the existence of memory traces can be demonstrated experimentally. This was referred to by Spitz (1965) as the beginning of learning according to the human pattern. Learning by conditioning is then gradually replaced by learning through experience. Here is then the first beginning of symbiotic relationship as well. We may say that, whereas during the quasi-prehistoric phase of magic hallucinatory omnipotence, the breast or the bottle *belongs* to the self, toward the third month, the object begins to be perceived as an *unspecific, need-satisfying part object* (A. Freud 1965).

When the need is not so imperative, when some measure of development enables the infant to hold tension in abeyance, that is to say, *when he is able to wait for and confidently expect satisfaction—*

only then is it possible to speak of the *beginning of an ego,* and of a symbiotic object as well. This is made possible by the fact that there seem to be memory traces of the *pleasures of gratification*—connected with the memory of the perceptual Gestalt of the mother's ministrations.

The specific smiling response at the peak of the symbiotic phase predicates that the infant is responding to the symbiotic partner in a manner different from that in which he responds to other human beings. In the second half of the first year, the symbiotic partner is no longer interchangeable; manifold behaviors of the five-month-old infant indicate that he has by now *achieved a specific symbiotic relationship with his mother* (Spitz 1965).

In 1954, Anna Freud reminded us that we may think of pregenital patterning in terms of two people joined to achieve what, for brevity's sake, one might call "homeostatic equilibrium" (see Mahler 1954a). The same thing may be referred to under the term "symbiotic relationship." *Beyond a certain, but not yet defined degree, the immature organism cannot achieve homeostasis on its own.* Whenever during the autistic or symbiotic phase there occurs "organismic distress"—that forerunner of anxiety proper— the mothering partner is called upon to contribute a particularly large portion of symbiotic help toward the maintenance of the infant's homeostasis. Otherwise, the neurobiological patterning processes are thrown out of kilter. Somatic memory traces are set at this time, which amalgamate with later experiences and may thereby increase later psychological pressures (Greenacre 1958).

Understanding of symbiotic phenomena, which I conceptualized initially through observation of mother-infant behavior in well-baby clinics, and also through reconstruction from systematic studies of severe symbiotic psychotic syndromes, I have since supplemented by way of our observational study of average mothers with their normal infants during the first three years of life, during the process of separation-individuation.

We have supplemented the understanding of these processes by way of following them in an observational study of *average* mothers with their *normal* infants during the first three years of life. We follow them from symbiosis to the process of separation-individuation, and up to the period of the establishment of libidinal object constancy in Hartmann's sense (1964).

OUT OF SYMBIOSIS THE INTRAPSYCHIC PROCESS OF SEPARATION-INDIVIDUATION EVOLVES

For more accurate conceptualization and formulation of these still (up to the third year) essentially preverbal processes, we have tried to determine characteristic behavioral concomitants of those intrapsychic events that seem to occur regularly during the course of separation-individuation. In previous papers, I have described the subphases of that process. The concept of subphases has been fruitful in that it has helped to determine the *nodal* points of those structuralization and developmental processes. We have found them to be characteristic at the crossroads of individuation. Their description has greatly facilitated the ordering of our data into the psychoanalytic frame of reference, in a meaningful way.

In the following, I wish to refer only to a few points that may illustrate and somewhat complement more recent metapsychological constructs. These have pointed to the significance of *optimal human symbiosis* for the vicissitudes of individuation and for the establishment of a *cathectically stable "sense of identity."*

I would like to mention a relevant physiological and experimental finding that bears upon the transition from the autistic to the symbiotic phase. These findings set the *beginning* of this transition at the *end* of the first month. There are corresponding findings—for example, by the late John Benjamin (1961)—which show that around three to four weeks of age a maturational crisis occurs. This is borne out in electroencephalographic studies and by the observation that there is a marked increase in overall sensitivity to external stimulation. As Benjamin said, "Without intervention of a mother figure for help in tension reduction, the infant at that time tends to become overwhelmed by stimuli, with increased crying and other motor manifestations of undifferentiated negative affect."

Metapsychologically speaking, this seems to mean that, by the second month, the quasi-solid stimulus barrier (negative, because it is uncathected)—*this autistic shell,* which kept external stimuli out—begins to crack. Through the aforementioned cathectic shift toward the sensory-perceptive periphery, a protective, but also receptive and selective, positively cathected stimulus shield now begins to form and to envelop the symbiotic orbit of the mother-child dual unity (Mahler 1967). This eventually highly selective boundary seems to contain not only the pre-ego self-representations, but also the not yet differentiated, libidinally cathected symbiotic part objects, within the mother-infant symbiotic matrix.

At the height of symbiosis—at around four to five months—the facial expression of most infants becomes much more subtly differentiated, mobile, and expressive. During the infant's wakeful periods, he reflects many more nuances of "states"—by now "ego states"—than he did in the autistic phase.

By the "states" of the newborn—which Peter Wolff (1959) has described—we gauge, in a very general way, the states of the sensorium. In the course of the symbiotic phase, we can follow by the "ego states" of the infant the oscillation of his attention investment between his *inner* sensations and the symbiotic, libidinal attractions. During his state of "alert inactivity" the infant's attention turns toward the outer world; this, however, as yet, comprises mainly percepts that are more or less *closely* related to the mother.

The indicator of outward-directed attention seems to be the prototypical biphasic visual pattern of turning to an outside stimulus and then checking back to the mother's Gestalt, particularly her face. From this kind of scanning, elements of strangeness reaction patterns will develop. Outward-directed perceptual activity gradually replaces the inward-directed attention cathexis that was, only recently, almost exclusively vested in symbiotically disoriented inner sensations. The process by which this occurs—and which might be appropriately termed *hatching*—can now begin.

The gratification-frustration sequences promote structuralization. It is important, however, as several writers have pointed out lately, that in the early months of life, tension should not remain on an inordinately high level for any length of time. If such stress traumata *do* occur during the first five months of life, the symbiotic partner—this *auxiliary ego*—is called upon to save the infant from the pressure of having to develop *his own resources prematurely*. As Martin James (1960) put it: "Premature ego development would imply that the infant—during the phase of primary narcissism—took over functions from the mother *in actuality*, or started *as though to do so*." Winnicott (1965) and other British analysts call such an occurrence development of a "false self"—by which I believe they mean *the beginning of "as if" mechanisms*.

When pleasure in outer sensory perceptions as well as maturational pressure stimulate outward-directed attention cathexis—while inside there is an optimal level of pleasure and therefore *safe anchorage* within the symbiotic orbit—these two forms of attention cathexis can oscillate freely (Spiegel 1959, Rose 1964). The result is an optimal symbiotic state from which smooth differentiation and *expansion beyond the symbiotic orbit* can take place.

The hatching process is, I believe, a gradual ontogenetic evolution of the sensorium—of the perceptual-conscious system—which leads to the infant-toddler's having a *permanently alert sensorium*, whenever he is awake.

It has been fascinating to observe how the prototype of outward-directed attention cathexis evolves—how the normal infant's differentiation process is guided by the pattern of "checking back" to the mother, as a point of orientation (Rose 1964). This pattern of checking back, and also the behavior termed "customs inspection" (Brody and Axelrad 1966), which consists in the baby's careful, more or less deliberate examination (visually and tactilely) of all features of the "not-mother's" face and comparing it point by point with the preobject or part-object representation of the mother—both these comparing and checking patterns recur, in an expanded, more complex edition, in the period from about ten to sixteen months of age, during the practicing subphase of separation-individuation. It then is supplemented by what Furer has called "emotional refueling."

THE SECOND MASSIVE SHIFT OF CATHEXIS

The peak point of the hatching process seems to coincide with the maturational spurt of active locomotion, which brings with it increased maturational pressure "for action," to practice locomotion and to explore wider segments of reality. From the fourth quarter of the first year on, this activity motivates the infant to separate in space from his mother, and to practice active physical separation and return. This will have a greatly catalyzing influence on further development of the ego.

The more nearly optimal the symbiosis, the mother's "holding behavior," has been, the more the symbiotic partner has helped the infant to become ready to "hatch" from the symbiotic orbit smoothly and gradually—that is, without undue strain upon his own resources—the better equipped has the child become to separate out and to differentiate his self-representations from the hitherto fused symbiotic self-plus-object representations. But even at the height of the second subphase of individuation—during the practicing period—neither the differentiated self-representations nor the object representations seem to be integrated as yet into a whole self-representation or a whole libidinal object representation.

Among the many elements of the mother-child relationship during early infancy, we are especially impressed with the mutual selection of cues. We observed that infants present a large variety of cues—to indicate needs, tension, and pleasure (SPII:2). In a complex manner, the mother responds selectively to only certain of these cues. The infant gradually alters his behavior in relation to this selective response; he does so in a characteristic way—the resultant of his own innate endowment and the mother-child relationship. From this circular interaction emerge patterns of behavior that already show certain overall qualities of the child's personality. What we seem to see here is the birth of the child as an individual (Lichtenstein 1964).

It is the specific unconscious need of the mother that activates, out of the infant's infinite potentialities, those in particular that create for each mother "the child" who reflects her own unique and individual needs. This process takes place, of course, within the range of the child's innate endowments.

Mutual cuing during the symbiotic phase creates that indelibly imprinted configuration—that complex pattern—that becomes the leitmotif for "the infant's becoming the child of his particular mother" (Lichtenstein 1961).

In other words, the mother conveys—in innumerable ways—a kind of "mirroring frame of reference," to which the primitive self of the infant automatically adjusts. If the mother's "primary preoccupation" with her infant—*her* mirroring function during earlier infancy—is unpredictable, unstable, anxiety-ridden, or hostile; if her confidence in herself as a mother is shaky, then the individuating child has to do without a reliable frame of reference for checking back, perceptually and emotionally, to the symbiotic partner (Spiegel 1959). The result will then be a disturbance in the primitive "self-feeling," which would derive or originate from a pleasurable and safe state of symbiosis, from which he did not have to hatch prematurely and abruptly.

The primary method of identity formation consists of mutual reflection during the symbiotic phase. This narcissistic, mutual libidinal mirroring reinforces the delineation of identity—through magnification and *reduplication*—a kind of echo phenomenon, which Paula Elkisch (1957) and Lichtenstein (1961) have so beautifully described.

In previous papers I have described, in some detail, the second massive shift of cathexis in ontogenetic development, which seems to take place when the practicing period begins (*SPII:5*). At that point, a large proportion of the available cathexis shifts from within the symbiotic orbit to investing the autonomous apparatuses of the self and the functions of the ego—locomotion, perception, learning.

In our study, we observe the intrapsychic separation-individuation process: the child's achievement of separate functioning in the presence and emotional availability of the mother. Even in this situation, this process by its very nature continually confronts the toddler with minimal threats of object loss. Nevertheless, through the predominance of pleasure in separate functioning, it enables the child to overcome that measure of separation anxiety that *is* entailed by *each new* step of separate functioning.

As far as the mothering partner is concerned, the practicing period confronts her with the impact of the toddler's spurt in individual autonomy, which is buttressed by the rapidly approaching occurrence—important for intrapsychic separation and self-boundary formation—of the negativistic behavior of the anal phase (A. Freud 1951a, Spock 1963).

The practicing period culminates around the middle of the second year in the freely walking toddler seeming to feel at the height of his mood of elation. He appears to be at the peak point of his belief in his own magic omnipotence, which is still to a considerable extent derived *from his sense of sharing in his mother's magic powers.*

CONCEPTUALIZATION OF THE INTRAPSYCHIC PROCESSES OF THE SECOND YEAR OF LIFE

Many mothers, however, take the very first unaided step of their toddler, who is, intrapsychically, by no means yet hatched, as heralding: "He is grown up now!" These mothers may be the ones who interpret the infant's signals according to whether they feel the child to be a continuation of themselves or a separate individual. Some tend to fail their fledgling, by "abandoning" him at this point, more or less precipitously and prematurely, to his own devices. They react with a kind of relative ridding mechanism, to the traumatization of their own symbiotic needs. These needs have been highlighted by the fact that maturational pressure has both enabled and prompted the child, at the very beginning of the second year, to practice the new "state of self": physical separateness.

One example of this is the case of Jay, who, at ten and a half months, had learned *precociously* to walk. At that time, his body schema and his spatial orientation were still at a stage of *symbiotic fusion* and *confusion.* One could see this by innumerable behavioral signs.

The infant of twelve to fourteen months, who is gradually separating and individuating, rises from his hitherto quadruped exercises, to take his first unaided steps—initially with great caution, even though exuberantly. He automatically reassures himself of some support within reach. He also relies on his own ability to slide safely down into the sitting position—when the going gets rough, so to say. Jay, however, even though he was most wobbly and unsure on his feet, did not do any of these.

Through maturation of the ego apparatuses—and facilitated by the flux of developmental energy (E. Kris 1955)—a relatively rapid, yet orderly process of separation-individuation takes place in the second year of life. By the eighteenth month, the junior toddler seems to be at the height of the process of dealing with his continuously experienced physical separateness from the mother. This coincides with his cognitive and perceptual achievement of the permanence of objects, in Piaget's sense (1936). This is the time when his sensorimotor intelligence starts to develop into true representational intelligence, and when the important process of internalization, in Hartmann's sense (1939)—very gradually, through ego identifications—begins.

Jay did not improve his skill in locomotion during his second year. He still impressed us with the impetuousness and repetitiveness of his locomotor activity, as well as with the frequency with which he got himself into dangerous situations and fell. He climbed onto high places and ran about, and peculiarly disregarded any obstacles in his way. All this time, his mother consistently and conspicuously made literally no move to protect him. Jay's behavior was, at least in the beginning, a tacit appeal to the mother. We assumed this because his falls definitely decreased when the mother was out of the room.

Jay's precocious locomotor maturation—with which the other developmental lines of his ego did not keep pace—should have made it even more imperative for the mothering partner to continue functioning as the child's auxiliary ego, in order to bridge the obvious gap between his motor and perceptual cognitive development.

The mother's inner conflicts, however, resulted in her appearing transfixed, almost paralyzed, at the sight of her junior toddler son's dangerous motor feats.

As I said before, many mothers fail their fledgling, because they find it difficult to strike intuitively and naturally an optimal balance between giving support—and yet at the same time knowing when to just be available and to watch from a distance. In other words, for many mothers in our culture, it is by no means easy to give up smoothly their "symbiotic holding behavior" and to provide, instead optimal support for the toddler on a higher emotional and verbal level, while allowing him to try his new wings of autonomy in the second year of life.

Jay's mother demonstrated this conflict to a bizarre degree; she continually watched from a distance like a hawk, but could not make a move to assist him. I believe that it was Jay's developmental lag—which the precocity of his locomotor maturation had created, combined with the mother's continued failure to protect Jay's body—that resulted in seemingly irreversible damage to each of the three essential structures of Jay's individuating personality.[1]

The sixteen- to eighteen-month level seems to be a *nodal* point of development. The toddler is then at the height of what Joffe and Sandler (1965) have termed "the ideal state of self." This is, I believe, the complex affective representation of the symbiotic dual unity, with its inflated sense of omnipotence—now augmented by the toddler's feeling of his own magic power—as the result of his spurt in autonomous functions.

THE SECOND EIGHTEEN MONTHS OF LIFE

In the next eighteen months, this "ideal state of self" must become divested of its delusional increments. The second eighteen months of life is *thus* a period of vulnerability. It is the time when the child's self-esteem may suffer abrupt deflation.

Under normal circumstances, the senior toddler's growing autonomy has already begun to correct some of his delusional overestimation of his own omnipotence. During the course of individuation, internalization has begun, by true ego identification with the parents.

Jay did not seem to be able to learn through experience. He continued to suffer his hard falls every so often, without appropriate affective reactions. He seemed to be peculiarly lacking in sensitivity to physical pain. This *denial of pain* appeared to be in compliance with his mother's reactive belief that her son was indeed impervious to pain. Jay thus earned, in addition to his mother's pride, the

---

1. Whether the obvious defect in his visual-motor coordination was on an organic or functional basis to begin with is a moot and at this point, I believe, indeterminable question, even though interesting.

epithet: "Jay, the Painless Wonder," from the mothers of other children in the group.

Even at twenty months, Jay was conspicuous for his poorly developed ability to "inhibit the immediate discharge of impulse, and the attack on materials." His behavior could be characterized as impulsive, repetitive, and disoriented in space; it seemed to lag in age-adequate reality testing. In pursuing a goal in space, he seemed to overlook obstacles that lay between his body and the point of destination he had set himself to reach—he bumped into them.

Examinations ruled out any neurological disturbance—a question which, of course, concerned us all along. Dr. Sally Provence, who examined and tested Jay, felt, as we did, that Jay was basically a well-endowed child whose intellectual development was being impaired by his psychological problems.

One of the crucial findings, if not *the main yield* of our study, concerns the *time lag that exists in normal intrapsychic development between object permanency (in Piaget's sense) and the attainment of libidinal object constancy,* in Hartmann's sense (*SPII:7*). Attainment of *libidinal object constancy* is much more gradual than the achievement of object permanency and, at least at the beginning it is a faculty that is waxing and waning and rather "impermanent." Up to about thirty months, it is very much at the mercy of the toddler's own mood swings and "ego states" and dependent on the actual mother-toddler situation of the moment.

In Jay's case it seemed there was by far too little *neutralized* cathexis available by the end of the fourth subphase of individuation—the subphase of the gradual attainment of *libidinal object constancy.*

To repeat: during the second half of the second year of life, the infant has become more and more aware of his physical separateness. Along with this awareness, the relative obliviousness of his mother's presence, which prevailed during the practicing period, wanes (*SPII:1*).

Instead, the toddler of sixteen to eighteen months may appear suddenly and quite conspicuously surprised by situations—for example, when he hurts himself—in which mother is not automatically at hand to prevent such an occurrence.

The previous relative obliviousness to mother's presence is gradually replaced by active approach behavior on a much higher level. As he realizes his power and ability to physically move away from his mother, the toddler now seems to have an increased need, and a wish, for his mother to share with him every new acquisition of skill and experience. We may call this subphase of separation-individuation, therefore, the period of *rapprochement* (*SPII*:1, *SPII*:4).

Jay's primary identity formation by thirty months of age showed, as if in a distorted mirror, the mother's unintegrated maternal attitudes, her schizoid personality traits.

The mother's perplexity seems to have been triggered by Jay's purely maturational spurt, in the physical sense, away from her. The mother was able to respond positively to Jay only when he went directly to her. But toddlers, especially in the period of rapprochement, do not run to their mothers to be hugged or picked up. Rather, they approach the mother on a higher emotional level by bringing things to her, making contact by gestures and words. Jay usually played at some distance from his mother, but would occasionally glance in her direction. Proximal contact between the two was quite infrequent. When it did occur, it was either that the mother went to Jay with an offer to read to him; or Jay, in turn, approached his mother with a book in his hand, which she would then read to him.

Thus, we could see Jay picking up, for example, this one cue, echoing and magnifying the mother's wish—which we knew from our intimate knowledge of the mother—that he be an "outstanding intellectual." One could almost predict one of the fateful variations of the *leitmotif* (Lichtenstein 1961) that is so frequently conveyed to the children of our time, and which Helen Tartakoff has dealt with in her paper: "The Normal Personality in Our Culture and the Nobel Prize Complex" (1966).

Already at the age of two, Jay had had great pleasure in the use of words. For a while, this acquisition of language had made for better communication between Jay and his mother. Yet, by the end of his third and *the beginning of his fourth year*, it became more and more apparent that there was a serious discrepancy in Jay's "lines of development" in Anna Freud's sense (1965)—both as to their rate of growth and as to their quality. Thus there ensued a serious deficit in the integrative and synthetic functions of Jay's ego. By that time, the counterphobic mechanism (which we saw in Jay's second year)—the impulse-ridden discharge behavior—had given way to phobic avoidance mechanisms.

The point that I wish to make in this presentation calls for conceptualization of certain elements of Jay's faulty individuation. The crucial deficiency was, we felt, Jay's disturbed body image, which robbed him of the core of primary identity formation, and, thus, of a reliably cathected self-feeling invested with neutralized energy. Furthermore, because the polarizing function of the symbiotic dual unity of this mother-child pair failed the individuating toddler, there was an obvious lack of a frame of reference for perceiving the extrasymbiotic external reality. In consequence, the intrapsychic representational world contained no clear boundaries between self and object—the boundaries between ego and id remained deficient and so did the boundaries and connections between the intersystemic parts of the ego. Thus, one might say, symbiotic confusion has been perpetuated. Two conspicuous behavioral signs were Jay's handling of his body in space and the disturbance he displayed, in words and actions, in projecting experiences in the dimension of time.

When Jay graduated from our study to nursery school, we predicted that he would attain a borderline adjustment with schizoid features—unless corrective emotional therapy in Alpert's (1959) sense could be instituted. We felt that he had no valid footing in the formation of his core identity; nor were the boundaries between id and ego and between self and object world structured firmly enough and sufficiently cathected with neutralized energy. Furthermore, there was not enough neutralized energy available for ego development; thus, the establishment of libidinal object constancy was also questionable. The possibility of secondary identity formation, by true ego identifications and internalization, was greatly reduced.

Our prediction *now* is that Jay will be compelled to develop as an adolescent and as an adult, as he has already started to do at age seven, "as if" mechanisms, in order to be able to function with his "false self" in his social environment. Suffice it to say that Jay reminded me of several patients in analysis, whose central problem was their incessant search for their place in life—their search for an identity (Ross 1967).

He reminded me especially of one analytic patient, whom I had treated as a child abroad and in his adolescence in this country. Charlie's developmental history I could reconstruct with fair accuracy through the material that his intermittent analyses have yielded, and with the aid of my intimate knowledge of his parents' personality.

I could reconstruct a very long symbiotic-parasitic phase with a narcissistic mother, who was highly seductive yet could accept Charlie only if she could regard him as a continuation of her own narcissistic self. She had no regard for the little boy as an individual in his own right. She constantly needed babies to cuddle and bore infants up to her climacterium.

After the symbiotic-parasitic relationship, the mother suddenly abandoned Charlie to his own devices, at the beginning of the third year. Subsequently, there was a strong mirroring identification on Charlie's part with his father. The latter, however, suffered from a paralyzing depression, and went into seclusion when Charlie was in his third year. This coincided with the time when the mother gave birth to one of her many babies. Thus, *both* primary love objects were unavailable to Charlie for object cathexis and for true ego identification, in the fateful second eighteen months of life.

Charlie never achieved libidinal object constancy. Instead, his identification with his mother was a total one—so much so that when his mother, while taking him by car to the kindergarten, accidentally hit a man, Charlie behaved as if *he* was the one who had *deliberately* hurt the man. He refused to go on to school: he was afraid that the police would arrest *him*. From then on, he insisted on wearing dark glasses to hide behind. He became intolerably destructive, and attacked his mother by throwing objects at her, obviously aiming at her eyes. At the same time, he developed a phobia of fire and a fear of going blind.

His symptoms were understood, in child analysis, as an attempt to reexternalize—to eject—the dangerous maternal introject. In view of the unavailability of the father figure, however, this left Charlie utterly depleted of object cathexis.

Between his child analysis and his early adolescence, I lost sight of Charlie for quite a while as he and his family continued to live abroad.

Charles was sixteen years old when his analysis was resumed, here in the States. During the interval he appeared to have undergone a profound personality change. The maturational and/or developmental process had changed, indeed, had transformed the exuberant, aggressive, and irrepressible Charlie of the prelatency and early latency period into a subdued, overcompliant, utterly passive and submissive youngster with a well-hidden cruel streak, which he tried strenuously to conceal even from himself.

He had a lofty—and not internalized—ego ideal, and imitated his father, parroting his sayings. Even though he seemed to try ever so hard to extricate himself from the actual influence of his mother, his analytic material revealed that he was forever searching for the "good" need-satisfying mother of his symbiotic phase! Yet, at the same time, he dreaded reengulfment in symbiosis. As soon as he found an object, he arranged somehow to lose her, out of fear that she would engulf him and that he would thus "lose himself." This was the same mechanism, I believe, with which he had so strikingly fought to eject the maternal introject, at the ages of five and six.

For lack of secondary—that is to say, true identity formation—through ego identifications, Charles seemed to be compelled to search for his identity to fill the painful void, the inner emptiness, about which he continually complained.

He set himself the goal—as several of these borderline cases do, either covertly or overtly—of becoming famous, or at least important. His quite good performance, however, measured up very unfavorably against his lofty ego ideal, with the result that Charles was left with an excruciatingly low self-esteem. For this discrepancy, Charles blamed his mother because she was the one who had made him believe, in his early childhood, that he was "a genius."

In adolescence, then, Charles displayed a peculiarly affectless state. He lacked the charm that Helene Deutsch and others have found to be one of the characteristics of true "as if" personalities (Ross 1967).

He repeatedly changed his allegiance to people and to groups, because he never did feel comfortable when he came close to them: *he could only long for them from a distance.* This intense longing was the strongest affect I have ever seen in Charles.

Like Greenson's patient (1958), Charles was continually seeking the company of others; he was quite incapable of being alone. *But he was also incapable of being "à deux" for any length of time!* What Charles kept seeking was experiences that would reunite him with the lost symbiotic mother, whom he had never renounced in the intrapsychic sense. His affectlessness seemed to be a deep defense against his anxiety, to ward off the feeling of emptiness at the loss of a part of himself, at a time when the loss of the symbiotic mother was still equivalent to losing part of the self.

I would like to close with a quotation from material during Charles's adolescent analysis. He complained: "I don't feel like anything. I start thinking a lot; and when I think, I am not very happy." At another time, he said: "I try to find out in how many ways we are alike with any person—anybody—but particularly with people I like and respect. First I did this with my parents, with their older friends, and now I do it usually with girls. I try to find out what kind of sports and songs they like."

Charles tried to compensate for the cathectic void by identification of the mirroring type. By literally mirroring others, and also himself, he tried to learn how to feel, how to have emotions. Here are some of the associations he made in analysis: "When I dance with a girl, she becomes just like all the other girls. I want to refresh myself that *she is the one who dances with me, and yet that she is still kind and sweet.* I put my head back to look at her face, and into her eyes." In another analytic hour Charles said: "I dance around by the mirror-glass door where I can look at my own face—see what I look like, *from the point of view of others;* and also I catch a glimpse of her face, to see whether she is enjoying the dance. One thing I notice—even if I enjoy dancing, I don't look too excited, so one cannot say whether I enjoy it. So perhaps this is not the way to find out about how the girl feels either."

This brief excerpt from Charles's analysis shows how he struggled with his lack of empathy and his lack of genuine affect. One can also see that he is searching incessantly for the girl who is still *kind* and *sweet*—the "good" symbiotic mother—whom he can reflect and whose eyes will reflect love for him.

SUMMARY

I have brought these clinical sketches of Jay and Charles, because I felt that these patients illustrated—through their developmental failure—the significance of normal symbiosis, and the crucial necessity of gradual individuation, particularly in the vulnerable second and third years of life.

In Jay's case we observed this developmental failure *in statu nascendi*. His traumatization occurred in the second year, and, as a result, *both* his reality constancy (Frosch 1966) and his object constancy suffered.

In Charles's case, we could fairly accurately reconstruct through analytic material the severe traumata, at vulnerable, nodal points of his separation-individuation process, particularly toward the end of it, when libidinal object constancy becomes established.

The fact that this traumatization occurred later than Jay's—in Charles's third year—is perhaps the reason why Charles's reality constancy remained fairly intact.

Both cases had to fall back to the primary mode—the "mirroring" kind of maintenance of identity—because of the failure of true identificatory and internalization processes.

Chapter 7

OBSERVATIONS ON ADAPTATION AND DEFENSE
IN STATU NASCENDI

[1968]

We address ourselves to the relationship between two of the four interdependent mental states of equilibrium described by Hartmann (1939)—the equilibrium between the individual and the environment, the young child's "preparedness for *average expectable* environmental situations and for *average expectable* internal conflicts" (p. 55). Although we realize that defensive processes may have the double function of warding off instinctual impulses and of serving adaptation to the external world (p. 50), there are nevertheless many adaptive phenomena whose function is broader and which do not serve a primarily defensive purpose.

Previous papers have discussed the fact that the "average expectable environment" to which the infant must at first adapt is the symbiotic milieu that includes the symbiotic partner in the undifferentiated stage. It might be said that during this phase the innate rhythms of the infant adjust automatically to those of the mother, and vice versa (Greene 1958).[1] Later, in the separation-individuation

1. Research into infantile psychosis suggests the hypothesis that early extreme incompatibilities may have existed in this respect in some cases of early infantile psychosis.

In collaboration with John B. McDevitt. M.D.

phase, the adaptive process is determined by the interaction between the child's innate and maturing equipment and the complex stimuli and responses received from his mother through the intricate function of her "mothering." The child's experiences over the course of time, on the basis of his drive and ego endowment, lead to more or less successful adaptation. His adaptive style contributes to his character traits, as do his defense behaviors. We have observed in our research the process by which these behaviors gradually become internalized as more or less successful defense mechanisms.

From birth to the end of the symbiotic phase, the child's development, including the adaptive process, is dependent primarily on the care which he passively receives from his mother. Of equal importance, from the second half of the first year, are the child's active efforts to obtain "good enough mothering" from his "ordinarily devoted mother" coinciding with his beginning differentiation. This is the first subphase of separation-individuation (SPII:3, SPII:4, SPII:5).

Our research procedure has been bifocal in providing (on the basis of at least twice-weekly observations) information about, first, the mother's functioning, particularly the degree and quality of her emotional availability to her child and the child's ability to make use of her throughout the separation-individuation process; and second, the behavior patterns of the child with respect to the changing state of his relatedness to his mother, as well as to the stage of his ego and psychosexual development. Of special importance to our investigation has been the child's active approach and passive appeal behavior, and his reactions to the structured separation experiences of our study. These provided behavioral data which facilitated our understanding of the intrapsychic processes underlying separation-individuation.

During the symbiotic phase and at the beginning of the individuation process, the mother is the one who chooses the degree and rhythm of closeness and separateness. From about the sixth month, once the child's coordination enables him to do so and particularly when he is able to crawl, he begins to determine the degree of closeness with and separateness from mother by means of his active distancing and approach behaviors. Thus, in the practicing period (ten to eighteen months), the child begins to explore beyond the threshold of our nursery, into a corridor, and sometimes by chance into an adjoining room. These first ventures into the toddler room are usually tentative and brief, but some babies even before toddler age begin to remain there for increasing lengths of time. By the beginning of the third year most senior toddlers are more or less firmly established in the toddler room. In other words, the accessibility of the infant room to the toddler room, and vice versa, through the corridor, permits us to observe systematically the frequent back-and-forth patterns between the child and his mother. Weekly interviews with the mother in a nearby room provide a passive separation experience for the child. His changing reactions to these brief separations are recorded in detail by participant and nonparticipant observers and periodically filmed as well.[2]

This preliminary contribution of a research project still in progress we hope will afford a glimpse into the workshop of psychoanalysts doing observational developmental research. We present a few selected behavioral phenomena observed in the early mother-child interaction, which we believe represent aspects of the obligatory adaptive process on the one hand, and precursors of intrapsychic defense mechanisms on the other.[3]

PHENOMENA OF DIFFERENTIATION

Typical behavior of the lap baby, such as molding and stiffening of the body, seems to facilitate libidinization of the surface of the body and thus serves delimitation of the body-self boundaries. However, in some infants this typical behavior may be exaggerated in the direction of increased molding or increased stiffening of the body and pushing away. Such behavior suggests a defensive warding off of symbiotic closeness or, the opposite, a disinclination to differentiate.

2. Many of the phenomena discussed were illustrated by films when this paper was presented at meetings.
3. We shall not review the existing literature on adaptation and on the prototypes and precursors of defense mechanisms.

Thus, even at the peak of the symbiotic phase (*SP*II:3), the differentiating infant's rudimentary ego is progressing against the regressive pull of symbiosis. Before clear differentiation of the ego has taken place, and throughout the period of the most rapid structuralization and organization process, particularly toward demarcation of the body image, behavioral phenomena seem to indicate conflicting tendencies toward differentiation and, concomitantly, toward symbiotic fusion with the object. The need to ward off envelopment in exclusive symbiosis with the mother can be observed as early as the fifth month. Such behavior not only includes stiffening rather than molding of the body when held but also turning, looking away, pushing away from the mother's body, or other gestural and affectomotor behavior (Spock 1963). These are sometimes accompanied by expressions of unpleasure and/or an increased attention cathexis directed beyond the confines of the mother-child dyad. Spock states: "The sixth- or seventh-month baby strives to outgrow the symbiotic enveloped relationship. . . . The child's developing nature is now obliging him to detach himself from his mother." The precious transitional object (Winnicott 1953) and especially the fetishlike adherence to the nighttime bottle are indications that displacement of libido onto the transitional object are important both as a defense against reengulfment in symbiosis and as a facilitation toward individuation and therefore structuralization and adaptation. In other words, we might say that adaptation and defense have common roots.

An example of exaggerated early defensive warding-off behavior is the case of Emmett. At eight to ten months, he showed a marked avoidance of eye engagement at close range with his mother as well as with others, although he responded appropriately at a distance. Evidence that this behavior can be described as defensive is the fact that visually and otherwise he explored with curiosity and competently manipulated objects in his inanimate environment, and that when approached slowly on his own visual level from a distance, he explored with interest the observer's mouth visually and tactilely while in his mother's lap.

Our knowledge of the mother—not only from observation of her mothering of Emmett but also of her mothering of her thirty-three-month-older first son, Stuart—provided us with some understanding of Emmett's warding-off behavior. The mother's inordinate symbiotic-parasitic needs and smothering body closeness (for example, she insisted on breast-feeding Stuart to sixteen and a half months and Emmette well into the second year) seemed to be related to Emmett's need to avoid proximal eye engagement, as if he were overwhelmed and needed to extricate himself visually and otherwise from the excessive symbiotic relationship. Could it be that the oversaturation with body and oral contact (for instance, hourly offering of the breast throughout the night) had to be counteracted by avoidance of visual perceptual contact? An additional contributing factor was the mother's intrusive and overbearing manner: she continually talked "at" Emmett though she seldom looked into his eyes. (A similar situation existed with Stuart. At the onset of crawling he deliberately avoided his mother and, in fact, if there were a choice he invariably went to the observer, the "other-than-mother.")

By thirteen months Emmett's avoidance of proximal eye engagement had markedly diminished. We would assume that this occurred with the libido-economic shifts that occur in the practicing subphase. The symbiotic tie had become less strong and the libido and attention cathexis had become more outwardly directed.

Another phenomenon of differentiation on the way to individuation is visual and tactile exploration of the face. This is the opposite of the warding-off behavior of Emmett. We saw this in Emmett in rudimentary form; he was able, when carefully approached by the observer, to explore his mouth. In doing so, he showed an individually characteristic pattern of a generally observable and important adaptive phenomenon which we encounter at the end of the third quarter and in the fourth quarter of the first year.

VISUAL AND TACTILE EXPLORATION

Once the infant is sufficiently individuated to recognize visually and tactilely the mother as his partner in the symbiotic dyad, he then turns with more or less wonderment and apprehension (commonly called "stranger reaction") to a prolonged visual and tactile exploration and study of the faces of others at close range. He seems to compare and check the features—appearance, feel, contour—of the face of the stranger with his mother's face and with his inner image of her.[4]

In children where the symbiotic phase is optimal and confident expectation maximal, curiosity and wonderment are the predominant elements of this inspection of strangers. In children whose basic trust is less than optimal, there may be an abrupt change to acute stranger anxiety; or there may be a prolonged period of mild stranger reaction which interferes with normal inspective behavior. The phenomenon and the factors underlying its variations are, we believe, an important aspect of and clue to evaluation of the evolution of the libidinal object, of socialization, and of progress toward eventual object constancy.

This phenomenon was observed and studied in Linda, who was fortunate in having had an especially gratifying and close relationship with her mother and who displayed at a very early age great interest in social contacts. To illustrate, we shall describe Linda's behavior at nine months of age when we observed her after her return with her mother following the summer vacation, a time when we would have expected her to be more wary of "relative stangers."

Soon after arrival, the mother placed Linda in a crib in a separate room for her nap. However, since Linda showed no signs of napping, one of us approached her. She smiled and indicated that she wanted to be taken out of the crib. When lifted from the crib she looked puzzled, although interested, as if only then was she aware that the observer was not her mother. She began to stroke the observer's face with her fingers, especially the nose and lips, and pinched her cheek—all the while accompanying her tactile exploration with her eyes and particularly looking with interest into the eyes of the observer. Her facial expression during this time was strikingly characteristic: sober, studious, and curious, but completely unafraid. When she heard her mother's voice from a distance, she seemed

4. Following Sylvia Brody, we have called this "customs inspection."

electrified and turned in the direction from which the voice came. Even before the mother appeared, Linda was smiling with anticipation, and when her mother took her into her arms her happiness was boundless. Linda did not need to inspect the familiar face of her mother; instead, in her exuberance and excitement she clutched her mother's neck so intensely that the mother cried out in pain. The observer then held her arms toward Linda, again inviting her to come to her. Unexpectedly, Linda did so without hesitation, revealing again her strong basic trust. At first Linda's smile persisted, carrying over from her reunion with her mother, but suddenly as she realized that the observer was not her mother, the sober-faced visual and tactile inspection began once again. When handed to a male observer, she readily accepted the change and repeated her study. But when offered the opportunity to go to a third observer, she demurred, not because of fear but because she had not yet completed her study of the second observer's face.

We have learned a great deal not only from Linda's behavior and development but also from comparing them with children of the same age, particularly with her sixteen-month-older brother, Peter, at about the same age. Peter's rapport with the mother had not been as satisfactory. In contrast to Linda's basic trust and minimal stranger anxiety at any age, by seven months Peter had developed marked stranger anxiety which lasted for several months. At that age, when he was approached with the utmost caution and mildest overtures as he stood on the chair in which his mother sat, he looked at the observer askance and was somewhat bewildered although quite interested. He felt the observer's arm, which rested on the chair next to him, patted it, and then looked at the face and the Gestalt to whom the arm belonged. His lower lip quivered, then, while still looking at the observer's face, he suddenly burst into tears and turned away.

From these and other less clear examples, we conclude that:

1. Visual and tactile inspection (of the human face in particular) is a characteristic complex behavioral phenomenon which is in the service of the infant's cognitive and emotional adaptive development at this age. It occurs at the time when others are recognized as different although similar to mother; that is, when the child has a

need to learn about persons other than the mother, and when he begins to recognize the mother as separate from himself, as a uniquely important and specific individual entity.

2. Within this phenomenon we can recognize confident expectation and its opposite, stranger reaction. In these observations the child's inspective studies would be considered adaptive behavior, the emotional concomitant of which is confident expectation. Stranger reaction, although still adaptive, would contain a strong defensive element. Although having different meanings, both the warding-off behavior of Emmett and the acute stranger reaction of Peter could be considered precursors to defense mechanisms such as denial, avoidance, restriction of the ego, repression, and reaction-formation.

Repeated inspections of persons other than the mother add to the child's adaptively useful differential image of his world. Toward the end of the first year this image consists of a much wider variety of familiar and less familiar animate and inanimate objects, and many elements which may be in varying degrees either directly related to the inner representation of the mother or recognized as belonging to mother, or as clearly "strange" individuals. With the beginning of this discrimination and coinciding with the specific attachment to the mother, we observe another interesting phenomenon.

NARCISSISTIC REGRESSIVE PHENOMENON[5]

A particularly interesting adaptive behavior that can also readily become defensive is a characteristic of the infant from the second half of the first year, after the specific tie to the mother has been established. This phenomenon, which continues with modifications until the child is able to function comfortably without mother's actual physical presence, is a characteristic response on the part of the child to brief separations from the mother. For example, we have observed that after the mother leaves the room for an interview, the child withdraws into himself, apparently concentrating on the memory of the previous state of oneness or closeness with mother; he

5. We have descriptively termed this phenomenon "low-keyedness."

seems to have a diminished interest in his surroundings, animate and inanimate. He may or may not appear bewildered. He seems to be preoccupied with his own thoughts, fantasies, or inner images, and endeavors to maintain his emotional balance by diminution of activity, by regression in relatedness, by underresponsiveness, by a reduction in his perceptual intake. This reaction to mother's brief absence is suggestive of an abortive and miniature anaclitic depression. It appears to be not only a reaction to being left by mother but also a defense of an internal libido-economic position. In this sense it resembles the conservation withdrawal in monkeys described by Kaufman and Rosenblum (1968).

If the child's equilibrium in this situation is precarious, as it often is, the active approach of an adult, even smiling at the child, may cause an end to this suspense—this quasi calmness before the storm—and distressed crying and other affectomotor behavior will ensue. The intruding adult, recognized as being "other" than mother, disturbs the precariously maintained adaptive and defensive balance. On the other hand, if the adult is quietly available to the child without intruding, this availability may offer comfort for which he may or may not reach out. Upon the mother's return, the child may cry even if he had not before; only then does he appear to realize acutely and more clearly the state of unpleasure he has experienced during her absence and permits himself to let go of the defense of low-keyedness.

Somewhat later in the child's development, as the representation of the love object becomes more distinct and intrapsychically available, and therefore sustains his emotional equilibrium, he may actively seek adults as substitutes and may turn his interest to play, first as a relief from longing and later as adaptation on a higher ego and socialization level.

To recapitulate, it is our assumption that the child, struggling to maintain the inner condition that exists when mother is in the room with him, must shut out affective and perceptual claims from other sources during her physical absence (Rubinfine 1961). We may say that this reaction is a narcissistic regressive phenomenon in the service of the development of the ego.

Linda's behavior at one year is a striking example of the adaptive phenomenon of this reaction. On a particular morning she was very cheerful prior to her mother's leaving the room for an interview. As her most familiar observer was absent, she was at first attended by a less familiar worker who reported that Linda gradually became sad, listless, slow-moving, and showed lack of interest and poise. Although she did not cry, she would not smile at the worker's friendly and passive overtures. She was about to lose her emotional equilibrium. At this point one of us took Linda quietly into her arms. Linda's posture and facial expression, particularly the look in her eyes, indicated inward-directed preoccupation with inner images or feeling states rather than her usual strong perceptual interest in the outside. (In such situations, it is necessary for the adult to be as unobtrusive as possible, to be merely anaclitically passively available.) From experience with other normal infants we knew that a smile or any active approach would be felt as an intrusion; it would upset Linda's equilibrium and she would burst into tears. Although she could not accept the observer as a substitute for her mother, after a short time she was able to use her to regress into a half-sleeping, quasi-symbiotic state. Her body relaxed, she put her finger into the observer's mouth, put her arms around her shoulders, and fell asleep. When placed in the crib, she awoke, cried, and required her transitional object, a diaper, for comfort. The change in her mood on her mother's return was striking. It is our impression that these reactions are an obligatory developmental phenomenon that is definitely adaptive during a certain age range but may become maladaptive if excessive and prolonged.

This phenomenon is seen in many variations and can in some children eventually and imperceptibly develop into a depressive mood, particularly by the end of the second or during the third year of life. We feel it is a precursor to depressive moods and is very much related to object loss and the loss of love. If it is mild or moderate at the appropriate age, and depending on the particular circumstances, it may be considered adaptive in that energy is conserved and the image of the mother is maintained and consolidated. However, if excessive or prolonged, it can become both a symptom of a depressive nature and a defensive behavior.

Similar behavioral precursors of adaptation and defense are the biphasic behaviors called ambitendency.

AMBITENDENCY[6]

Ambitendency appears to be a surface manifestation of the child's coping with obligatory developmental conflicts, indicating steps on the way to intrapsychic compromise solutions, and thus to internalization. It demonstrates with particular clarity, and thus is a paradigm of, the common root of adaptation and defense.

In the spontaneous behavior of the junior toddler, one can often see actions that can be interpreted as the result of two opposite impulses in rapid succession—smiling and crying, stroking and hitting, kissing and biting. This is true also of more complex biphasic behavior which does not alternate in such rapid succession but is perhaps aimed at cancelling out, undoing the first phase, and finally, coping with the conflict by nonbiphasic internalized defense mechanisms—for instance, denial, reaction-formation, or turning into the opposite.

The vicissitudes of this ambitendency are interesting to pursue. They appear to be a kind of experimentation of the ego in the direction of integration. One of the clearly adaptive manifestations of ambitendency is the obligatory alternation of the typical approach and distancing behavior to and from mother of the junior toddler. However, the same degree of ambitendency may also be a precursor of heightened ambivalence, giving rise to exaggerated approach and clinging, to distancing and ignoring, as well as to longer than optimal and somewhat facile splitting of the "good" and "bad" objects. The latter is the precursor and part of the mechanism of projection which, if persistent and augmented, becomes the basis for maladaptive defense mechanisms.

Hence, ambitendent behaviors may be seen as: (1) promoting the integrative function of the ego; (2) as the model on which heightened

6. The term *ambitendency* (like autism also) was first used by Bleuler in an entirely different context—not of development but of psychopathology.

ambivalence is based; and (3) when acquiring a maladaptive quality, as giving rise to mechanisms of splitting and of projection.

Ambitendency is a concept parallel and related to the mechanism of splitting of the object world. The mechanism consists of splitting of the "good" and "bad" object representations, and of separating and partly isolating from each other the respective libidinal and aggressive drives. It does not necessarily involve the pathological process of splitting of the self-representation. We have observed such splitting of the "good" and "bad" object representation in children who have had an unsatisfactory relationship with their mothers during the first two years of life. In one of our mother-child pairs, we observed a too-exclusive parasitic relationship; in another there was an emotional unavailability on the part of the mother. In both cases, the child's basic mood was angry and depressive.

For such children the smallest, most routine separations are reacted to by an immediate splitting of the object representations. Libido is displaced onto the image of the absent mother, while the mother substitute and particularly any unfamiliar adult present draws upon herself the entire negative affect. It seems that in her absence, the "good" mother image can be preserved against the ensuing destructive aggression only by splitting off the "bad" image and displacing the aggression onto persons other than the mother. But when the real mother reappears, the entire ambivalence may become centered upon her once again.

CLINGING VERSUS TURNING AWAY FROM MOTHER

From our studies so far it would seem that the adaptive use of ambitendency depends to a great extent on the course and outcome of the symbiotic phase and the first subphase of separation-individuation (differentiation) of the mother-child relationship. Previous publications (SPII:1, SPII:2) have described the child's normal need to reestablish periodically contact with the mother, first by physical "refueling,"[7] later by visual and auditory contact, and

7. As the child, through the maturation of his locomotor apparatus, begins to venture farther away from the mother's feet, he is often so absorbed in his own activity that he seems oblivious to the mother for long periods of time. However, he returns to the mother periodically, seeming to need her physical proximity. This phenomenon was termed "emotional refueling" (M. Furer 1964).

finally by emotional, vocal, and verbal rapprochement. These phenomena occur typically in an atmosphere of the usual emotional availablity of the mother, at a time when the child is moving away from her in order to explore wider segments of reality.

In situations of less or more than optimal emotional availability of the mother, or in cases of unpredictability, confident expectation does not develop into what Erikson has called "basic trust." Heightened ambivalence and/or excessive separation anxiety ensues and may be observed at first in the back-and-forth movements of mother and child. These contacts may be fraught with anxiety and aggression; that is, moved from the fairly neutralized ego sphere into the conflictual sphere of the ego. In the observable behavior of the child, as well as in his first vocal and verbal utterances, the defensive aspect becomes predominant. Here we have in mind the exaggerations of behaviors like shadowing and darting away from the mother, characteristic of the third subphase from eighteen to twenty-four months and well into the third year (*SP*II:1).

Clinging behavior interferes with the child's normal adaptive and enriching experiences with his animate and inanimate environment. Contrariwise, the child may consistently reduce contacts and interaction with his mother, avoiding and ignoring her, literally denying the mother's presence, seeming to look through her. As an example, when asked in the toddler room, "Where is Mommy?" the child may not react or answer. Many children use such denial in a mild form; they are increasingly involved in fantasy play and with toys in order to cope with separation from the mother in progressive and adaptive ways. But if denial is massive and continual, it becomes maladaptive.

As early as fourteen months we saw in Peter's relation to his mother the beginning of excessive avoiding and denying the mother's presence and a veering away from her when he had seemingly started out to go to her. During the same developmental period we noticed marked unhappiness and narcissistic regressive reactions to the mother's brief absences. This occurred prior to the birth of his sister, Linda, when Peter was sixteen months old. After Linda's birth, Peter clung to his mother for a while but then, after a brief period of only veering away from her, he showed increased avoidance and rejection of the mother. This behavior persisted with variations throughout the third and into the fourth subphase of the separation process. As Peter functioned independently in the toddler room, he seemed to have no need of his mother. He played well, with good use of his imagination and his autonomous ego functions; but he appeared subdued, sober, and at times depressed, and unlike the other toddlers, he did not seek out his mother from time to time, especially when fatigued or in need of bodily care. On the contrary, Peter unmistakably avoided his mother and when her name was mentioned he did not seem to listen. He exhibited an absence of appropriate affect and a denial of any pleasure when his mother returned to the room; this sometimes caused the mother to complain, "Peter doesn't care."

For some time Peter seemed to be completely involved in his fantasy play and showed little interest in the people around him. He was far too introverted for his age and lacked the vivaciousness and "motor luxury" characteristic of his age (Homburger 1923). Denial of the disappointing and ambivalently cathected inner image of the mother seemed to have hampered Peter in working through the experience of separateness. Only gradually did he begin to acknow-ledge her presence and occasionally to go to her when he experienced need or longing. This is again at variance with most of the other toddlers observed; they go readily to their mothers, talk about her whereabouts, and thus openly indicate that she is missed. It is interesting to note, however, that Peter, though more slowly than the other toddlers, gradually worked through and accepted the fact of separateness.

THE ONSET OF REPRESSION

Peter's behavior and play activity are also illustrative of the development of the classical defense mechanism of repression. He had been an active and alert infant who had manifested much ambitendency. Small sadomasochistic actions were characteristic of both his and his mother's behavior. At sixteen months when his sister, Linda, was born, if not prevented he acted on the impulse to hit and bite her; yet, at the same time or in rapid alternation, he liked to touch, stroke, and pet her, and seemed to be fascinated by her.

Slowly but within six weeks, one could see week-by-week a definite change in Peter's behavior toward the baby. At first, although he would still raise his arm, he would inhibit the action of hitting; finally we saw the twenty-month-old boy only petting his sister. The mother who had earlier felt that she could not safely leave him alone with the baby after a few months had no hesitation in doing so. It is reasonable to assume that the mother's admonitions through the fear of loss of love had become internalized.

Peter's behavior, and information from the mother, suggested that repression had occurred in the sense that Peter was no longer aware of his anger and that his aggression had been turned into affection. The earlier ambitendency, indicating both aggression and libidinal interest, gave way to an internalized conflict, the resolution of which left no sign of direct aggressive behavior. Hence, we conclude that repression had occurred. Something that had been there, that one could expect to be there, was no longer discernible; it was replaced by a change in behavior indicating that the mechanism of repression was aided and maintained by the additional use of the mechanisms of reaction-formation and reversal of affect.

Although the behavior described here may be considered a precursor of repression, from our observations and knowledge of Peter's development we see no reason not to speak, even at this early age, of the defense mechanism of repression.[8] Peter, who had been a conspicuously aggressive infant and small toddler, became and continued to be a more than optimally reflective, subdued, and passive little boy during the first three-quarters of his third year.

In his clash with the external world, Peter internalized the mother's prohibitions. His greater than average aggression became muted by repression which, before our own eyes, was reenforced by reaction-formation and by turning into the opposite. In the individuation of Peter, we could follow the establishment of these defense mechanisms which, on the one hand, warded off aggressive

8. As early as 1935, Bornstein described early repression in the case of Lisa.

impulses, and, on the other hand, modified Peter's behavior, including his relationships with people.

As a consequence, there was a marked change in the pattern of his adaptation to his mother as well as to others, and he also displayed a different basic mood. Thus, we were able to see in a sixteen- to twenty-month-old child: (1) the common roots of defense and adaptation; (2) the early internalization of a conflict; (3) the establishment of classical defense mechanisms, as well as precursors to superego development; and (4) the manner in which defensive processes may have the double function of warding off instinctual impulses and, at the same time, of serving adaptation to the external world.

From our observations we have come to expect not only continual change but also sudden spurts in development. Thus, we were not completely surprised when in the last quarter of the third year, at the advent of the phallic phase, Peter's behavior changed. He became cavalierlike and friendly toward his mother, even though at the same time he was quite self-assertive and independent. He also showed signs of the beginnings of oedipal behavior, objecting to intimacies between his parents. We have every reason to believe that this change resulted from the flux of developmental energy generated by the phallic phase (E. Kris 1955).

Despite the described variations in Peter's behavior, we believe that it is within the range of normal. In contrast, we would like to describe phenomenologically somewhat similar behavior (for example, ignoring of the mother) in Harriet. However, it should be noted that the mechanisms underlying Harriet's behavior deviated from the norm and, we believe, were prognostically more malignant.

Excessive narcissism could be observed in Harriet. As early as at eight months, she consoled herself and enjoyed nothing more than rocking back and forth before a large mirror in an autoerotic fashion, watching herself and thus reenforcing the kinesthetic sensations of her body reflected in the mirror. Her preference for inanimate objects over people was striking. Her identifications were with dolls, or at best, with the family dog with which she shared her food and which she mirrored in many ways; she would often urinate by lifting her leg or she would try to retrieve objects inside the playpen with her mouth. This mechanism of anthropomorphizing the dog, so to speak, or animating the doll, and particularly the erotic overstimulation, led to defensive behavior that observers described as avoidance, suspiciousness, coyness, obliqueness, withdrawal, and inhibition of approach and appeal. There were signs of a defense which have been described as deanimation (*SPI*:6, *SPI*:11) and of massive denial.

From the beginning of her life the interaction between Harriet and her mother was anything but satisfactory. The mother lacked empathy as well as the capacity for emotional modulation, creating that sort of symbiotic atmosphere in which ministrations were neither in response to cues nor spontaneous—they were dispensed mechanically, doled out, as it were. Cuddling and, later on, quite grossly sexualized petting were "bestowed" upon the sixteen- to twenty-month-old child unpredictably and impulsively. In her mother's words, Harriet was being conditioned to be a mother to her doll, because the mother herself was expecting another baby. The not-yet fourteen-month-old little girl seemed to oblige mechanically.

CONCLUSIONS

We have attempted to describe, within our psychoanalytic genetic frame of reference, some surface behavioral phenomena that we have observed. These appear to fit into this frame of reference and thus tend to verify the psychoanalytic hypotheses arrived at through reconstruction and extrapolation.

To paraphrase Fenichel's words when he appraised Anna Freud's (1936) classic, *The Ego and the Mechanisms of Defense,* psychoanalysts, even when they investigate the psychic surface, remain nonetheless depth psychologists. Further, we believe that psychoanalytically oriented work of the kind we are conducting demonstrates how the surface differentiates itself from the depths, how the individuating infant-toddler emerges out of the hazy orbit of his symbiotically fused existence, and finally, how these observations of behavioral and transactional phenomena can be related to intrapsychic events or processes.

A few examples of surface phenomena—typical and general

behavior as well as individually varied behavior—have been presented, but we can do no more than suggest their relevance to character formation with regard to the adaptive aspects of internalization, organization, and structuralization. Some examples of the modes in which these phenomena relate to the defensive organization of the ego have been given. We have attempted to demonstrate, by way of prototypes of our observational research data, how these data provide referents for such processes as structure formation and defense mechanisms. It has been illustrated, we believe, how these structures come about as a result of the action upon the infant's and toddler's innate givens by the mothering partner, the most important single factor of the average expectable environment. A certain degree of extrapolation and reconstruction is, of course, necessary in order to form psychoanalytically meaningful hypotheses about these observational data.

We agree with Loewald, Lampl-de Groot, and Tartakoff that the organizing—more specifically, the internalizing—progressive developmental processes and their resultant structures are far broader in scope and significance than the defensive processes were believed to be in their original, limited, and clinical sense.

Some of the behavioral sequences discussed may appear from the start to serve adaptation; some serve a primarily defensive function, or may be initially adaptive and later, through a change of function, become true defense mechanisms of the ego, and vice versa. Such defense mechanisms as repression, reaction-formation, denial, and turning into the opposite have been observed *in statu nascendi* in Peter, Harriet, and other children.

It should be stressed that phenomena such as learning the mother's and others' faces, the libido-economic regulatory function of narcissistic regressive reactions, the alternation of approach and distancing behavior, even ambitendency to a degree, like the manifestations of play activity, serve primarily adaptive, integrative, and organizing purposes. We believe that it is an important step toward clarification of psychoanalytic theory if these processes are kept apart—are not equated or confused with and are as clearly distinguished as possible—from the defensive functions of the ego.

Although we keep in mind Anna Freud's statement that "the

defensive measures of the ego against the id are carried out silently and invisibly," we feel that, under the conditions of a study such as ours, a good many steps in the process by which these measures come into being can be traced.

We also hope that observational studies of normal early development may further contribute to those which Ernst Kris envisaged— namely, to furnish data and thus provide answers to such questions as genetic and adaptive aspects of the total personality and to psychoanalysis as a general psychology.

Chapter 8

ON THE FIRST THREE SUBPHASES OF THE
SEPARATION-INDIVIDUATION PROCESS

[1972]

I have based this presentation upon two thoughts of Freud—two pillars of psychoanalytic metapsychology. The first is that, at the time of his biological birth, the human being is brought into the world in an immature state. (This is due to the fact that the over-development of his CNS requires a large cranial cage.) Hence he is *at first absolutely,* and remains later on—even "unto the grave"—*relatively* dependent on a mother.

The second Freudian tenet, which is probably a result of the first, is his emphasis that *object relationship*—i.e., one person's endowing another with object libido—is the most reliable single factor by which we are able to determine the level of mental health on the one hand and, on the other, the extent of the therapeutic potential.

Object relationship develops on the basis of, and *pari passu* with, differentiation from the normal mother-infant dual unity, which Therese Benedek (1949) and I, independently of each other, have designated as the *normal phase of human symbiosis (SPI:6).*

"Growing up" entails a gradual growing away from the normal state of human symbiosis, of "one-ness" with the mother. This process is much slower in the emotional and psychic area than in the physical one. The transition from lap-babyhood to toddlerhood goes through gradual steps of a separation-individuation process, greatly facilitated on the one hand by the autonomous development of the ego and, on the other hand, by identificatory mechanisms of different sorts. This growing away process is—as Zetzel, Winnicott and also Sandler and Joffe indicate in their work—a lifelong mourning process. *Inherent in every new step of independent functioning is a minimal threat of object loss.*

Following my work with a few psychotic latency children, whom I tried to help with the traditional child analytic method in Vienna back in the 1930s—and on the basis of engrams left in my mind as a pediatrician and head of a well-baby clinic, after having studied tics and early infantile psychosis from the early 1940s on—I decided to look more closely at the *fountainhead*—to examine the phenomena that those two Freudian thoughts I mentioned earlier entail. I decided to study the earliest average mother-infant and mother-toddler interaction *in situ.*

The biological birth of the human infant and the psychological birth of the individual are not coincident in time. The former is a dramatic and readily observable, well-circumscribed event; the latter, a slowly unfolding intrapsychic process.

For the more or less normal adult, the experience of being both fully "in" and at the same time basically separate from the "world out there" is among the givens of life that are taken for granted. Consciousness of self and absorption without awareness of self are the two polarities between which we move, with varying ease and with varying degrees of alternation or simultaneity. This too is the result of a slowly unfolding process. In particular, this development takes place in relation to *(a)* one's own body, and *(b)* the principal representative of the world, as the infant experiences it, namely, the primary love object. *As is the case with any intrapsychic process, this one reverberates throughout the life cycle.* It is never finished; it can always become reactivated; new phases of the life cycle witness new derivatives of the earliest process still at work (cf. Erikson 1968). However, the principal psychological achievements in this process take place, as we see it, in the period from about four or five to thirty or thirty-six months of age, a period that we refer to—at Dr. Annemarie Weil's helpful suggestion—as the *separation-individuation phase.*[1]

1. Personal communication.

In the course of our rather unsystematic naturalistic *pilot study,* we could not help but take note of certain *clusters of variables* at certain crossroads of the individuation process, insofar as they *repeated themselves.* This strongly suggested to us that it would be to our advantage to subdivide the data that we were collecting on the intrapsychic separation and individuation process, in accordance with the *repeatedly observable, behavioral and other surface referents of that process.* Our subdivision was into four subphases: differentiation, practicing, rapprochement, and "on the way to libidinal object constancy." (The timing of these subphases is still inaccurate, and we are still working on the timetable as we go along with the processing of our data.)

I should also mention in passing that I have described an objectless phase, *the phase of normal autism;* and the phase corresponding to Anna Freud's "need-satisfying" and Spitz's "preobject" phase—which I like to call *the symbiotic phase.* Both these precede the first subphase of separation-individuation—that of *differentiation.*

DIFFERENTIATION

At about four to five months of age, at the peak of symbiosis, the behavioral phenomena seem to indicate the beginning of the first subphase of separation-individuation—called *differentiation.* It is synonymous in our metaphorical language with "hatching from the mother-infant symbiotic common orbit." During the symbiotic months, through that activity of the pre-ego, which Spitz has described as *coenesthetic receptivity,* the young infant has familiarized himself with the mothering half of his symbiotic self, indicated by the unspecific, social smile. This smile gradually becomes the specific (preferential) smiling response to the mother, *which is the supreme sign that a specific bond* between the infant and his mother has been established.

When inner pleasure, due to safe anchorage within the symbiotic orbit—which is mainly entero-proprioceptive and contact perceptual—continues, and pleasure in the maturationally increasing outer sensory perception stimulates outward-directed attention cathexis, these two forms of attention cathexis can oscillate freely (Spiegel 1959, Rose 1964). The result is an optimal symbiotic state, out of which smooth differentiation—and *expansion beyond the symbiotic orbit*—can take place. This hatching process is, I believe, a gradual ontogenetic evolution of the sensorium—the perceptual-conscious system—which leads to the infant-toddler's having a more *permanently alert* sensorium, whenever he is awake (cf. also Wolff 1959).

In other words, the infant's attention—which during the first months of symbiosis was in large part *inwardly* directed, or focused in a coenesthetic and somewhat vague way *within the symbiotic orbit*—gradually gains a considerable accretion through the coming into being of a perceptual activity that is outwardly directed during the child's increasing periods of wakefulness. This is a change of degree rather than of kind, for during the symbiotic stage the child has certainly been highly attentive to the mothering figure. But gradually that attention is combined with a growing store of memories of mother's comings and goings, of "good" and "bad" experiences; the latter were altogether unrelievable by the self, but were predictably relieved by mother's ministrations.

Six to seven months is the peak of the child's hair-pulling, face-patting, manual, tactile and visual exploration of the mother's mouth, nose, face, as well as the covered (clad) and unclad *feel* of parts of the mother's body; and furthermore the discovery of a brooch, eyeglasses or a pendant attached to the mother. There may be engagement in peek-a-boo games in which the infant still plays a passive role. This later develops into the cognitive function of checking the unfamiliar against the already familiar—a process that Sylvia Brody termed "customs inspection."

It is during the first subphase of separation-individuation that all normal infants achieve their first tentative steps of breaking away, in a bodily sense, from their hitherto completely passive lap-baby-hood—the stage of dual unity with the mother. They stem themselves with arms and legs against the holding mother, as if to have a better look at her as well as at the surroundings. One was able to see their individually different inclinations and patterns, as well as the general characteristics of the stage of differentiation itself. They all like to venture and stay just a bit away from the enveloping arms of the mother; if they are motorically able to slide down from mother's lap, they tend to remain or to crawl back as near as possible and play at the mother's feet.

Once the infant has become sufficiently individuated to recognize the mother, visually and tactilely, he then turns, with greater or less wonderment and apprehension (commonly called "stranger reaction"), to a prolonged visual and tactile exploration and study of the faces of others, from afar or at close range. He appears to be comparing and checking the features—appearance, feel, contours and texture—of the stranger's face with his mother's face, as well as with whatever inner image he may have of her. He also seems to check back to her face in relation to other interesting new experiences.

In children for whom the symbiotic phase has been optimal and "confident expectation" has prevailed (Benedek 1938), curiosity and wonderment are the predominant elements of their inspection of strangers. By contrast, among children whose basic trust has been less than optimal, an abrupt change to acute stranger anxiety may make its appearance; or there may be a prolonged period of mild stranger reaction, which transiently interferes with pleasurable inspective behavior. This phenomenon and the factors underlying its variations constitute, we believe, an important aspect of and clue to our evaluation of the libidinal object, of socialization, and of the first step towards emotional object constancy.

THE BEGINNING PRACTICING PERIOD

The period of differentiation is followed—or rather, is overlapped—by a practicing period. This takes place usually from about seven to ten months, up to fifteen to sixteen months of age. In the course of processing our data we found it useful to think of the practicing period in two parts: (1) the early practicing phase—overlapping differentiation—characterized by the infant's earliest ability to move away physically from mother by crawling, climbing and righting himself, yet still holding on; and (2) the practicing period proper, characterized by free, upright locomotion.

At least three interrelated, yet discriminable, developments contribute to and/or, in circular fashion, interact with the child's first steps into awareness of separateness and into individuation. They are: the rapid *body differentiation* from the mother; the establishment of a *specific bond* with her; and the *growth and functioning of the autonomous ego apparatuses in close proximity to the mother.*

It seems that the new pattern of relationship to mother paves the way for the infant to spill over his interest in the mother on to inanimate objects—at first those provided by her—such as toys which she offers, or the bottle with which she parts from him at night. The infant explores these objects visually with his eyes, and their taste, texture and smell with his contact perceptual organs, particularly the mouth and the hands. One or the other of these objects becomes a transitional object. Moreover, whatever the sequence in which these functions develop in the beginning practicing period, the characteristic of this early stage of practicing is that, while there is interest and absorption in these activities, interest in the mother definitely seems to take precedence. We also observed in this early period of practicing that the "would-be fledgling" likes to indulge in his budding relationship with the "other than mother" world.

For instance, we observed one child, who during this period had to undergo hospitalization of a week's duration. During that period, it seems, he was frustrated *most* by his confinement to a crib, so that he welcomed *anyone* who would take him out of it. When he returned from the hospital, the relationship to his mother had become less exclusive, and he showed no clinging reaction or separation anxiety; his greatest need now in the Center and at home was to be taken for walks, with someone holding his hand. While he continued to prefer his mother to do this—with and for him—he would readily accept substitutes.

The optimal psychological distance in *this early practicing subphase* would seem to be one that allows the moving, exploring child freedom and opportunity for exploration at some physical distance from mother. It should be noted, however, that during the entire practicing subphase mother continues to be needed as a stable point—a "home base" to fulfill the need for refueling through physical contact. We see seven- to ten-month-olds crawling or rapidly paddling to the mother, righting themselves on her leg, touching her in other ways, or just leaning against her. This phenomenon was termed by Furer "emotional refueling." It is easy to observe how the wilting and fatigued infant "perks up" in the shortest time, following such contact; then he quickly goes on with his explorations, and once again becomes absorbed in his pleasure in functioning.

Mark was one of those children who had the greatest difficulty in establishing a workable distance between himself and mother. His mother was ambivalent as soon as Mark ceased to be part of herself, her symbiotic child. At times she seemed to avoid close body contact; at other times she might interrupt Mark in his autonomous activities to pick him up, hug him and hold him. She did this, of course, when *she* needed it, not when *he* did. This ambivalence on mother's part may have been what made it difficult for Mark to function at a distance from his mother.

During the early practicing subphase, following the initial push away from mother into the outside world, most of the children seemed to go through a brief period of increased separation anxiety. The fact that they were able to move independently, yet remain connected to mother—not physically, but through the distance modalities, by way of their seeing and hearing her—made the successful use of these distance modalities extraordinarily important for a while. The children did not like to lose sight of mother; they might stare sadly at her empty chair, or at the door through which she had left.

Many of the mothers seemed to react to the fact that their infants were moving away by *helping* them move away, that is, by giving them a gentle, or perhaps less gentle, push. Mothers also became interested in and sometimes critical of their children's functioning at this point; they began to compare notes, and they showed concern if their child seemed to be behind. Sometimes they hid their concern in a pointed show of nonconcern. In many mothers, concern became especially concentrated in eagerness that their children should begin to walk. Once the child was able to move away some distance, it was as if suddenly these mothers began to worry about his being able to "make it" out there, in the world, where he would have to fend for himself. In that context, walking seemed to have great symbolic meaning for both mother and toddler: it was as if the walking toddler had proved by his attainment of independent upright locomotion that he had already graduated into the world of fully independent human beings. The expectation and confidence that mother exudes that her child is now able to "make it out there" seems to be an important trigger for the child's own feeling of safety and perhaps also for his exchanging some of his magical omnipotence for autonomy and developing self-esteem (Sandler, Holder, and Meers 1963).

THE PRACTICING SUBPHASE PROPER

With the child's spurt in autonomous functions, especially upright locomotion, the "love affair with the world" (Greenacre 1957) is at its height. During these precious six to eight months (from ten-twelve to sixteen-eighteen months), for the junior toddler the world is his oyster. Libidinal cathexis shifts substantially into the service of the rapidly growing autonomous ego and its functions; the child seems intoxicated with his own faculties and with the greatness of his world.

At the same time, we see a relatively great imperviousness to knocks and falls and other frustrations, such as a toy being grabbed by another child. As the child, through the maturation of his locomotor apparatus, begins to venture farther and farther away from the mother's feet, he is often so absorbed in his own activities that for long periods of time he appears to be oblivious of the mother's presence. However, he returns periodically to the mother, seeming to need her physical proximity and refueling from time to time.

It is not at all impossible that the elation of this subphase has to do not only with the exercise of the ego apparatuses, and the body feeling of locomotion in the upright position like the bipedal grown-up dashing through the air, but also with the elation of escape from absorption into the orbit of mother. From this standpoint, we might say that, just as the infant's peek-a-boo games seem to turn from passive to active—the losing and then regaining of the love object— the toddler's constant running off, to be swooped up by mother, turns his fear of reengulfment by mother from passive to active. This behavior also, of course, guarantees that he *will* be caught, that is, it confirms over and over again that he is connected to mother, and that he still wishes to be. We need not assume that the child's behavior is intended to serve these functions when it first makes its appearance; but it is necessary to recognize that it produces these effects, which can then be repeated intentionally.

Phenomena of mood are of great importance at this stage. Most children in the practicing subphase appeared to have major periods of exhilaration, or at least of relative elation; they became *low-keyed* only when they became aware that mother was absent from the room. At such times, their gestural and performance motility slowed down; their interest in their surroundings diminished; and they appeared to be preoccupied once again with inwardly concentrated attention, with what Rubinfine (1961) called "imaging."

LOW-KEYEDNESS

Our inferences about the low-keyed state start from two recurrent phenomena: (1) if a person other than mother actively tried to comfort the child, he would lose his emotional balance and burst into tears; and (2) the visible termination of the child's "toned-down" state, at the time of his reunion with the briefly absent mother. Both these phenomena heightened our awareness that, up to that point, the child *had been* in a special "state of self." This low-keyedness and inferred "imaging" of mother are reminiscent of a miniature anaclitic depression. We tend to see in it the child's effort to hold on to a state of mind that Joffe and Sandler (1965) have termed "the ideal state of self," similar to the condition that Kaufman and Rosenblum (1968) have termed "conservation withdrawal" in monkeys.

THE SUBPHASE OR RAPPROCHEMENT

The third subphase of separation-individuation (from about sixteen to twenty-five months) begins hypothetically by *mastery* of upright locomotion and consequently less absorption in locomotion *per se.*

By the middle of the second year of life, the infant has become a toddler. *He now becomes more and more aware, and makes greater and greater use of his awareness of physical separateness.* Yet, side by side with the growth of his cognitive faculties and the increasing differentiation of his emotional life, there is a noticeable waning of his previous imperviousness to frustration, as well as of his relative obliviousness to the mother's presence. Increased separation anxiety can be observed—a fear of object loss inferred from the fact that when he hurts himself he discovers, to his perplexity, that his mother is not automatically at hand. The relative lack of concern about the mother's presence that was characteristic of the practicing subphase is now replaced by *active approach behavior,* and by a seemingly constant concern with the mother's whereabouts. As the toddler's awareness of separateness grows—stimulated by his maturationally acquired ability physically to move away from his mother, and by his cognitive growth—he now seems to have an increased need and wish for his mother to *share with him* every new acquisition on his part of skill and experience. We call this subphase of separation-individuation, therefore, *the period of rapprochement.*

The earlier "refueling" type of contact with mother, which the baby sought intermittently, is now replaced by a quest for constant interaction of the toddler with mother (and also with father and familiar adults) at a progressively higher level of symbolization. There is an increasing prominence of language, vocal and other intercommunications, as well as symbolic play.

In other words, when the junior toddler grows into the senior toddler of eighteen to twenty-four months, a most important emotional turning point is reached. The toddler now begins to experience, more or less gradually and more or less keenly, the obstacles that lie in the way of his anticipated "conquest of the world." Side by side with the acquisition of primitive skills and perceptual cognitive faculties, there has been an increasingly clear differentiation between the intrapsychic representation of the object and the self-representation. At the very height of mastery—towards the end of the practicing period—it has already begun to dawn on the junior toddler that the world is *not* his oyster; that he must cope with it more or less "on his own," very often as a relatively helpless, small and separate individual, unable to command relief or assistance, merely by feeling the need for them, or giving voice to that need.

The quality and measure of the wooing behavior of the toddler during this subphase provide important clues to the assessment of the normality of the individuation process.

Incompatibilities and misunderstandings between mother and child can be observed even in the case of the normal mother and her normal toddler, these being in part specific to certain seeming contradictions of this subphase. Thus, in the subphase of renewed, active wooing, the toddler's demand for his mother's constant participation seems contradictory to the mother: while he is now not as dependent and helpless as he was six months before, and seems eager to become less and less so, nevertheless he even more insistently expects the mother to share every aspect of his life. During this subphase some mothers cannot accept the child's demandingness; others cannot face the fact that the child is becoming increasingly independent and separate.

In this third subphase, while individuation proceeds very rapidly and the child exercises it to the limit, he also becomes more and more aware of his separateness and employs all kinds of mechanisms to resist separation from the mother.

But no matter how insistently the toddler tries to coerce the mother, she and he no longer function effectively as a dual unit; that is to say, he can no longer participate in the still maintained delusion of parental omnipotence. Verbal communication becomes more and more necessary; gestural coercion on the part of the toddler, or mutual preverbal empathy between mother and child, will no longer suffice to attain the goal of satisfaction, of well-being (Joffe and Sandler 1965). The junior toddler gradually realizes that his love objects (his parents) are separate individuals with their own individual interests. He must gradually and painfully give up his delu-

sion of his own grandeur, often with dramatic fights with mother—
less so, it seemed to us, with father.

This is the crossroad that my co-workers and I termed the *rap-prochement crisis.*

According to Annemarie Weil's suggestion, at this point the three basic anxieties of early childhood so often coincide. There is still a fear of object loss, more or less replaced by a conspicuous fear of loss of love and, in particular, definite signs of castration anxiety.

Here, in the rapprochement subphase, we feel is the mainspring of man's eternal struggle against both fusion and isolation.

One could regard the entire life cycle as constituting a more or less successful process of distancing from and introjection of the lost symbiotic mother, an eternal longing for the actual or fantasied "ideal state of self," with the latter standing for a symbiotic fusion with the "all good" symbiotic mother, who was at one time part of the self in a blissful state of well-being.

Chapter 9

RAPPROCHEMENT SUBPHASE OF THE
SEPARATION-INDIVIDUATION PROCESS

[1972]

From our studies of infantile psychosis, as well as from observations in well-baby clinics, we have already learned that the human infant's physiological birth by no means coincides with his psychological birth. The former is a dramatic, readily observable, and well-defined event; the latter is a slowly unfolding intrapsychic process.

For the more or less normal adult, the experience of being both fully "in" and at the same time basically separate from the world "out there" is one of the givens of life that is taken for granted. Consciousness of self and absorption without awareness of self are the two poles between which we move with varying degrees of ease and with varying alternation or simultaneity. This, too, is the result of a slowly unfolding process. In particular, this development takes place in relation to (a) one's own body; and (b) the principal representative of the world as the infant experiences it (the primary love object). As is the case with any intrapsychic process, this one continues to reverberate throughout the life cycle. It is never finished; it can always be reactivated; new phases of the life cycle witness later derivatives of the earliest process still at work (cf. Erikson 1959). However, as we see it, the principal psychological achievements in this process take place in the period from about the fourth or fifth to the thirtieth or thirty-sixth month of age, a period that we refer to, in accordance with Annemarie Weil's helpful suggestion,[1] as the separation-individuation phase.

During the course of a rather unsystematic, naturalistic pilot study, we could not help taking note of certain clusters of variables, at certain crossroads of the individuation process, in so far as they repeated themselves at certain points of the maturational timetable. This strongly suggested to us that it would be to our advantage to subdivide the data that we were collecting on the intrapsychic separation and individuation process in accordance with the behavioral and other surface referents of that process that we had found to be repeatedly observable (SPII:1, SPII:4). Our subdivision was into four subphases: *differentiation, practicing, rapprochement,* and a fourth subphase, occurring during the third year, which, the longer we studied it, the more cautiously did we have to designate it as *the child on the way to object constancy.* And according to my definition, it should be regarded as the stage in which a unified representation of the object becomes intrapsychically available, as the love object had been available to the child in the outside world during his complete and later partial need-satisfying object relationship stage.

When inner pleasure prevails as the result of the child's being safely anchored within the symbiotic orbit (which is mainly proprioceptive and contact perceptual) and when pleasure in the maturationally widening outer sensory perception (as, for example, vision) stimulates outward-directed attention cathexis, these two forms of attention cathexis can oscillate freely (Spiegel 1959, Rose 1964). The result is an optimal symbiotic state out of which expansion beyond the symbiotic orbit and smooth differentiation from the mother's body can take place. This process, to which I gave the name "hatching out," may be looked upon as a gradual ontogenetic evolution of the sensorium—the perceptual conscious system—a "tuning in" process that leads to the infant's having a more permanently alert sensorium when he is awake (cf. Wolff 1959).

It is during the first subphase of separation-individuation that all

1. Personal communication (1954).

normal infants achieve, through maturation of apparatuses, their first tentative steps of breaking away, in a bodily sense, from their hitherto completely passive lap-babyhood—the stage of dual unity with the mother. They push themselves with arms, trunk, and legs against the holding mother, as if to have a better look at her, as well as the surroundings. One is able to see their individually different inclinations and patterns, as well as the general characteristics of the stage of differentiation itself. All five- to six-month-old infants like to venture and stay just a bit of a distance away from the enveloping arms of the mother; as soon as their motor function permits, they like to slide down from mother's lap, but they tend to remain as near as possible to her and to play at her feet.

Once the infant has become sufficiently individuated to recognize the mother, visually and tactilely, as not just part of the symbiotic dyad but as his partner in it, the fact that he is ready to take this step is indicated by his preferential, specific smiling response to and for mother. At about the same time, or perhaps within an interval of a few weeks, he then turns, with greater or less wonderment and apprehension (commonly called "stranger reaction"), to a prolonged visual and tactile exploration and study of the faces of others, from afar or at close range. He appears to be comparing and checking the features—appearance, feel, contour, and texture—of the stranger's face with his mother's face, as well as with whatever inner image he may have of her. He also seems to check back, apparently to compare all other interesting new experiences with the mother's gestalt, her face, in particular.

It should be emphasized that we view separation and individuation as intertwined developmental processes, rather than as a single process. And they may proceed divergently, as the result of a developmental lag of one or the other. We have observed that children who achieve premature locomotor development, and are therefore able and prompted to separate physically from their mothers, may become prematurely aware of their own separateness much before their individuation (reality testing, cognition, etc.) has given them the means with which to cope with this awareness. On the other hand, we have found that in infants with overprotective and infantilizing mothers, individuation may develop well ahead, and may result in a lag of boundary formation and a lag in readiness to function as a separate individual without undue anxiety.

The period of differentiation is followed or, we might better say, is overlapped by a practicing period. This takes place usually from about seven to ten months, and continues to fifteen or sixteen months of age. In the course of processing our data, we found it useful to think of the practicing period in two parts: (a) the early practicing subphase, which overlaps with differentiation and is ushered in by the infant's earliest ability to physically move away from mother through crawling, climbing, and righting himself, yet still holding on; and (b) the practicing period proper, phenomenologically characterized by free upright locomotion.

During the early practicing subphase, throughout which crawling, paddling, pivoting, climbing, and righting himself are practiced by the infant, usually with much glee, these functions widen the child's world. Not only can he take a more active role in determining closeness and distance to mother, but the perceptual modalities that had up till then been used to explore the relatively familiar environment are suddenly exposed to a wider world; the sensorimotor intelligence, in Piaget's sense, takes a big step forward.

The optimal psychological distance in this early practicing subphase would seem to be one that allows the infant, whose movements are mostly quadrupedal, freedom and opportunity for exploration at some physical distance from mother. It should be noted, however, that during the entire practicing subphase mother continues to be needed as a stable point, a "home base" to fulfill the need for refueling through physical contact. We have seen seven- to ten-month-old infants crawling or rapidly paddling to the mother, righting themselves on her leg, touching her in other ways, or just leaning against her. This phenomenon was termed by Furer[2] (1959/1960) "emotional refueling." It is easy to observe how the wilting and fatigued infant "perks up" in the shortest time, following such contact, after which he quickly goes on with his explorations, once again absorbed in pleasure in his own functioning.

2. Personal communication (1959/1960).

THE PRACTICING SUBPHASE PROPER

With the spurt in autonomous functions, such as cognition, but especially upright locomotion, the "love affair with the world" (Greenacre 1957) begins. The toddler takes the greatest step in human individuation. He walks freely with upright posture. Thus, the plane of his vision changes; from an entirely new vantage point he finds unexpected and changing perspectives, pleasures, and frustrations. At this new visual level there is more to see, more to hear, more to touch, and all this is experienced in the upright bipedal position. How this new world is experienced seems to be subtly related to the mother, who is the center of the child's universe from which he gradually moves out into ever-widening perimeters.

During this precious six-to-eight-month period, for the junior toddler (ten-twelve to sixteen-eighteen months) the world is his oyster. Libidinal cathexis shifts substantially into the service of the rapidly growing autonomous ego and its functions, and the child seems to be intoxicated with his own faculties and with the greatness of his world. It is after the child has taken his first upright independent steps (which, by the way, more often than not he takes in a direction away from mother, or even during her absence) that one is able to mark the onset of the *practicing period par excellence* and of reality testing. Now, there begins a steadily increasing libidinal investment in practicing motor skills and in exploring the expanding environment, both human and inanimate. The chief characteristic of this practicing period is the child's great narcissistic investment in his own functions, his own body, as well as in the objects and objectives of his expanding "reality." Along with this, we see a relatively great imperviousness to knocks and falls and to other frustrations, such as a toy being grabbed away by another child. Substitute adults in the familiar setup of our nursery are easily accepted (in contrast to what occurs during the next subphase of separation-individuation).

As the child, through the maturation of his locomotor apparatus, begins to venture farther away from the mother's feet, he is often so absorbed in his own activities that for long periods of time he appears to be oblivious to the mother's presence. However, he returns periodically to the mother, seeming to need her physical proximity from time to time.

The smoothly separating and individuating toddler finds solace for the minimal threats of object loss that are probably entailed in each new stage of progressive development in his rapidly developing ego functions. The child concentrates on practicing the mastery of his own skills and autonomous capacities. He is exhilarated by his own capacities, continually delighted with the discoveries he is making in his expanding world, quasi-enamored with the world and with his own omnipotence. We might consider the possibility that the elation of this subphase has to do not only with the exercise of the ego apparatuses, but also with the infant's delighted escape from reengulfment by the still-existing symbiotic pull from the mother.

Just as the infant's peek-a-boo games seem to turn at this juncture from passive to active, to the active losing and regaining of the need-gratifying love object, so too does the toddler's constant running off (until he is swooped up by his mother) turn from passive to active the fear of being reengulfed by, or fused with, mother. It turns into an active distancing and reuniting game with her. This behavior reassures the toddler that mother will want to catch him and take him up in her arms. We need not assume that this behavior is intended to serve such functions when it first emerges, but quite clearly it produces these effects and can then be intentionally repeated.

Most children, during the practicing subphase proper, appear to have major periods of exhilaration, or at least of relative elation. They are impervious to knocks and falls. They are low-keyed only when they become aware that mother is absent from the room, at which times their gestural and performance motility slows down, interest in their surroundings diminishes, and they appear to be preoccupied with inwardly concentrated attention and with what Rubinfine (1961) calls "imaging." During this period, the toddler's sensorimotor intelligence imperceptibly develops into representational intelligence and into concomitant emotional growth that characterizes the third subphase of the separation-individuation process—the period of rapprochement.

THE PERIOD OF RAPPROCHEMENT

The rapprochement subphase (from about fifteen to twenty-two months, and very often far beyond the second birthday) begins hypothetically with the mastery of upright locomotion and the consequent diminishing absorption in locomotion and other autonomous functioning.

By the middle of the second year of life, the infant has become a toddler. He now becomes more and more aware of and makes greater and greater use of his physical separateness. Side by side with the growth of his cognitive faculties and the increasing differentiation of his emotional life, there is also, however, a noticeable waning of his previous imperviousness to frustration, as well as of his relative obliviousness to the mother's presence. Increased separation anxiety can be observed—a fear of object loss that can be inferred from many behaviors; for example, from the fact that when the child hurts himself, he visibly discovers to his perplexity that his mother is not automatically at hand. The relative lack of concern about the mother's presence that was characteristic of the practicing subphase is now replaced by active approach behavior, and by a seeming constant concern with the mother's whereabouts. As the toddler's awareness of separateness grows, stimulated by his maturationally acquired ability physically to move away from his mother and by his cognitive growth, he now seems to have an increased need and wish for his mother to share with him his every new acquisition of skill and experience. These are the reasons for which I called this subphase of separation-individuation, the period of rapprochement.

Now after mastery of free walking and beginning internalization, the toddler begins to experience, more or less gradually and more or less keenly, the obstacles that lie in the way of what was, at the height of his "practicing" an omnipotent exhilaration, a quite evidently anticipated "conquest of the world." Side by side with the acquisition of primitive skills and perceptual cognitive faculties, there has been an increasingly clear differentiation, a separation, between the intrapsychic representation of the object and the self-representation. At the very height of mastery, toward the end of the practicing period, however, it has already begun to dawn on the junior toddler that the world is *not* his oyster; that he must cope with it more or less "on his own," very often as a relatively helpless, small, and separate individual, unable to command relief or assistance merely by feeling the need for them or giving voice to that need.

The quality and measure of the *wooing* behavior of the toddler toward his mother during this subphase provide important clues to the assessment of the normality of the individuation process. We believe that it is during this rapprochement subphase that the foundation for subsequent relatively stable mental health or borderline pathology is laid.

Incompatibilities and misunderstandings between mother and child can be observed at this period even in the case of the normal mother and her normal toddler, these being in part specific to certain seeming contradictions of this subphase. Thus, in the subphase of renewed, active wooing, the toddler's demands for his mother's constant participation seem contradictory to the mother: while the toddler is now not as dependent and helpless as he was half a year before, and seems eager to become less and less so, he even more insistently expects the mother to share every aspect of his life. During this subphase, some mothers are not able to accept the child's demanding behavior; others cannot tolerate gradual separation— they cannot face the fact that the child is becoming increasingly independent of and separate from them, and is no longer a part of them.

In this third subphase, while individuation proceeds very rapidly and the child exercises it to the limit, he is also becoming more and more aware of his separateness and is beginning to employ all kinds of partly internalized, partly still outwardly directed and acted out coping mechanisms in order to resist separation from the mother. No matter how insistently the toddler tries to coerce the mother, however, she and he no longer function effectively as a dual unit; that is to say, he can no longer get her to participate with him in his still maintained delusion of parental omnipotence. Likewise, at the other pole of the erstwhile dual unity, the mother must recognize a separate individual, her child, in his own autonomous right. Verbal communication has now become more and more necessary; gestural coercion on the part of the toddler, or mutual preverbal empathy between mother and child, will no longer suffice to attain the child's goal of satisfaction, of well-being (Joffe and Sandler 1965). Similarly, the mother can no longer make the child subservient to her own predilections and wishes.

The junior toddler gradually realizes that his love objects (his parents) are separate individuals with their own individual interests. He must gradually and painfully give up his delusion of his own grandeur, often through dramatic fights with mother—less so, it seemed to us, with father. This is a crossroad that we have termed the "rapprochement crisis."

Depending upon her own adjustment, the mother may react either by continued emotional availability and playful participation in the toddler's world or by a gamut of less desirable attitudes. From the data we have accumulated so far, we would state strongly that the mother's continued emotional availability is essential if the child's autonomous ego is to attain optimal functional capacity. If the mother is "quietly available" with a ready supply of object libido, if she shares the toddling adventurer's exploits, playfully reciprocates and thus helps his attempts at imitation, at externalization and internalization, then the relationship between mother and toddler is able to progress to the point where verbal communication takes over, even though vivid gestural behavior, that is, affectomotility, still predominates. By the end of the second or the beginning of the third year, the predictable emotional participation of the mother seems to facilitate the rich unfolding that is taking place in the toddler's thought processes, reality testing, and coping behavior.

The toddler's so-called "shadowing" of the mother at fifteen to twenty months of age (an often encountered phenomenon that is characteristic of this subphase) seems obligatory, except in the cases of those mothers who, by protracted doting and intrusiveness which spring from their own symbiotic-parasitic needs, become themselves the shadowers of the child. In normal cases, a slight shadowing by the toddler after the hatching process gives way to some degree of object constancy in the course of the third year. However, the less emotionally available the mother has become at the time of rapprochement, the more insistently and even desperately does the toddler attempt to woo her. In some cases, this process drains so much of the child's available developmental energy that, as a result, not enough may be left for the evolution of the many ascending functions of his ego. We shall illustrate the characteristics and certain typical conflicts of the rapprochement subphase with a few vignettes.

During the period of rapprochement Barney behaved with particular poignancy. He had gone through a typical, although precocious, "love affair with the world" in which he would often fall and hurt himself and always react with great imperviousness. Gradually he became perplexed to find that his mother was not on hand to rescue him, and he then began to cry when he fell. As he became aware of his separateness from his mother, his previous calm acceptance of knocks and falls began to give way to increased separation anxiety.

Early maturation of Barney's locomotor function had confronted him with the fact of physical separateness from his mother, before he was fully ready for it at nine to ten months of age. For this reason, we believe, he displayed to an exaggerated degree during his period of rapprochement the opposite of "shadowing." He would challenge mother by darting away from her, confidently and correctly expecting her to run after him and sweep him into her arms; at least momentarily he had undone the physical separateness from her. The mother's own increasingly frantic response to the dangerous darting made Barney, in turn, intensify and prolong this behavior so that his mother for a while despaired of being able to cope with Barney's "recklessness." We see this behavior as the result of the precocious maturation of the child's locomotor functions coupled with the relative lag in maturation of his emotional and intellectual functions. Hence, he could not properly evaluate, or gauge, the potential dangers of his locomotor feats.

The imbalance between the developmental line of separation and that of individuation, causing a jumbled intermeshing of factors of the second, the practicing, and the third, the rapprochement subphases, appeared to have set an overdetermined pattern of accident proneness in this child (Frankl 1963). Barney's reckless behavior had introjective qualities as well. It was, as every symptomatic behavior is, overdetermined. It no doubt also derived from identification with, or better stated, from introjection of his father's sports-loving nature. (The children were permitted to watch and admire, and, at times, to participate in their father's highly risky athletic feats.)

Barney's mother, whom we observed as the ideal mother during Barney's early practicing subphase, now at his chronological age of the rapprochement subphase would alternately restrict Barney or, from sheer exhaustion, give up altogether her usual alertness to his needs and her previous high level of attunement to his cues. She would either rush to him in any situation, whether or not his need was real, or she would find herself keeping away from him at a time when she was really needed; in other words, her immediate availability became unpredictable to her, no less than to him.

The disturbance of the relationship between Barney and his mother during this period was not total, however, nor did it, we believe, inflict permanent damage on Barney's personality development. Neither hostility, splitting, nor increased and more permanent ambivalence resulted. Barney continued to bring everything within reach to his mother to share, filling her lap. He would have periods in which he sat quietly and did jigsaw puzzles or looked at picture books with his mother, while remaining full of confidence and basic trust toward the world beyond the mother.

This mother-child relationship became mutually satisfactory again with the advent of the fourth subphase, as a result of which Barney in the third year became a patient, well-functioning, and, within normal limits, more sedentary child. I believe that Barney's very satisfactory symbiotic differentiation, and early practicing subphases, as well as the fact that his father (with whom he roughhoused and whom he hero-worshipped) became an important part of his world during his second year of life, were all favorable factors in his development.

A different manifestation of the crisis of the third subphase was observable in Anna. Her mother's marked emotional unavailability made Anna's practicing and exploratory period brief and subdued. Never certain of her mother's availability, and therefore always preoccupied with it, Anna found it difficult to invest libido in her surroundings and in her own functioning. After a brief spurt of practicing, she would return to her mother and try to engage her with greater intensity by all possible means. From such relatively direct expressions of the need for her mother as bringing her a book to read to her, or hitting at the mother's ever-present book in which she was engrossed, Anna turned to more desperate measures, such as falling or spilling cookies on the floor and stamping on them, always with an eye to gaining her mother's attention, if not involvement.

Anna's mother was observed to be greatly absorbed in her own interests which were anything but child-centered. She emphasized with seeming satisfaction and with some mock self-depreciation that both her older children seemed to have preferred their father, who had apparently shared the mother's task in diapering and bottle-feeding the babies.

We observed in Anna, as early as the ninth and tenth month, increased clamoring for closeness to mother, refusal to accept any substitutes in the mother's presence let alone in her absence, and greatly reduced pleasure in and diminution of activity. She had far too little investment of libido in practicing the autonomous partial functions of her individuating ego; approaching, even beseeching, behavior toward mother far outweighed any involvement in activity away from mother. Hence there was a complete overlapping and intermingling of characteristics of both the practicing and rapprochement subphases.

Whereas all the landmarks of individuation—the development of partial motor skills, of communication, of imitation and identification, and of defenses—appeared at appropriate times, there was minimal progress toward object constancy (in Hartmann's sense).

Concomitant with Anna's inability to let mother out of sight, her activities and movements were low-keyed: they lacked the vivacity and luster that was characteristic of the behavior of her practicing contemporaries. Her happier moods and greater vivacity, which coincided with the achievement of free walking, were fleeting. On the other hand, her language development was even precocious.

Anna's chronic frustration in her attempt to win her mother's love had noticeably impaired the amalgamation of libido and aggression. Her ambivalence visibly affected her mood, which was characterized by ready smiles when her mother or a father substitute approached her, but which was quite readily switched to the opposite—moroseness, unhappiness, and even despair. This reminded us of the mood swings and fluctuations of self-esteem that we observe so conspicuously in borderline phenomena in the psychoanalytic situation.

In our study we had a fairly good setup, we feel, for gauging the junior and later the senior toddler's capacity to function in the mother's presence, and to compare it with his functioning during the brief periods of her physical absence. The latter situation varies from the mother's just being in the adjacent nursery, or in the nearby interviewing room, to being out of the building. The toddler stays within a familiar setting, with familiar adults and contemporaries.

It may be of interest for me to relate a few details of Anna's personality development in the fateful "second eighteen-month period of her life." It had already been observed by us that Anna's play had a quality of early reaction-formation. The mother reported that Anna had shown disgust when she gave her a portion of her older brother's clay to play with, and this had been at as early as eighteen or nineteen months. Anna's toilet training started at about twenty months, seemingly without pressure. Anna was already saying the word "do-do" at that age, and at first her mother was quite well attuned to cues from her concerning her toilet needs. She praised Anna whenever the latter produced either urine or feces. From her twentieth month on, Anna was repeatedly heard saying, "bye-bye, wee wee," as she pulled the chain to flush the toilet. Soon, however, many observers noted that Anna was beginning to request bathroom trips whenever she wanted her mother's attention, or whenever she wanted to prevent mother from leaving the room for an interview— in any event, more frequently than she could actually have had a bowel or urinary urge.

Anna was bowel trained by twenty-two months, and at that age she went for days without wetting. At the beginning of toilet training (particularly bowel training), we saw that Anna was willing and able to oblige her mother so that both mother and daughter found in the toileting an emotionally positively charged meeting ground. But within two months, toileting had been drawn into the conflictual sphere of this mother-child interaction. At around twenty-three months of age, Anna used wetting all across the room as a weapon. Her mother was then pregnant and, as time went on, her pregnancy caused her to become narcissistically self-absorbed. She had fewer and fewer positive reactions to Anna's demands to accompany her to the upstairs bathroom at home. In fact, she told us that she asked her then four-year-old son to substitute for her in taking Anna to the toilet. The boy, we later learned, did not miss the opportunity to provocatively and aggressively display his manly prowess, his penis, to his little sister. Anna's penis envy thus gained momentum, as did her defiance of mother.

A battle around toilet training ensued between Anna and her mother. At around two years of age (twenty-four to twenty-seven months, to be exact) Anna started to use her sphincter control to defy her mother. From twenty-two months on, severe constipation developed in the wake of Anna's deliberate withholding of her feces.

We did not see Anna for about three months (from her twenty-fifth to her twenty-eighth month) during which time a sister was born.

Anna returned at twenty-nine months of age. Her mother carried the baby sister, Susie, with Anna following close behind. The mother looked harassed and tired as she entered the room, and, with a tight smile, exclaimed, "I feel filthy dirty, and so mad, mad, mad!" She complained that Anna "is driving me crazy." Anna had indeed been very difficult, whining, and demanding, but, in addition, for the past two or three days had been withholding her feces and had not had a bowel movement. The mother mimicked Anna as she held her thighs tightly together and stamped her feet. She also said that Anna was in pain most of the time and actually very uncomfortable. The pediatrician, she reported, had assured her that this was a normal occurrence after the birth of a new baby and that she should take it calmly and pay no attention to Anna's toileting at this time. Making a hopeless gesture, she said "But I simply can't do it; I just get so mad."

Anna was observed in the toddler's room playing with water. This, however, was not the kind of play that children her age usually enjoy, but it appeared to us to be of a compulsive nature. She began to scrub a bowl to which flour had stuck and was very determined to scrub it clean, becoming annoyed when she could not do so. She looked up at the observer and said, "Bowl not clean." All this while Anna seemed most uncomfortable. She obviously needed to defecate and was under continual bowel pressure. Beads of perspiration appeared on her forehead and the color would come and go from her face. Twice she ran to the toilet. She sat on the toilet and urinated;

then she got up and became preoccupied with flushing the toilet. She went back to the toddler room and listlessly played with dough, but again, and all during her play, Anna was in discomfort and kept jiggling and jumping, with the color repeatedly draining from her face. Finally, she jumped up and ran to the toilet, sat down on it, and said to the observer, "Get me a book." Sitting and straining, she looked up at the observer with a rather painful expression on her face, and said, "Don't let Mommy in, keep Mommy out, keep Mommy out." The observer encouraged her to talk about this some more, and she said, "Mommy would hurt me." She then looked at the book, at the pictures of the baby cats and baby horses, and as the observer was showing the pictures of the baby farm animals, Anna began to look as though she was particularly uncomfortable. She looked down at her panties, which had become stained, and said she wanted clean ones. Finally, in extreme discomfort, she seemed unable to hold back the feces any longer, and called out, "Get me my Mommy, get me my Mommy." Her mother came quickly, sat down beside her, and Anna requested that she read to her.

A participant observer watched from the booth, and noted that the mother was reading the same book about farm animals that the first observer had previously read to Anna. Pointing to the animals, the toddler was heard to say, "My Poppy has a piggy in his tummy." Her mother looked perplexed and asked Anna, "What?" Anna repeated the sentence. The mother seemed distraught as her daughter was now talking gibberish. She felt Anna's forehead to see whether she was feverish, but the child smiled, pointed to the book again, and said, "No, it's a baby horse." At this point, with a blissful expression on her face, Anna defecated. After her bowel movement, Anna was more relaxed; she played peek-a-boo with the door, asking the observer to stand behind it.

In this episode, the sequence of behaviors and verbalizations enabled us to draw conclusions, to reconstruct, as it were, the development of Anna's early infantile neurosis *in statu nascendi*. With her deficient emotional supplies from maternal support, the development of autonomy had not been enough to gradually replace the obligatory early infantile symbiotic omnipotence. In spite of her excellent endowment, Anna was unable to ward off the onslaught of separation anxiety and the collapse of self-esteem. Her anger at mother for not having given her a penis was unmistakable in her verbal material. She coveted those gifts that mother received from father, among which was a porcelain thimble which she was allowed to keep. Anna turned in her disappointment to father, and, when mother became pregnant, in a perplexed way she obviously equated gift with baby, with feces, and with penis. She showed great confusion about the contents of the body: her own pregnancy fantasies were quite evident, but she was unclear as to who had what in his or her belly. She seemed to expect a baby in the belly of her father, as well as in her mother's. The equation of feces = baby = phallus was explicitly expressed in her behavior and verbal utterances.

The mother-toddler relationship was such that Anna had to defend the good mother against her destructive rage. This she did by splitting the object world into good and bad. The good was always the absent part object, never the present object. To clarify this, let me describe another sequence of events and verbalizations in Anna's third year. Whenever her mother left, she had temper tantrums and would cling to her beloved and familiar play teacher, but not without verbally abusing her while still keeping her arms around her neck. When they read a book together, Anna found fault with every picture and every sentence that the playroom teacher offered; she scolded the teacher, everything was the opposite of what the teacher said, and she was "bad, bad, bad."

I watched this behavior from the observation booth and ventured quietly into the playroom where I sat at the farthest corner from Anna and her loved-and-hated teacher. Anna immediately caught sight of me and angrily ordered me out. I softly interpreted to Anna that I understood: Anna really wanted nobody else but her Mommy to come back in through that door and that was why she was very angry. She was also very angry because not Mommy but the observer was reading to her. I said that she knew that Mommy would soon come back. With my quasi interpretation, some libidinal channels seemed to have been tapped; the child put her head on the observer's shoulder and began to cry softly. Soon, the mother came back. It was most instructive to see, however, that not a flicker of radiance or happiness was noticeable in Anna at that reunion. Her very first words were, "What did you bring me?" and the whining and discontent started all over again. For quite a while Anna did not succeed in attaining a unified object representation or in reconciling the synthesized good and bad qualities of the love object. At the same time, her own self-representation and self-esteem suffered.

By contrast, what we saw in Barney's case was merely a transitional developmental deviation in the form of a rapprochement crisis. In Anna we observed a truly neurotic symptom-formation, developing on the basis of a rather unsatisfactory mother-child relationship yet activated and, to a great extent, produced by accumulated traumata.

Until way beyond the fourth subphase, Anna's relationship to her mother remained full of ambivalence. Her school performance was excellent, however. Constipation continued as a symptom for several years. Her social development was good. Our follow-up study will tell us more about the fate of her infantile neurosis.[3]

SUMMARY

In our observation of two toddlers, we saw why the rapprochement crisis occurs and why in some instances it becomes and may remain an unresolved intrapsychic conflict. It may set an unfavorable fixation point interfering with later oedipal development, or at best add to the difficulty of the resolution of the oedipus complex.

The developmental task at the very height of the separation-individuation struggle in the rapprochement subphase is a tremendous one. Oral, anal, and early genital pressures and conflicts meet and accumulate at this important landmark in personality development. There is a need to renounce symbiotic omnipotence, and there is also heightened awareness of the body image and pressure in the body, especially at the points of zonal libidinization.

Three great anxieties of childhood meet at this developmental stage. (1) While the fear of object loss and abandonment is partly relieved, it is also greatly complicated by the internalization of

3. [See the source notes appended to this volume.]

parental demands that indicate beginning superego development. In consequence, we observe an intensified vulnerability on the part of the rapprochement toddler. (2) Fear in terms of loss of the love of the object results in an extrasensitive reaction to approval and disapproval by the parent. (3) There is greater awareness of bodily feelings and pressures, in Greenacre's sense. This is augmented by awareness of bowel and urinary sensations during the toilet training process, even in quite normal development. There is often displayed, in some instances quite dramatically, a reaction to the discovery of the anatomical sex difference with prematurely precipitated castration anxiety.

Chapter 10

SYMBIOSIS AND INDIVIDUATION: THE PSYCHOLOGICAL BIRTH OF THE HUMAN INFANT

[1974]

I would like to start on a somewhat personal note, to indicate how, amidst my reconstructive studies in the psychoanalytic situation, this observational, normative work, one of whose yields is the present paper, came about.

During my own formative years when I was still a trainee at the Psychoanalytic Institute in Vienna, my experiences as head of a well-baby clinic in the late 1920s brought the (albeit preconscious) impression again and again to my mind that the human infant's *biological, actual birth experience* did not coincide with his "psychological birth." The sensorium of the newborn and very young infant did not seem to be "tuned in" to the outside world; he appeared to be in a twilight state of existence.

Then, in the 1930s, when I had a number of neurotic child and adult psychoanalytic patients, there happened to be among them two latency-age patients whom I found myself unable to treat with the traditional psychoanalytic method. One of them, a highly intelligent eight-year-old boy, was referred by the parents and the school because he did not seem to comprehend the necessary requirements of the

The fifteenth Sophia Mirviss Memorial Lecture, November 1973.

reality situation in the classroom, nor was he able to listen to and act upon the reality requirements of family life.

He needed his mother's almost continual attendance. She had to—and sometimes did—guess his primary process thoughts and wishes; otherwise, the patient—with or without an initial temper tantrum—retreated into a bizarre dreamworld of his own. The contents of this dreamworld were discernible in those instances in which he acted out his delusional fantasies; for example, he donned his father's derby hat and walking stick, fully believing that appropriating these paraphernalia of his father actually made him the father, and in addition made him the absolute ruler of the universe.

The analyst was permitted, I soon discovered, to play one of two roles only: either I had to act as an inanimate extension of the patient's ego, a quasi-tool of the delusionary aggrandized self of the patient, or else I had to be completely passive—quasi-deanimated, another (albeit somewhat more significant) piece of furniture in the room.

The animate and individuated existence of the human objects— father, brother, analyst, classmates, and even mother—was blotted out as far as possible. If these deanimation and dedifferentiation mechanisms (SPI:10) did not work, every so often the patient fell into a panic-stricken rage attack, and then slumped into the twilight state of the psychotic.

In spite of the immense difference between these two groups of human beings—the very young infant and the psychotic child—one basic similarity between the two groups made a great impression on me: neither seemed to have been *psychologically* born, that is to say, "tuned in" to the world of reality. What the youngest babies have *not yet* achieved, the psychotics have *failed to* achieve—psychological birth: that is to say, becoming a separate, individual entity, acquiring an, albeit primitive, first level of self-identity.

This common feature of a perceptual twilight state of the two groups of human beings slowly percolated in my mind, with the result that I asked myself two questions: (1) How do the vast majority of infants manage to achieve the obligatory second, the psychic birth experience? How do they emerge from what is obviously a twilight state of symbiotic oneness with the mother—an innate given—that gradually allows them to become intrapsychically separated from her, and to perceive the world on their own? (2) What are the genetic and structural concomitants that prevent the psychotic individual from achieving this second birth experience, this hatching from the symbiotic "common boundary with the mothering one?"

After another decade of experience with psychotic children I embarked in the late 1950s on a systematic study of "The Natural History of Symbiotic Child Psychosis,"[1] which used a tripartite design.

We attempted to establish what Augusta Alpert would have called a "corrective symbiotic relationship" between mother and child, with the therapist acting as a bridge between them. We became more and more convinced that the "basic fault" in the psychotic was his inability to perceive the self and the mother as separate entities, and thus to use the mother as a "beacon of orientation in the world of reality," as his "external ego." This is in contrast to normal children or to children whose disturbances belong to other categories of pathology.

Soon after initiating the psychosis project (and almost parallel with it), we started a pilot study, in which we endeavored to find out how *differentiation* and *self-boundary formation* do develop in most human beings! (Practically no specific data were available about this at that time.) This pilot study was a bifocal observational study of randomly selected mother-infant pairs, who were compared with each other and compared with themselves over time. The pilot study of the average mother-infant pairs was undertaken with the hypothesis that "there exists a normal and universal intrapsychic separation-individuation process in the average child, which is preceded by a normal symbiotic phase."

It is my conviction that, in the *normal individual,* the sociobiological utilization of the mother, of the "outer half of the self" (Spitz 1965), and later on, the emotional availability of the love object—the postsymbiotic partner—are the necessary conditions for an *intrapsychic* separation-individuation process. This is, in fact, synonymous with the *second,* the psychological birth experience: a rather slow and very gradual *hatching out process,* as it were.

1. [See the source notes appended to this volume.]

As the result of my clinical work in the psychoanalytic situation, and my observational studies of the first years of life, I am now able to state with a fair degree of accuracy what many of my colleagues have found in their mainly reconstructive work: namely, that milder than outrightly psychotic clinical pictures are derived from disturbances in the orderly progression of the subphases of the separation-individuation process. Hence, I shall briefly review that orderly developmental process.

I

The biological unpreparedness of the human infant to maintain his life separately is the source of that species-specific, prolonged, absolute dependence on the mother (Parens and Saul 1971), which has been designated by Benedek (1949) and myself as "the mother-infant symbiosis." I believe that it is from this symbiotic state of the mother-infant dual unity that those experiential precursors of individual beginnings are derived which, together with inborn constitutional factors, determine every human individual's unique somatic and psychological makeup.

The symbiotic patterning, such as the molding or stiffening of the body when it is held, as well as the specific and characteristic nursing situations and countless other variables within the symbiotic dyad, give us some clues as to what is going on in the infant; but translation of the observable phenomena of early pre-ego states—in our terms, the autistic and early symbiotic periods—into psychological terms is exceedingly difficult. Extrapolations drawn from preverbal behavioral data are even more precarious than the use of hypotheses deduced from observational data of later periods of life. To understand *preverbal* phenomena, as Augusta Bonnard (1958) succinctly stated, "We are . . . compelled to seek out their connotations, either through their pathological or normal continuance in somewhat older individuals than an infant, or else through their regressive manifestations" (p. 583).

As I have described in many of my publications, we have learned a great deal about the symbiotic nature of human existence by intensively studying the preverbal phenomena of symbiosis in their pathological and regressive manifestations.

In our normative study, however, we have tried not only to validate our hypothesis of the *symbiotic origin of human existence,* but to follow development into that period of early life that I named the separation-individuation phase. We studied randomly selected infant-mother pairs, and observed their interaction *beyond* the normal symbiotic phase.

As soon as signs of differentiation appear, the data are considerably easier to read—and constructions appear to be more reliable. This is because the infant's behavior has been polarized and rendered more meaningful through the presence and availability or lack of availability of the mother. The mother's presence and her interaction with the child furnish a circular yet bipolar frame of reference: baby and mother, transacting with each other in a more readable way.

This has enabled us to study the psychological birth of the human infant, the main dynamics of which are: the major shifts of libidinal and aggressive cathexis in the bodily self; and the changing nature and level of the approach and distancing behaviors between infant and mother during the course of the developmental process, from biological birth till the open-ended phase of libidinal object constancy.

In the weeks preceding the evolution to symbiosis, the newborn's and very young infant's sleeplike states far outweigh the states of arousal. They are reminiscent of that primal state of libido distribution that prevailed in intrauterine life, which resembles the model of a closed monadic system, self-sufficient in its hallucinatory wish fulfillment.

Ribble (1943) has pointed out that it is by way of mothering that the young infant is gradually brought out of an inborn tendency toward vegetative-splanchnic regression and into increased sensory awareness of and contact with the environment. In terms of energy or libidinal cathexis, this means that a progressive displacement of drive energy has to take place from the inside of the body (particularly from the abdominal organs) toward its periphery. *The shift from predominantly proprioenteroceptive toward sensoriperceptive cathexis of the periphery*—the rind of the body ego (as Freud called it)—is a major step in development.

The well-known peripheral pain insensitivity as well as the panic-creating hypersensitivity to enteroceptive ("gut") sensations, which are equated with bad introjects in psychosis, bear witness to the fact that this important and massive cathectic shift has failed to occur.

I believe that this major cathectic shift marks the progression from the normal autistic to the normal symbiotic phase.

The main task of the autistic phase is that with predominantly physiological mechanisms, the homeostatic equilibrium of the organism be maintained, under the changed postpartum conditions.

Through the inborn and autonomous perceptive faculty of the primitive ego (Hartmann 1939), deposits of memory traces of the two primordial qualities of stimuli of "good"—that is, pleasurable—and "bad"—that is, painful—occur. We may further hypothesize that these are cathected with primordial undifferentiated drive energy.

John Benjamin (1961) found that an interesting physiological maturational crisis occurs at around three to four weeks. This is borne out in electroencephalographic studies, and by the observation that there is a marked increase in overall sensitivity to external stimuli. "Without intervention of a mother figure for help in tension reduction," Benjamin says, "the infant tends to become overwhelmed by stimuli, with increased crying and other motor manifestations of undifferentiated negative affect" (p. 27).

I believe that this crisis—from our developmental point of view—marks the cracking of the "autistic" shell, the beginning dissolution of the negative, that is to say, uncathected, stimulus barrier. It marks the beginning of its replacement—through the aforementioned cathectic shift—by a positively cathected *protective* and *selective* stimulus barrier which creates a common "shield," as it were, a quasisemipermeable membrane enveloping both parts of the mother-infant dyad.

The symbiotic phase is marked by the infant's increased attention to and perceptual-affective investment in stimuli that *we* (the adult observers) recognize as coming from the world outside, but which (we postulate) the infant does not recognize as having a clearly outside origin. Here begins the establishment of "memory islands" (*SPI*:6), but not as yet a differentiation between inner and outer, self and other. The principal psychological achievement of the symbiotic phase is that the specific bond between infant and mother is created, as is indicated by the specific smiling response (Spitz 1946a).

The period of five to seven months is the peak of manual, tactile, and near-visual exploration of the mother's mouth, nose, face, as well as the "feel" of the mother's skin. With these behaviors, the infant seems to begin to distinguish between contact-perceptual experiences and those originating in his own body, and to single out experiences of the hitherto completely coenesthetic global sensory experiences of mother's and his own bodies. Furthermore, these are the weeks during which the infant discovers with fascination inanimate objects worn by the mother—a brooch, eyeglasses, or a pendant. He begins looking around within the symbiotic dual unity by straining away from the mother's body as if to have a better look at her, and also to look beyond the symbiotic orbit—for example, in the pursuit of toys. There may be engagement in peek-a-boo games, in which the infant still plays a passive role (Kleeman 1967). These explorative patterns later develop into the cognitive function of checking the unfamiliar against the already familiar.

It is during the first, the differentiation subphase (four-five to ten months of age), that all normal infants achieve their initial tentative steps of breaking away, in a bodily sense, from their hitherto completely passive lap-babyhood—the stage of dual unity with the mother. One can observe individually different inclinations and patterns as well as the general characteristics of the *stage of differentiation itself.* All infants like to venture and stay just a bit of a distance away from the enveloping arms of the mother; and, as soon as they are motorically able to, they like to slide down from the mother's lap. But they tend to remain or crawl back, as near as possible, to play at the mother's feet.

The baby now begins "comparative scanning," "checking back to mother." He becomes interested in and seems to compare "mother" with "other," the familiar with the unfamiliar, feature by feature, it would seem. He appears to familiarize himself more thoroughly, as it were, with what *is* mother; what feels, tastes, smells, looks like, and has the "clang" of mother. *Pari passu*, as he learns the "mother *qua* mother," he also finds out what belongs and what does not belong to mother's body (such as a brooch, the eyeglasses). He starts to discriminate between mother and whatever it is—he or she or *it*—that looks, feels, moves differently from or similarly to mother.

In children for whom the symbiotic phase has been optimal and "confident expectation" has prevailed, curiosity and wonderment—discernible through the "checking back" pattern—are the predominant elements of the inspection of strangers. By contrast, among children whose basic trust has been less than optimal, an abrupt change to acute stranger anxiety may make its appearance; or there may be a prolonged period of mild stranger reaction, which transiently interferes with pleasurable inspective behavior. This phenomenon and the factors underlying its variations constitute, we believe, an important aspect of and a clue to our evaluation of the libidinal object, of socialization, and of the first step toward emotional object constancy. This inverse relation between basic confidence and stranger anxiety deserves to be emphasized and further verified (*SPII:7*).

In cases in which the mother showed ambivalence or parasitism, intrusiveness, or "smothering," differentiation in the child was disturbed to various degrees and in different forms. The seeking of distance from the symbiotic partner appeared in some of our babies surprisingly early—at the *peak* of the symbiotic phase. During the differentiation subphase, this distance-seeking seemed to be accompanied by greater awareness of mother as a special person (full establishment of the libidinal object [Spitz 1965]), even though in very rare cases this awareness may already have been suffused at that stage with negative aggressive affect. This we were able to deduce from primitive, but sometimes quite unmistakable avoidance behaviors.

The differentiation subphase overlaps with the practicing period, which is the second subphase of the separation-individuation process. In the course of processing our data, we found it useful to think of the practicing period in two parts: the *early* practicing phase—overlapping differentiation, and ushered in by the infant's earliest ability to move away from the mother, by crawling, paddling, climbing, and righting himself—yet still holding on; and the practicing period proper, phenomenologically characterized by free, upright locomotion. At least three interrelated, yet discriminable developments contribute to and, in circular fashion, interact with the child's first steps into awareness of separateness and into individuation. They are: the rapid *body differentiation* from the mother; the establishment of a *specific bond with her;* and the *growth and functioning of the autonomous ego apparatuses in close proximity to the mother.*

It seems that the new autonomous achievements, plus the new pattern of relationship to mother, together pave the way for the infant to spill over his interest in the mother onto inanimate objects, at first those provided by her, such as a blanket, a diaper, a toy that she offers, or the bottle with which she parts from him at night. The infant explores these objects near-visually with his eyes, and "tests" their taste, texture, and smell with his contact-perceptual organs, particularly the mouth and hands (Hoffer 1949). One or the other of these objects may become a transitional object (Winnicott 1953). Moreover, whatever the sequence in which the infant's functions develop during the differentiation subphase, the characteristic of this early stage of practicing is that, while there is interest and absorption in these activities, interest in the mother definitely seems to take precedence.

Through the maturation of his locomotor apparatus, the child begins to venture farther away from the mother's feet. He is often so absorbed in his own activities that for long periods of time he appears to be oblivious to the mother's presence—yet he returns periodically to the mother, seeming to need her physical proximity.

The optimal distance in the *early practicing subphase* would seem to be one that allows the moving, exploring quadruped infant freedom and opportunity to exercise his autonomous functions at some physical distance from mother. At the same time, however, mother continues to be needed as the "home base," for what Furer named "emotional refueling."

It is worth noting, however, that despite the children's apparent obliviousness to their mothers during the early practicing period, most of them seemed to go through a brief period of increased separation anxiety. The fact that they were able to move away independently, yet remain connected with their mother—not physically, but by way of their seeing and hearing her—made the successful use of these distance modalities extraordinarily important. The children did not like to lose sight of mother; they might stare sadly at her empty chair, or at the door through which she had left.

We had not expected and were surprised by the finding that the advent of the capacity of free upright locomotion seems to take place in a direction not *toward* but *away from* mother, or even in the absence of mother. This is, we feel, an indicator that the normal infant is endowed with an innate given that prompts him at a certain point of his autonomous maturation to separate from mother—to further his own individuation. Walking makes possible for the toddler an enormous increase in reality discovery and the testing of his world through his own control, as a quasi-magic master. It coincides with the upsurge of goal-directed active aggressiveness.

The mother's renunciation of possession of the body of the infant boy or girl, at this point of the toddler's development, is the sine qua non requirement for normal separation-individuation. Most mothers recognize—empathically or even verbally—that this quasi-altruistic surrender of the infant's body to himself is a deplorable but necessary step in promoting the infant's autonomous growth. This, I feel, is also the first prerequisite for the development of the child's self-esteem. The practicing toddler's self-love and love of the object world, both his narcissism and his potential object love, are at their acme.

The child is exhilarated by his own capacities—he wants to share and show. He is continually delighted with the discoveries he makes in the expanding world; he acts as though he were enamored of the world and with his own grandeur and omnipotence.

The obligatory exhilaration of the practicing period seems to hinge upon the ascendancy of the infant's upright free locomotor capacity. In those children in whom locomotion is delayed, this obligatory exhilaration is also delayed, seems to be of shorter duration, and is much less in evidence. Besides being the function by which the child can physically distance himself from mother or approach her at will, locomotor capacity provides him with a variety of other experiences. His body is more exposed, but his plane of vision and the relation of his upright body in space enable him to see the world from a different—and relatively grown-up—angle. We know from Piaget that sensorimotor intelligence at this point is supplemented by a beginning representational intelligence; thus, symbolic thinking and upright free locomotion herald attainment of the first level of self-identity, of being a separate individual entity.

Even though some children were further advanced in their perceptual, cognitive, and other autonomous functions of the ego; more advanced in their reality-testing function—that is to say, in their autonomous individuation—locomotion was the behavioral sign which indicated most visibly to the observer the end of the "hatching process," that is to say, *psychological birth.*

II

Success in goal-directed activity seemed in inverse relation to the manifestations of hostile aggression, which was also involved in this, the second great shift of cathexis in the growing-up process.

Not only is the child in love with himself (narcissism); substitute familiar adults in the familiar setup of our nursery were easily accepted and even engaged. This was in contrast to what occurred during the next subphase, the subphase of rapprochement.

During the entire practicing subphase, the child has evoked the delighted and automatic admiration of the adult world, specifically of his average "ordinary devoted mother" (Winnicott 1960). Her admiration, when it is forthcoming, augments the practicing toddler's sound narcissism, his love of himself. Every new achievement, every new feat of the fledgling elicits admiration, at first unsolicited, later more or less exhibitionistically provoked by him from the entire adult object world around him. This kind of admiration, which does not even need to be expressed in words or gestures, may be one of the feeding lines that on the one hand promotes progression of the ego's autonomous functioning, and on the other furnishes a great accretion to the practicing toddler's feeling of grandeur—often exalted self-esteem.

In a circular fashion, the mirroring admiration also seems to augment the budding ego's readiness for mirroring the love object. Along with the rapid growth of cognition, it gradually leads to internalization processes of the *now fully born* (structured) *ego*. Eventually, these result in true ego identifications, in Jacobson's sense (1954).

Now, however, the price of this precious progress in development of autonomy has to be paid! As the sixteen- to eighteen-month-old's cognitive development progresses, he becomes more and more aware of his loss of the "ideal sense of self"—of well-being—when he notices his mother's absence from the room. At such times, we observed what we came to call *low-keyedness:* the toddler's gestural and performance motility slowed down, his interest in his surroundings diminished, and he appeared to be preoccupied with an inwardly concentrated attention. It was as if he wished to "image" another state of self—the state that he had felt at the time when the symbiotically experienced partner had been "one" with him.

As the toddler's awareness of separateness grows—an awareness stimulated by his maturationally acquired ability physically to move away from his mother and by his *cognitive growth*—he seems to experience an increased need and wish for his mother to *share* with him his every new acquisition of skill and experience. These are the reasons for which I called this subphase of separation-individuation the period of *rapprochement.*

At the very height of mastery, toward the end of the practicing period, it begins to dawn on the junior toddler that the world is *not* his oyster; that he must cope with it more or less "on his own," very often as a relatively helpless, small, and *separate* individual, unable to command relief or assistance merely by feeling the need for them or even by giving voice to that need. The quality and measure of the *wooing* behavior of the toddler toward his mother during this subphase provide important clues to the assessment of the normality of the individuation process.

The junior toddler gradually realizes that his love objects are separate individuals with their own individual interests. He must gradually and painfully give up his delusion of his own grandeur and participation in the still delusionally believed-in omnipotence of mother and father. Dramatic fights may ensue with mother, and temper tantrums might be the order of the day. (Many years ago, I recognized the significance of temper tantrums as a behavioral indication by which outward directed aggression is turned back onto the "self." Therefore, this mechanism may be looked upon as a precursor of internalization of aggression, and also as a precursor of superego formation.)

Be that as it may, as far as our observational research indicated, this phase of development is a *crossroads* that my co-workers and I termed the *rapprochement crisis*.

From around eighteen months on, we observed that our toddlers were quite eager to exercise their rapidly growing autonomy. Increasingly, they chose not to be reminded of the times when they could not manage on their own. On the other hand, the desire to be separate, grand, and omnipotent often conflicted with the desire to have mother magically fulfill all one's wishes—without the need to recognize that help was *actually coming from the outside*. Thus, in a majority of cases, the prevalent mood swung to that of general dissatisfaction and insatiability, and there developed a proneness to rapid swings of mood and to temper tantrums. The period of rapprochement was thus characterized by a sometimes rapid alternation of the desire to reject mother, on the one hand, and to cling to her with coercive, determined tenacity in words and acts on the other hand, a behavioral sequence that the word *ambitendency* describes most accurately. But often at that age there already was a *simultaneous* desire in both directions—i.e., the characteristic *ambivalence* of the eighteen- to twenty-two-month-olds.

In the rapprochement period which follows the earlier described psychological birth, the source of the child's greatest pleasure shifts from independent locomotion and exploration of the expanding inanimate world to *social interaction*. Peek-a-boo games as well as games of imitation become favorite pastimes. Recognition of mother as a separate person in the large world goes parallel with awareness of other children's separate existence, their being different from the own self. This was evidenced by the fact that children now showed a greater desire to *have* or to *do* what another child had or did—that is, a desire for mirroring, imitating, and coveting what the other child had. For example, the desire to acquire a "second belly button" (a penis) was sometimes quite openly expressed by girls. Along with this important development, there appeared the "no" along with definitely goal-directed anger, aggressiveness, if the desired aim could not be obtained. We are not, of course, losing sight of the fact that these developments take place in the midst of the anal phase, with its characteristics of anal acquisitiveness, jealousy, envy, and negativism, but also with a much earlier detection than we had previously believed of the anatomical sexual difference.

Depending upon her own adjustment, the mother may react either by continued emotional availability and playful participation in the toddler's world, or by a gamut of less desirable attitudes. If the mother is "quietly available" with a ready supply of object libido, if she shares the toddling adventurer's exploits, playfully reciprocates and thus helps his attempts at imitation, externalization, and inter-nalization—then the relationship between mother and toddler is able to progress to the point at which verbal communication takes over, even though vivid gestural behavior (this is, affectomotility) still predominates. By the end of the second or the beginning of the third year, the predictable emotional participation of the mother seems to facilitate the rich unfolding that is taking place in the toddler's thought processes, reality testing, and coping behavior. In most favorable cases, the toddler is, at this point, on the way to emotional object constancy in our and (I believe) in Hoffer's sense.

III

I should like to conclude my paper with some general statements, which may go beyond the topic that the title of my paper implied.

It is a generally accepted hypothesis among psychoanalysts that unless the child successfully traverses the symbiotic phase, and that first subphase of separation-individuation termed *differentiation*, psychosis will ensue (Mahler 1968).

Milder than psychotic disturbances, I believe, occur in children who, though they have passed through a separation-individuation process, have shown ominous deviations from the orderly progression of the subphases. If there is too much overlapping, or other serious disturbances in the differentiation and practicing subphases, and if the rapprochement crises were extreme and did not give way to any degree of object constancy, which is the open-ended fourth subphase of the separation-individuation process, fixation points are created. What may thus ensue is: narcissistic character formation and/or borderline pathology (with splitting mechanisms of the self and of the object world).

More and more, psychoanalysts have become aware of the fact that the pathologies of many of their adult (and, of course, also child) patients derive from the earliest years of life. Either deliberately or without full knowledge of their significance, analysts have been trying to reconstruct not only the preoedipal but also the preverbal genetic roots of their patients' greater or lesser failure to separate intrapsychically.

In my Freud Anniversary Lecture (*SP*II:11), I gave a vignette of one of my adult patient's borderline features of his analytic material, as I was able to reconstruct it from his dreams and fantasies, from his symbolic or symptomatic behavior, and especially from his body feelings, which he was able to put into words. It had become quite clear that his pathology derived from partial failures of the separation-individuation process.

Many more case histories and vignettes are contained in the works of psychoanalysts who have been the authors of recent books and articles. The most widely read and most influential in this direction are the works of Kernberg (1967, 1970) and Kohut (1971). It has become quite fashionable to compare, juxtapose, or polarize *The Analysis of the Self* with Kernberg's equally important work on the borderline patient, and it is also fashionable now to hint, as a sort of side issue, at certain observational and experimental data of Spitz, Mahler and her co-workers, as well as those of Judith Kestenberg, John Benjamin, T. Gouin-Décarie (1963), and many others. It would seem as if those developmental data had *something* to do with psychoanalytic propositions and constructs; but they are referred to as if they were *purely observational*—or *sociobiological* at best. They are not integrated, either as germinal or fundamental, with the lately quite obviously widening scope of psychoanalytic theory and practice. Only a few of my psychoanalytic colleagues have become fully aware that, for this widening scope of psychoanalytic theory, those hypotheses that have been derived from psychoanalytic observational data of the preverbal phase have made meaningful, and indeed indispensable contributions to their own reconstructive work, and offer the promise of further progress in psychoanalytic metapsychology and practice.

Even though most analysts, especially and particularly analysts of adults, may daily encounter material that has the flavor and the patterning of the preverbal, earliest primary-process-dominated phases in the lives of their patients, they shy away from attempts at correlation, let alone from integration of their reconstructive work with those developmental data that Spitz, myself and my co-workers, and others have found. These data, we have postulated, pertain to that period of life which is, especially lately, brought up in the literature as the "unrememberable" and the "unforgettable," (Frank 1969, Anthony 1961, Lampl-de Groot 1973).

Freud himself clearly implied that we will remain handicapped in our efforts at reconstruction unless we learn more and more how to decipher the prehistoric phase of human development. I believe, like Ernst Kris and others, that unless we try to integrate consensually validated preverbal data with the constructs of psychoanalytic theory—which derives from reconstructive material learned in the psychoanalytic situation—we shall remain handicapped in making progress. (It should not be overlooked that even *our* developmental hypotheses are to an extent reconstructive—our constructions and reconstructions, inductive and deductive methods are intertwined all along in both the analytic and the observational situations.)

In a recent discussion of "On the Current Status of the Infantile Neurosis"[2] (*SPII*:12), I took the standpoint that psychoanalytic metapsychology and our technique would gain greatly if, side by side with the drive theory and our newer structural theory—both of which will remain the foundations of psychoanalysis—we would let ourselves be guided by the steadily growing psychoanalytic developmental theories. These theories have already put at our disposal many consensually validated data of infant observation, which have

2. See also Ritvo (1974) and Loewald (1974).

proved to be of value in reconstructing the data gained in the psychoanalytic situation with regard not only to the oedipal and the preoedipal stages, but also to much that is capable of validation from the preverbal stage.

We are still underestimating the pathogenicity, but also the character-building, the personality-integrative role of preverbal levels of development; and we are underestimating in particular the importance of ego and superego precursors—and especially their capacity for creating hard-to-decipher proclivities to intrapsychic conflicts!

Part Two

THE CLINICAL APPLICATION OF THE THEORY OF SEPARATION-INDIVIDUATION TO INFANTILE NEUROSES AND BORDERLINE CONDITIONS

Chapter 11

A STUDY OF THE SEPARATION-INDIVIDUATION PROCESS AND ITS POSSIBLE APPLICATION TO BORDERLINE PHENOMENA IN THE PSYCHOANALYTIC SITUATION

[1971]

The question of the kind of inferences, if any, that can be drawn from preverbal material in and outside the psychoanalytic situation is a most controversial one. It is, I feel, a very interesting issue, yet quite difficult to deal with. Precisely because verbal means lend themselves only very poorly to the translation of such material, most researchers have seen fit to create a new language, often filled with metaphors, in order to communicate their findings to others.

EARLY DEVELOPMENT IN OBSERVATIONAL RESEARCH

Psychoanalytic observational research of the first years of life touches on the essence of reconstruction and on the problem of coenesthetic empathy, both so essential for the clinical efficiency of psychoanalysis.

At one end of the spectrum of opinion on these questions stand those who believe in innate, complex oedipal fantasies, those who, like Melanie Klein and her followers, assume and rely on earliest

The Twentieth Freud Anniversary Lecture, April 1970.

extrauterine (human) mental life. They believe in a quasi-phylogenetic memory, an inborn symbolic process. For them, no phenomenological, behavioral data can have sufficient validity to refute their *a priori* convictions about complex mental positions, such as the schizoid position in the fourth month of life, or the depressive position at eight months.

At the other end of the spectrum stand those among us Freudian analysts who look with favor on stringent verbal and reconstructive evidence. We organize these on the basis of Freud's metapsychological constructs; yet some of us seem to accord preverbal material no right to serve as the basis for even the most cautious and tentative extension of our main body of hypotheses, unless these, too, be supported by reconstruction, that is to say, by clinical and, of course, predominantly verbal material.

Yet Freud's hope was that his fundamental body of theory—that truly monumental basis of clinical and theoretical work—would remain a *living heritage*. Even his genius could not work out every detail in one lifetime; these, added bit by bit, should eventually coalesce to form a general psychology.

Instead of entering into the controversy as to whether preverbal infant observation has any validity for drawing inferences about the evolution of *intrapsychic* human life, I would like to present an account of one such effort. I do so in order to show what possible inferences were permitted from some of the repetitive, fairly regularly occurring clusterings of the data, which we accumulated around our tentative working hypotheses.

I will put aside the history of my work and descriptions of our methods and proceed to some observations made, and inferences drawn, from my more recent studies at the Masters Children's Center and in the psychoanalytic situation.[1]

Beyond the conceptualization of the subphases of the separation-individuation[2] process, we have made additional observations relevant to substantive issues of the study. They are repetitive, if not

1. [See source notes appended to this volume.]
2. I owe the term *separation-individuation* to Dr. Annemarie Weil's suggestion to point out clearly the two aspects of this intrapsychic process (personal communication, 1954).

ubiquitous, age-specific clusterings of behavioral sequences and affective reactions found in our children between five and thirty-six months of age. These were polarized by the mother-child interaction during their coenesthetic[3] period of life, and continued in individually more and more differentiated sequences and reactions into the period Spitz has called the "diacritic organization."[4]

First substantive issue: We observed the bridge function of mother-related parts of the familiar inanimate surroundings of our nursery of our infants—for example, the chair on which mother habitually sat, or her handbag, and so on. The infant, within a certain age span, turned to these objects as substitutes for the mother when she left the room, rather than to another adult. This mechanism we recognized as a transitional phenomenon between Kestenberg's (1971) organ-object bridges, Winnicott's (1953) transitional, and Greenacre's (1969, 1970) fetishlike objects.

Second substantive issue: We observed in life and on film a differential, truly coenesthetic response to the *warmth* and *turgor*, to the "feel" of the human body (molding phenomena [*SPII:3*], tactile and visual exploration of the human face and similar behaviors) quite different from their handling of inanimate objects (*SPII:7*). The inverted and grossly distorted response to the animate and inanimate object world in psychosis was described by Sechehaye (1947), Mahler (*SPI:10*), Searles (1960), and others.

Third substantive issue: Our data have indicated the importance of the "carrying power," as it were, of the young child's "confident expectation" (Benedek 1938) as contrasted with some children's "basic mistrust," to use Erikson's term (1950). This we saw in some children as early as six or seven months. We observed children of the same mother at comparable ages, one of whom showed minimal stranger anxiety and optimal basic trust; the other, increased stranger anxiety and a lack of basic trust.

One tries to understand these variations by way of the siblings'

3. *Coenesthesia* is defined in Drever's *Dictionary of Psychology* as: common sensibility, the total undifferentiated mass of sensations derived from the body as a whole, but more particularly, the internal organs.

4. *Diacritic*—from the Greek—is "to distinguish, to separate across" (cf. Spitz 1945).

different endowments on the one hand and, on the other, through the prevalent emotional climate of the particular mother-infant relationship, as observed in their interaction and through interviews with the mother (cf. Weil 1970).

This phenomenon of "confident expectation," as well as its opposite—more than optimal stranger anxiety and "basic mistrust"—contributes and relates to later attitudes in life, even though intervening drive and defense vicissitudes will, of course, greatly influence and may even change these patterns.

Fourth substantive issue: The basic mood, our study indicated, appeared to have its beginning as early as the last half of the second year. It seemed to derive substantially from this very "basic trust" or, in contrast, from "basic mistrust"; as I have described (*SP*II:5), it also derived from a too sudden deflation of the obligatory infantile belief in its own and borrowed magic omnipotence (Jacobson 1953b).

Our research design had built into it brief, passive separation experiences, experiments as it were. Once a week, a senior worker assigned to a particular mother-child pair interviewed the mother in a room outside the nursery.

From the infant's reactions to these brief separations I believe that we were able to judge fairly how the infant's "need" became a "wish" in Max Schur's sense (1966). Our data indicated the phenomenological concomitants of the development from an "unspecific craving" to the specific "object-bound" affect of "longing" (*SP*I:15, *SP*II:1). This seemed to occur gradually and had, at first, a "waxing and waning" quality. It had its beginnings at the height of bodily differentiation from the love object and continued into the practicing period of ten to fifteen months. At that age "longing" is indicated by the phenomenon of *low-keyedness* during brief separations. This culminates—during the *rapprochement* period at fifteen to twenty-five months—in impressive, individually different reactions to mother's absences, which are much more specific and readable.

The smoothly separating and individuating toddler easily finds solace in his rapidly developing ego functions. The child concentrates on practicing mastery of his own skills and autonomous capacities.

During this practicing subphase of separation-individuation, one can occasionally see with particular clarity that the intrapsychic process of separation and individuation runs on two intertwined, but not always synchronized developmental tracks: one is *individuation*—the evolution of intrapsychic autonomy; the other is the intrapsychic *separation* process, which runs along the track of differentiation, distancing, boundary-structuring, and disengagement from mother.

As I indicated elsewhere, in a study such as ours, one learns most when elements of the process are "out of kilter."

BRIEF COMPARATIVE DEVELOPMENTAL HISTORIES OF BARNEY AND SAMMY

I shall illustrate this with two brief vignettes.

Barney, whose maturational process enabled him to achieve upright locomotion precociously at nine months of age, had the opportunity, by endowment and by the nature of the mother-child relationship, to take into and integrate in his early ego structure certain patterns of the mother-child relationship, and eject, that is, externalize, others. He also seemed to have ample opportunity to emulate and eventually to identify with his father, who was very much a hero for him by the last half of the second year. Barney's mother emphasized this again and again.

Barney's early darting away from his mother with the expectation of being chased by her had interesting components of the mother-child as well as of the father-child relationship.

The contrasting mother-child pair, *Sammy* and his mother, had a greatly prolonged symbiotic and—on the mother's part—parasitic relationship. His mother breast-fed Sammy for one and a half years. Both parents kept him in continual dependency. Confined to a small area by his own, partly constitutional, partly environmental, delay in locomotor capacity, Sammy made the most extensive use of his visibly emerging perceptive, cognitive, and prehensile faculties. He occupied and amused himself alone in our playpen for long periods of time when his mother was out of the room. This he did at an age when children of comparable age would vigorously protest against such confinement. He willingly engaged others and accepted their active comforting, which other children would not. He did not show any sign of low-keyedness or of specific longing at the age at which we observed such phenomena in other children. (Such behavior appeared delayed in Sammy.)

The normal child's early defensive struggle against interferences with his autonomy was, however, amply exemplified by Sammy. He valiantly struggled, from an early age, in fact, from the fifth month on and attempted to extricate himself from the smothering grip of his mother (cf. Spock 1963).

Most of the time children in the practicing period appeared relatively elated and self-sufficient. They became low-keyed only when they became aware that mother was absent from the room. In those instances their gestural and performance motility slowed down, their interest in their surroundings diminished; they appeared to be preoccupied with inwardly concentrated attention, with what Rubinfine (1961) called "imaging." This we were permitted to assume from behavioral evidence: (1) when another person than the mother actively tried to comfort the child, he would lose his intrapsychic balance and burst into tears; and, of course, also from (2) the child's reaction to reunion with the briefly absent mother. The low-keyedness and apparent "imaging" of mother, I tend to interpret as the attempt to hold on to a state of mind that Sandler, Holder, and Meers (1963) have termed "the ideal state of self." This seems to consist of a symbiotic closeness, completeness, a coenesthetically sensed dual unity with mother.

SEPARATION ANXIETY

Some children transiently appeared quite overwhelmed by fear of object loss, so that the "ego-filtered affect of longing" was in danger of very abruptly turning into desperate crying. This was the case with Barney for a short time at a period when his "individuation" had not yet caught up with his maturational spurt of locomotion, serving separation. He was unable to cope emotionally, for a while, with the experience of the self-induced separations from mother in space. He was visibly bewildered when he hurt himself and noticed that his mother was not, automatically, close.

Our data, in their rich detail, have unmistakably shown regularly occurring combinations of factors from which we were permitted to conclude that there was a dawning awareness that the still-symbiotic mothering half of the self was missed. The ensuing behavior of low-keyedness had different shadings in individual children compared with each other and with themselves over time. In a paper written with McDevitt (*SP*II:7) I likened this initial "low-keyedness" with the "conservation-withdrawal" of monkeys as described by Charles Kaufman and L. A. Rosenblum (1968).

This longing for the state of well-being and unity, or closeness, with mother we found peculiarly lacking in children whose symbiotic relationship had been an unduly prolonged or a disturbed one: in Sammy, who had an exaggeratedly close, parasitic symbiosis with his mother; in another child, a little girl (Harriet), in whom the mother-infant relationship was what Robert Fliess (1961) termed *asymbiotic*. It seemed diminished and irregular in children in whom the symbiotic relationship with mother was marred by the unpredictability and impulsivity of a partly engulfing and partly rejecting mother.

In the course of the practicing period, we were impressed by the tremendously exhilarating, truly dramatic effect that upright locomotion had on the hitherto also very busy quadruped infant's general mood. I became aware of its importance for the achievement of the "psychological birth experience," the "hatching," through unexpected, regularly occurring observations of behavioral sequences, comparing them with Phyllis Greenacre's work (1957) on the childhood of the artist. It seemed to me that most practicing toddlers had a "love affair with the world" as well.

This exhilaration occurred later than usual in those cases where the ascendancy of the child's free locomotor capacity was delayed. Thus, this phenomenon seemed definitely connected with and dependent on the function of free locomotor activity of the ego.

With this acquisition of exhilarating upright, free locomotion and the closely following attainment of that stage of cognitive development that Piaget (1936) regards as the beginning of representational intelligence, the human being had emerged as a separate and autonomous being. These two powerful "organizers" (Spitz 1957) seem to be the midwives of *psychological birth*. With this "hatching" process the toddler reaches the first level of identity, that of being a separate individual entity (Mahler 1958b).

Now that the child has come to be more aware of his separate self, he has once again an increased need to seek closeness with mother. This had been, so to speak, held in abeyance throughout the practicing period. That is why I gave this subphase the name *rapprochement.*

IMPORTANCE OF THE EMOTIONAL AVAILABILITY OF MOTHER AND DISENGAGEMENT FROM HER IN THE RAPPROCHEMENT SUBPHASE

One cannot emphasize too strongly the importance of the optimal emotional availability of the mother during this subphase. The value of the father in this period has been stressed by Loewald (1951), Greenacre (1966), and Abelin (1971).

The refueling type of bodily approach described by Furer[5] which characterized the practicing infant, was now replaced in the period between fifteen and twenty-five months by interaction of toddler and mother on a much higher level; symbolic language, vocal and other intercommunications, as well as play became increasingly prominent (Galenson 1971).

We observed separation reactions in all our children during this rapprochement subphase. And I would venture the hypothesis that it is in those children whose separation reactions are characterized by moderate and ego-filtered affects, in which the libidinal valence— love instead of aggression—predominated, that subsequent development is more likely to be favorable.

Through this rapprochement process, the sense of identity, the self-representation as distinct from the object representation, begins to become consolidated.

5. Personal communication.

Two characteristic patterns of behavior—the shadowing of mother and the darting away from her with the expectation of being chased and swept into her arms—indicate the toddler's wish for reunion with the love object, and, side-by-side with this, also a fear of reengulfment. One can continually observe the warding-off pattern against impingement upon the toddler's recently achieved autonomy. Moreover, the incipient fear of loss of love represents an element of the conflict on the way to internalization. Some toddlers of rapprochement age already seem to be rather sensitive to disapproval. Autonomy is defended by the "no" as well as by the increased aggression and negativism of the anal phase. (One is reminded of Anna Freud's classic paper on negativism and emotional surrender [1952a].)

In most mother-toddler pairs, these rapprochement conflicts, which McDevitt calls the *rapprochement crises,* do finally come to an end. This is helped by the developmental spurt of the conflict-free parts of the autonomous ego (Hartmann 1939). These then, in the third year, help the child in his progress toward the attainment of libidinal object constancy, in Hartmann's sense (1952).

During the time of normal symbiosis, the narcissistically fused object is felt to be "good," that is, in harmony with the symbiotic self, so that primary identification takes place under a positive valence of love. Later on, after separation, the child may have encountered "bad," frustrating, unpleasurable, even frightening experiences in his interaction with mother and "other," so that the image of the object may have assumed a "negative emotional valence" (Heimann 1966).

THE ROLE OF AGGRESSION AND THE DEFENSE MECHANISM OF SPLITTING THE OBJECT WORLD INTO "GOOD" AND "BAD"

The less gradually the intrapsychic separation-individuation process takes place, and the less the modulating, negotiating function of the ego gains ascendancy, the greater the extent to which the object remains an unassimilated foreign body, a "bad" introject in the intrapsychic emotional economy. In the effort to eject this "bad" introject, derivatives of the aggressive drive come into play and there seems to develop an increased proclivity to identify with, or to confuse, the self-representation with the "bad" introject. If this situation prevails during the rapprochement subphase, then aggression may be unleashed in such a way as to inundate or sweep away the "good" object, and with it the "good" self-representation. This would be indicated by early, severe temper tantrums, for example, in children in whom the too sudden and painful realization of their helplessness results in the too abrupt deflation of their previous sense of their own and shared magic omnipotence (in Edith Jacobson's sense, 1964).

I observed many of our normal children recoil, or show signs that had to be interpreted as a kind of erotized fear, on being cornered by an adult who wanted to seek, often playfully, bodily contact with the child. This seemed to be felt as overwhelming by the toddler because of the adult's sheer bodily size and strength.

These behaviors remind us of the fear of reengulfment by the already somehow contaminated, dangerous "mother of separation" in whose omnipotence the child still believes, but who does not seem to let him share in her omnipotence any more.

There were other early constellations of variables, which may represent fixation points for pathological regression, such as the precocious differentiation of a "false self" (Winnicott 1962a) by a little girl (Heather), who played peek-a-boo with herself when her mother rejected her because she was a late walker; or the narcissistic hypercathexis of the body ego in the case of Harriet, a child whose mother did not seem to have enough tender emotion for her children, but rather overstimulated them. All these constellations of factors are possible contributories to borderline features in personality development.

In incipient infantile neurosis, conflict is indicated by coercive behaviors directed toward the mother, designed to force her to function as the child's omnipotent extension. This alternates with signs of desperate clinging. In other words, in those children with less than optimal development, the ambivalence conflict is discernible during the rapprochement subphase in rapidly alternating clinging and increased negativistic behaviors. This may be in some cases a reflection of the fact that the child has split the object world, more permanently than is optimal, into "good" and "bad." By means of this splitting, the "good" object is defended against the derivatives of the aggressive drive.

These mechanisms, coercion and splitting of the object world, are characteristic in most cases of borderline transference. We were able to study these in the verbal, primary process material of a few children at the end of their second and during their third year of life. These mechanisms, along with the problem of finding what the late Maurice Bouvet (1958) described as the "optimal distance," may prevail as early as in the fourth subphase of separation-individuation at a time when "libidinal object constancy" should have been achieved and separation reactions should be receding.

Disturbances during the rapprochement subphase are likely to reappear in much more definite and individually different forms during the final phase of that process in which a unified self-representation should become demarcated from a blended and integrated object representation.

The clinical outcome of these rapprochement crises will be determined by: (1) the development toward libidinal object constancy; (2) the quantity and quality of later disappointments (stress traumata); (3) possible shock traumata; (4) the degree of castration anxiety; (5) the fate of the oedipus complex; and (6) the developmental crises of adolescence—all of which function within the context of the individual's constitutional endowment.

TWO IMPORTANT FINDINGS

During the years of our data collection, we classified and sorted the material and ordered it into distinct categories that were relevant to our working hypotheses.

One interesting yield of our data processing was the finding that, from sixteen or seventeen months on, the data no longer "fit" comfortably into discrete categories. It began to appear increasingly arbitrary to describe any one item of behavior without referring to more and more of the total array of behaviors that were to be seen in the child at a particular period of time. It seemed that the behavior of the child was becoming increasingly integrated.

That also meant that early affectomotor and preverbal sensorimotor patterns had already been integrated by the middle of the second year, solidly enough, so that derivatives could not be reconstructively traced back, step-by-step, by means of deduction. In other words, we learned inductively that in most individuals the derivatives of the early, preverbal, sensorimotor period became integrated into character structure.

The second observation during data processing had to do with sex differences. Until this point, the children often seemed to us to fit into various subgroups from the separation-individuation point of view—subgroups containing both boys and girls. But now while, on the one hand, the complexity of the children made it difficult to group them, on the other hand, those common traits that existed were suggestive of a growing trend toward sexual differentiation and identity formation.

In average development, as I indicated in my Brill Memorial Lecture (SPII:1), the progressive forces of the growing ego are astonishingly successful. Often they tend to even out most of the discrepancies and minor deviations.

It is precisely the deficiencies of integration and internalization which will leave residua, and thus may manifest themselves in borderline mechanisms, which indicate a degree of failure of the synthetic function of the ego.

EARLY DEVELOPMENT RECONSTRUCTED

I should emphasize, however, as others and I myself have done before, that in terms of reconstruction in the psychoanalytic situation in general, none of the phenomena that can be reconstructed from unintegrated residua will be an equivalent repetition, a replica as it were, of early developmental sequences of the preverbal phase. One must expect that reconstructions will always contain telescoped screen memories and defense formations that have been altered by subsequent progressive development, as well as by regressive changes in the instinctual drives, in the ego, and in the superego. These may, or may not, make their appearance in the verbal and nonverbal material.

For many borderline phenomena, one can apply what is learned from observation, not so much to content as to general behaviors and attitudes of the patient in the psychoanalytic situation, that is to say, to certain configurations, persistent transference or acting-out patterns which seem to be the outcome of unresolved conflicts of the separation-individuation process.

My intention, at first, was to establish in this paper linking up, in neat detail, the described substantive issues with specific aspects of borderline phenomena shown by child and adult patients in the psychoanalytic situation. But I have come to be more and more convinced that there is no "direct line" from the deductive use of borderline phenomena to one or another substantive finding of observational research.

It cannot be accidental, however, that in the literature it is the borderline pathology that authors single out as paradigmatic of fixation or regression, traceable to certain aspects of the formative events of the separation and individuation process (Kohut 1966, Tartakoff 1966, Kernberg 1967, Frijling-Schreuder 1969).

The literature abounds in papers and symposia dealing with the sequelae of the failure of internalization, increased separation anxiety, and other clinical signs that indicate, for example, the following: that the blending and synthesis of "good" and "bad" self and object images have not been achieved; that ego-filtered affects have become inundated by surplus unneutralized aggression; that delusions of omnipotence alternate with utter dependency and self-denigration; that the body image has become or remains suffused with unneutralized id-related erogeneity and aggressive, pent-up body feelings, and so on.

Before I proceed to my case illustration, I would like to single out two main additional propositions which seem to me relevant for the understanding of borderline phenomena in the psychoanalytic situation. One is the importance of reconciliation and, thus, of integration of the image of the erstwhile "good" symbiotic mother, whom we long for "from the cradle on to the grave," this image to become blended with the representation of the ambivalently loved—dangerous because potentially reengulfing—"mother after separation."

I also wish to point out my impression—just an impression—gained of the importance of the preoedipal father's role in the sample that we have studied. We gained the impression that he was not only the "awakener from sleep" (Lewin 1952), but also the protector from the by-then, in so many cases, contaminated (Kris et al. 1954), potentially overwhelming "mother of separation."

The second proposition refers to the erogeneity of the body image, its suffusion with narcissistic cathexis (Schur 1955). This seems to be due to a disturbed cathectic balance of libido distribution between the self and the object. I found a group of borderline phenomena which seems to be related to heightened body narcissism, focal and diffuse erogeneity of the body image, prevalent in many borderline features of male and female patients alike.

If there was major failure of integration during the first three subphases of separation-individuation, particularly on the level of gender identity, the child might not have taken autonomous, representationally clearly separated possession of his or her own bodily self, partly because he or she did not experience the mother's gradual relinquishing possession of her toddler's body (A. Freud 1952b, 1953, Hoffer 1950a, 1950b, Greenson 1954). Such male and female patients alike will ever so often act out in the transference and in life, especially in marriage, the unconscious role of a cherished or rejected part of the parent's hypothetical body-self ideal, or treat the spouse's body as a cherished or rejected organ of their own self (Stein 1956).

Let me cite only one example of borderline phenomena in the psychoanalytic situation.

Mr. A., an unmarried man in his late twenties, and an only child, was one of those patients who demonstrated, as well as unconsciously acted out, man's eternal search for the "good symbiotic mother," so as to latch on to her, to be united with her, to be "safe" with her. The basic importance of this archaic mechanism has been described by the Hungarian analyst Imre Hermann (1936). In many cases the so-called primordial transference (Stone 1961) is found to contain this basic longing for reunion with the symbiotic mother— with the search for her in fantasy after intrapsychic separation had severed the tie with her.

My patient, Mr. A., after a period of analysis, during which he occasionally complained bitterly that he could not feel close to or relate to the analyst, or to anybody else, gave vent to his great resentment, and every so often his rage against his superiors, his contemporaries, his father, his mother, and of course also his analyst. They had all "let me down; they just expected too much of me." His mother, in particular, was impossible to please, she was unloving, undemonstrative, and so on. His anger was readily turned back upon the self.

In the midst of these "grievance sessions," in which self-accusations and self-denigration played just as prominent a role as his complaints about people, there were, by contrast but only on rare occasions, hours in which he saw the object world and himself in a rather rosy light. On those days his grandiose fantasies (Kohut 1968) easily came through, and his transference feelings swung from despondency and self-denigration to childlike admiration for and unqualified overestimation of others—particularly his analyst (Greenacre 1966). In real life he showed a more adequate evaluation of his real worth and of his truly excellent endowment, but in his transference neurosis his mood swings were extreme, as was his belief in his own magic omnipotence and that of analysis itself, although both collapsed from one day to another. (We owe the description of this mechanism to Edith Jacobson 1953b, 1957b, 1964, 1967.)

During a long stretch of analysis, two screen memories stood out. I believe that these will be better conveyed if they are interwoven with and discussed in the light of the working-through process.

In one of these all-too-rare "good hours" (Kris 1956b), the patient brought out—this time with an amazing array of rather libidinally cathected strong affects dominated by muted anxiety and longing— the helplessness and misery of the episodes that we knew so well as screen memories: his helplessness and lonesome desperation when as a schoolboy he had been wheeled away from his parents into the operating room and another traumatic episode when he had been banished from the parental bed.

The impact of his upsurging affects was connected in the transference with his apprehension about being taken from and thus losing the analyst by the demands of his job.

He indicated that when he was lying on the couch, he would feel himself floating far away into space. He associated this feeling with those he had had when he was anesthesized and also with man's flight into space away from his safe anchorage on earth. Both groups of associations shook him up considerably. At the end of the hour he seemed to be literally collapsed and miserable. In spite of his tall, imposing stature he became little more than a small heap of misery— an abandoned child. His body narcissism was greatly increased, and counterphobic mechanisms became prominent as a way of fending off his hypochondriacal preoccupations.

In one of the succeeding hours, the patient, in one of his characteristic mood swings, announced that he definitely wanted to sit up; he said this with what was for him unusual determination. "When I lie down, I get this floating feeling again, as if I am floating far away from you into space." The feeling he experienced during anesthesia, of the stars and rockets overhead falling upon him, piercing his skin, was related to the prickly feeling in his limbs that he had felt before falling asleep at the onset of anesthesia. He considered man's ambition to land on another planet to be the culmination of his detachment from earth, a demonstration of the possibility that man would never achieve anchorage again.

These fantasies were associated with the other affect-laden screen memory as well: his mother, who had until then allowed him to snuggle up to her and occupy his father's bed, had told him one day that he was now too big a boy for such intimacy. He insisted that this had occurred when he was not yet three years old.

The predominant nightly fear of his early childhood had reappeared during his anesthesia. There was the little dark man of his early nightmares, sitting on his shoulder, grinning unmercifully and thus indicating that "he was about to kidnap me." He desperately wanted his father—not his mother—to come to his rescue with a flashlight, as he had indeed done during the patient's early childhood, so as to dispel his son's night terrors.

During the hour in which he sat up, the patient, with averted gaze, expressed his past longing to throw his arms around his mother's neck and to be told by her that everything will be all right! He now felt the same way about his analyst, and he dreaded, when lying down, the vivid sensation that he was about to float away into space. At times, he said, the distance between the analyst and himself became too threatening.

Fear of the grinning, dark little man who had perched on his shoulder during anesthesia, seemed to have originated at the height of the phallic phase; it occurred coincidental with or subsequent to the time when he had been banned by his mother from his snuggling position beside her. The fear of the little dark man was, of course, overdetermined. The homunculus symbolized his body as a whole, detached—banished—from his anchorage at his mother's body. It also symbolized many other elements.

Ever since that very early occurrence of being banished, the patient felt that he could not approach his mother; she was hard, forbidding, and critical of him. He could not share with her. He had had the urge to run away from home and search—but *for what* and *where?* Until his analysis during his adult life he used to wander aimlessly in the streets or take endless drives without any goal—away from people.

Fixation to the rapprochement subphase of development seemed to be quite obvious and convincing. His splitting of the object world was overdetermined; it consisted basically of searching for the good symbiotic mother as contrasted with the forbidding "bad" mother after separation. The bad castrated and castrating, yet phallic woman's forbidding quality was projected onto the "bad outside world," and his relationships with women were marred by a fear of being engulfed by them. The competitive, but admired, protective, "good" masculine world as represented by his father was pitted against this "bad mother of separation."

After this sequence of analysis he again brought out, but with attenuated guilt feelings, his death wishes concerning the "mother of separation." She was standing in the way of his pal-like relationship to his father. This came to the fore with appropriate affective cathexis and could be connected by him with many of the subsequent vicissitudes of his instinctual drives, conflicts around the two levels of his identity, and the adverse fate of his originally quite adequate "basic trust" (Mahler 1958b).

His main primordial transference began to change when, after we had worked through his utter dependency needs, he exclaimed that, for the first time, he felt that the analyst was his friend.

I think these are the instances to which Winnicott (1969) was referring when he spoke of his patients' long-standing inability and then their final ability to use the object, the analyst, in the transference.

It was clear that the patient felt an intense longing for the symbiotic mother—not just the need-satisfying one—the symbiotic half of the self, the longing for the probably still coenesthetically remembered harmony of the dual-unity stage. Side by side with this there was the impotent rage, hatred that the patient felt toward the depreciated, castrated, and castrating "mother of separation." This was connected, of course, with the patient's feeling that sexuality was dirty and that because mother and father had indulged in it, the product would inevitably have to be an anal monster—the little dark homunculus—he himself.

It befits this Freud Anniversary Lecture that I conclude by quoting Freud himself, by citing from *Civilization and Its Discontents* (1930), which bears on his implicit recognition of the importance of the coenesthetic realm of human experiences.[5] He said:

> Through a deliberate direction of one's sensory activities and through suitable muscular action, one can differentiate between what is internal . . . and . . . what emanates from the outer world. In this way one makes the first step towards the introduction of the reality principle which is to dominate future development. This differentiation, of course, serves the practical purpose of enabling one to defend oneself against sensations of unpleasure which one actually feels or with which one is threatened. In order to fend off certain unpleasurable excitations arising from within, the ego can use no other methods than those which it uses against unpleasure coming from without. . . .

5. I am grateful to Dr. Kestenberg (1971) for drawing my attention to this quotation.

In this way then, the ego detaches itself from the external world. Or, to put it more correctly, originally the ego includes everything, later it separates off an external world from itself. Our present ego-feeling is, therefore, only a shrunken residue of a much more inclusive—indeed, an all-embracing—feeling which corresponded to a more intimate bond between the ego and the world about it. If we may assume that there are many people in whose mental life this primary ego-feeling has persisted to a greater or less degree, it would exist in them side by side with the narrower and more sharply demarcated ego-feeling of maturity, like a kind of counterpart to it. In that case, the ideational contents appropriate to it would be precisely those of limitlessness and of a bond with the universe—the same ideas with which my friend [Romain Rolland] elucidated the "oceanic" feeling. [p. 67f.]

Chapter 12

ON THE CURRENT STATUS OF
THE INFANTILE NEUROSIS

[1975]

As Anna Freud (1936, 1962, 1965) expressed it—and as Ritvo (1974) and Lebovici (1973) have said—our current view on the concept of infantile neurosis differs considerably from that which prevailed at the time of Little Hans and the Wolf Man.

I would like to briefly discuss how the concepts of *infantile neurosis,* of *object relations,* and of *narcissism* might be clarified by including in their consideration the symbiotic and separation-individuation phases of human development. I believe if these considerations were to become integrated into our thinking in terms of assessing the widening scope of neurotic and other disturbances of childhood (cf. also Nagera 1966), it might help us to comprehend such issues as the parallel existence, the simultaneous development, and the interrelationships of what we call object relationship and narcissism—or transference neurosis and narcissistic disturbances—and also borderline symptomatology.

The change in our thinking since the 1920s is attributable to the fact that before Freud gave us the structural theory, we had only the libido theory as our guide; nowadays, we employ the structural theory intensively to aid us in our formulations. In addition, however, we have, thanks to Spitz, to the work of the Hampstead

Clinic, and to many others, a growing psychoanalytic developmental theory at our disposal, concerned mainly with the evolution of object relationship.

Much of the empirical data available to us reveals that, while the concept of infantile neurosis derives from the prototypic source of intrapsychic conflict at its most complex state—the oedipus complex—there is much in the neurotic development we see daily that derives as well from the prephallic, preoedipal periods, during which crucial forms of psychic organization and reorganization are structured.

As I see it, much of our understanding may depend on developmental aspects in which most important are the qualitative assessment of residues of the symbiotic as well as the separation-individuation periods.

Through cross fertilization of the structural and refined psychoanalytic developmental theories, we today possess *instruments* which, if used to amplify the libido theory, might bring us further in our understanding of the widening scope of neurotic symptoms in childhood as well as during the entire life cycle.

As early as 1924, Abraham apparently was concerned with the lack in the concomitant status of object relations when he formulated the concepts of the *preambivalent, ambivalent,* and *postambivalent object.* We easily forget the fact that the apex of the libido theory which holds the key to neurosis, the oedipus complex itself, is not only a drive theory but, equally importantly, an object relations theory. In this regard, Rangell (1972), has suggested that the oedipus complex may be viewed as another organizer (in Spitz's sense).

A number of problems remain unsettled because of a tendency to underestimate the potentiality of the ego and the superego precursors at early levels of development to create intrapsychic conflicts.

I also feel that our understanding of infantile neurosis might profit by integration of data gained by observation and reconstruction of the very first phases of the child's extrauterine existence. This, I believe, may be achieved by observing the path of the infant's differentiation and disengagement from the symbiotic matrix—and tracing the first steps of internalized conflict.

In our clinical and normative observational work with mother-child pairs, we came across—to our own surprise—*developmental conflicts* that are *phase specific*, yet individually variable as well. These occurred—with amazing regularity—from the second half of the second year on (*SPII*:8, 9, 10).

As I have earlier described (*SPII*:6), it is precisely at the point when the child is at the peak of his delusion of omnipotence—at the height of the practicing period—that his narcissism is particularly vulnerable to the danger of deflation, because the maturational and developmental progression of the locomotor and cognitive functions of his ego confront him with a new and disturbing reality.

In these early months (from about the fifteenth or sixteenth month) the toddler develops a dawning awareness of his own separateness. As a result of the maturational achievement of the ego, culminating in free upright locomotion and advanced cognitive development, the toddler is no longer able to maintain the delusion of his omnipotent grandeur.

In the following, third subphase of the separation-individuation process, the rapprochement period, while individuation proceeds rapidly and the child exercises it to the limit, he becomes more and more aware of his separateness and begins to employ all kinds of partly internalized, partly still outwardly acted-out coping mechanisms in order to deny separateness. One of the often seen coping behaviors is the toddler's insistent claim for the mother's attention and participation.

But no matter how insistently the toddler tries to coerce the mother, he and she no longer function effectively as a dual unit; that is to say, he can no longer enforce her participation in his persisting delusion of parental omnipotence. Simultaneously the other half of the erstwhile dual unity, the mother, must recognize her child as a separate, autonomous individual in his own right. Verbal communication becomes more and more necessary; gestural coercion on the part of the toddler or mutual preverbal empathy between mother and child will no longer suffice for the child to attain his goal of satisfaction, of well-being (Joffe and Sandler 1965).

The junior toddler gradually realizes that his love objects (his parents) are separate individuals with their own interests. He must gradually and painfully give up both the delusion of his own

grandeur and the participation in his persistently believed-in omnipotence of mother. The result is heightened separation anxiety as
well as coercive dramatic fights with mother, less so, it seemed to us,
with father. This is the crossroad that we have termed the "rapprochement *crisis.*"

This rapprochement struggle has its origin in the *species-specific*
human dilemma that arises out of the fact that, on the one hand, the
toddler is obliged by the rapid maturation of his ego—the consolidation of his individuality (individuation)—to recognize his separateness—while, on the other hand, he is as yet unable to stand alone but
will continue to need his mother for many years to come (Parens and
Saul 1971).

Three paramount anxieties of childhood converge in the rapprochement period, which may continue far past the second year of
life: (1) The fear of object loss is partly relieved by internalization, but
it is also complicated by the introjection of parental demands; this
not only indicates the beginning of superego development, but also
expresses itself in the fear of *losing the object's love,* an intensified
vulnerability on the part of the rapprochement toddler, which
manifests itself in a highly sensitive reaction to approval and disapproval by the parent. (2) A greater awareness of bodily feelings and
pressures, augmented by awareness of bowel and urinary sensations
during the toilet training period. (3) In some instances, a reaction
occurs to the discovery—rather earlier than we thought—of the
anatomical sex difference which prematurely precipitates castration
anxiety and penis envy respectively (*SP*II:1, Roiphe and Galenson
1972).

In many of our normal children, the developmental forces enabled them to resolve the rapprochement conflict and proceed to
higher and broadened levels of object relationship and ego functioning, even though some may have developed transient neurotic symptoms; in some cases, however, the rapprochement crisis led to great
ambivalence and even to splitting of the object world into good and
bad, with consequences that later may become organized into neurotic symptoms of the narcissistic variety; in still other children, islands
of developmental failures may lead to borderline symptomatology in
latency and adolescence (*SP*II:11, Frijling-Schreuder 1969).

Fixation at the level of rapprochement may be seen every so often in the widening range of child and adult patients who nowadays seek our help. Their most pervasive anxiety is separation anxiety—their affects may be dominated by narcissistic rage with temper tantrums which may subside and give way to altruistic surrender (A. Freud 1936). Their basic conflict is to be sought and found, it seems to me, in the primitive narcissistic struggle that surfaced or was acted out in the rapprochement crisis.

What I wish to indicate in closing this brief discussion are several points connecting the rapprochement crisis to the infantile neurosis as it has been classically conceived: (1) Understanding of the rapprochement crisis throws some light, it would seem, on the genesis of neurosis of those patients in whom the main technical problem is that which the late Dr. Bouvet (1958) described—namely, the finding of the "optimal distance" between the self and the object world. Oscillation between longing to merge with the good object representation, with the erstwhile (in one's fantasy at least) blissful union with the symbiotic mother and the defense against reengulfment by her (which could cause loss of autonomous self-identity)—these mechanisms are the outcome of the basic conflict which exists in a more primitive form in the rapprochement subphase. The complex developmental processes of the rapprochement subphase undoubtedly affect the manner in which the child will subsequently negotiate the oedipal crisis.

A tendency toward splitting of the object world may ensue as the child's solution to the pain of longings and losses of the rapprochement crisis. This must, it seems to me, make for greater difficulty in the resolution of the complex object-related conflicts of the oedipal period, promoting ambivalence and throwing an ominous cast on the oedipal and postoedipal personality development.

In these, and perhaps other diverse ways, the infantile neurosis becomes manifestly visible at the oedipal period, but may be shaped by the rapprochement crisis *that precedes it.*

Chapter 13

DEVELOPMENTAL ASPECTS IN THE ASSESSMENT OF NARCISSISTIC AND SO-CALLED BORDERLINE PERSONALITIES

[1977]

We believe the outstanding feature of narcissistic as well as borderline personalities is that they do not proceed in the ordinary way through the developmental process that culminates in a well-defined oedipus complex and in neurosis. We agree with Rangell (1972) that the oedipus complex—the core of neurosis—may be regarded as the fourth psychological organizer. Its shape, resolution, and mode of dissolution can restructure earlier developmental events. The oedipus complex represents the acme not only of infantile psychosexual development but also of object relations. It transforms the previous mainly external regulation of narcissism into internal self-esteem regulation by the superego.

Many of our colleagues have found the symbiosis and separation-individuation frame of reference useful in their work with child and adult patients in general, and narcissistic and borderline patients in particular. Nevertheless, although we have delineated the subphases of separation-individuation and come to some general hypotheses about subphase vulnerabilities, we are increasingly aware of the need to be more precise and detailed in our evaluation of what we call

In collaboration with Louise Kaplan, Ph.D.

subphase adequacy. Such an extension can only be achieved by consideration of the interlocking strands of narcissism and psychosexual development (Spruiell 1975), in addition to that of object relations of the separation-individuation process. We hope that this broader perspective of the subphase theory will facilitate the assessment of narcissistic and borderline personality organizations.

Eventually it should be possible to determine the progressive subphase adequacy in all three areas of development, and in the second half of the third year perhaps gauge whether the preconditions for normal oedipal development and the infantile neurosis prevail. These preconditions entail that self-constancy, that is, individual entity and identity, should be achieved at the end of the rapprochement subphase, in addition to a level of object constancy that facilitates triangular whole-object relations cathected with neutralized libido and aggression. In the psychosexual sphere an emerging and flexible narcissistic genital orientation should be evident. Repression is the main defense mechanism in these important developments.

As we emphasized in the book *The Psychological Birth of the Human Infant* (Mahler, Pine, and Bergman 1975), a predominantly observational study of the preverbal and primary-process phases of development, the subphase-related progress in object relations could be fairly reliably studied through its *referents*. These referents were furnished by observation of interactive behaviors of the mother-child unit over the course of time, polarized by the two partners of the dual unit. In contrast to progress in object relations, the building of a cohesive, separate, and whole self-representation is elusive. What the infant feels subjectively eludes the observing eye; that is, behavioral referents are barely existent. We may assume, however, that the earliest perceptions are those of bodily sensations. Freud (1923) described the ego as "first and foremost a body-ego" (p. 27).

What we have in mind then is to consider the subphase adequacy or subphase inadequacy of all three strands of preoedipal development. Consideration of the traditional hierarchic psychosexual stages is implicit in the separation-individuation subphase theory; here we will stress this issue somewhat more than previously.

As for narcissism, in our observational study and later in our film analyses we noted episodes in which the differentiating five- to eight-month-old, surrounded by approving and libidinally mirroring friendly adults, seemed electrified and stimulated by this reflecting admiration. We recognized that an important source of narcissistic libido, the quantity and quality of libidinization of the body ego or body self, is dependent upon early narcissistic supplies. These supplies are contributed in the symbiotic phase as well as in the differentiation and early practicing subphases by fueling by the environment. Imbalances in fueling by the environment will be described in our two sample cases.

Each subphase makes its particular contribution to healthy or pathological narcissism; narcissistic reserves are still being built up, to a great extent, by subphase-adequate mothering in the later subphases The *autonomous achievements* of the practicing subphase are the main source of narcissistic enhancement from *within*. Most infant-toddlers of the practicing stage show three contributories to narcissism at their peak. These are (in an exaggerated way and in individually different proportions): self-love, primitive valuation of their accomplishments, and omnipotence. During the rapprochement subphase, prior to and dependent on the resolution of the rapprochement crisis, narcissism (particularly omnipotence shaken by the coming of age of representational intelligence) is subphase-specifically vulnerable.

We shall describe below the diametrically opposite vicissitudes of infantile omnipotence, body self-love, self-esteem regulation, and self- and gender formation in two children. These two case studies illustrate what we mean when we speak of the broad spectrum of borderline phenomena. Furthermore, these examples point out the relevance of the subphase hypothesis for the understanding of both borderline and narcissistic phenomena in future investigations.

The sketches of Sy's and Cathy's development have been drawn from *carefully processed*, voluminous observational data of their first three years of life, occasional follow-up material of their nursery and kindergarten and school years, and finally a more systematic follow-up study undertaken at latency age and early adolescence, respectively. We shall not of course regard our project as satisfactorily terminated until we have had the opportunity to analyze two to three children and at least one mother.

SY

We begin with the subphase developmental history of one of our study children in whom, by the middle of the third year, we already found such severe disorders in all three aspects of the separation-individuation process that we predicted borderline personality development.

Sy's innate ego endowment was better than average, as our controlled observational data and the developmental tests unequivocally indicated. From his sixth or seventh month until the last quarter of his second year, Sy's life was a saga of daytime attempts to extricate himself from his mother's suffocating envelopment and intrusiveness. During the night, on the other hand, he behaved or was seduced into behaving as the "child-lover at the breast." At seven to nine months, when normally the specific bond with mother is at its peak and stranger anxiety appears, Sy strained *away* from his mother's body when she held him.

Sy's slow locomotor maturation complicated matters. Moreover, the mother discouraged every attempt at locomotion as well as other autonomous functions. Phase-specific stranger anxiety was replaced by *stranger preference*. By twelve months of age Sy used his newly emerged ego function of crawling to crawl rapidly away from mother. And if a stranger and mother were to beckon simultaneously, he would unhesitatingly go to the "non-mother." As soon as Sy mastered rapid crawling, Sy's mother redirected his course incessantly—intruding and forcing him to interact with her continually.

Sy had no opportunity to experience the obligatory forms of separation reactions that the other children showed at subphase-adequate times. His differentiation, practicing, and rapprochement subphases were rudimentary and distorted and the subphase characteristics highly confused.

Sy's symbiotic phase pervaded the differentiation process; it interfered with and crowded out the ego-building contributions that the practicing and rapprochement subphases furnish to psychic structuralization. *It was the all-important, almost purely maturational, species-specific emergence of free upright locomotion, as late as at seventeen months, that made Sy suddenly aware that he might suffer object loss.*

The sudden onset of the rapprochement conflict, which Sy experienced without his ego having been prepared for functioning separately (in a clearly delineated practicing subphase), was one of the roots of his deviational development. The absence of a definitive practicing subphase deprived his ego of the capacity to mitigate gradually the impact of his pregenital instinctual drives and deprived him as well of *both* the internal source of narcissism derived from the autonomous ego sphere and the narcissistic enhancement afforded by the normal active, aggressive spurt of practicing.

The period from his seventeenth to twentieth month was a particularly unstable and stormy one. At the beginning of his rudimentary rapprochement subphase, Sy would go to his mother somewhat more often with requests and demands. More often than not his mother completely ignored these requests. At seventeen to eighteen months Sy refused the breast, and promptly developed a sleep disturbance, which allowed his mother to rationalize the reintroduction of her dried breast—a "giant pacifier." At the same time the need for mother increased. Sy clung to her after each nap, cried in the morning, and continued to have difficulty in falling asleep.

By his twentieth month, whatever relation Sy had developed to the object world at large became actively split off as all "bad." He became aggressive to the other children and suspicious toward those at the Center who were previously his friends. Up to then he had been fairly exuberant and trusting. Now he became somber, depressed, and moody.

From the moment he weaned himself, Sy's separation-individuation process was corroded in all three areas previously cited by his excessive castration anxiety, which later amounted to mutilation anxiety. This anxiety was so overwhelming because his ego did not experience the obligatory and normal subphase-adequate fears of object loss, stranger anxiety, separation anxiety, and fear of loss of the object's love at subphase-adequate times. In the psychosexual sphere anal concerns and severe castration anxiety overlapped. Such overlapping was augmented by massive, visual exposure to the sexual organs of nude men, his father's included, in the locker room. At the same time, Sy was permitted to perceive in equally traumatic proportion sights that brought home to him, out of phase, the danger of castration. He would go to urinate in the bathroom but instead would masturbate. He was unable to sit down for fear that his feces, and possibly his penis, would be flushed away. His predilection to expose his penis and frequent utterances, such as "nice penis," "you nice people," indicated, among other signs, the precocious onset and prolonged adherence to the narcissistic-phallic phase of libido development.

The father's dictum was: a baby belongs to the mother as long as he wants her breast. As soon as the son rejects the breast he belongs to the father. Sy's castration anxiety increased significantly in his third year when Sy's father took him over, body and soul. The father duplicated the mother's overstimulation of the first two years. The father's behavior was described thus: "He at once threatens and cajoles, manhandles and caresses, slams about and seduces Sy. When the father's rage reaches a peak, he switches to seductive kissing and tickling. The whole thing is sadistic, sexualized, and hysterical." At the birth of his brother in Sy's thirty-fourth month his mother was in the hospital for a prolonged stay and his father was his only caretaker. Sy was in a frenzied, panicky state. He talked incessantly in gibberish, expressing primary-process ideation.

By age four, Sy had turned violently against his mother and emulated his father's degrading of her. He totally rejected her in his attempt to become big and manly like his father. Sy began to vomit food his mother wanted him to eat and developed an eating problem. During Sy's struggle with identification with father, he turned all his crude aggression against his mother—kicking and biting and shouting at her. In the midst of this turnabout in Sy's fifth year, another fateful traumatization occurred. Sy's father exchanged him for his younger brother, who was at the very age at which the father had taken Sy over from the mother. Whereas Sy had been aggressive, elated, and rather manic in nursery school, now at kindergarten age everybody noted that the sparkle in his eye was gone. Sy turned once again to his mother and became her quasi satellite, in an anxious but subdued alliance against the younger brother and father.

Sy's subphase developmental history was characterized by prolongation up to his twentieth month of the nocturnal "child-lover-at-the-breast" symbiosis. This, without more than a nominal experiencing of the practicing and rapprochement subphases of separation-individuation, was overlapped by and continued as a bizarrely frank oedipal relation with his mother and later with his father.

From the time he weaned himself and walked, Sy was treated by the mother as her "man," with reciprocal behavior on his part. It is a demonstration *in statu nascendi* and step by step of what Kernberg (1967) describes as the genetic-dynamic analysis of the borderline personality's oedipus complex. He says: "What is characteristic of the borderline personality organization . . . is a specific condensation between pregenital and genital conflicts, and a *premature* development of oedipal conflicts . . . " (p. 678).

We could follow, in the second part of Sy's third as well as in his fourth, fifth, and sixth years, the vicissitudes of the failure of the ego's function of normal repression. There were many instances of this failure, but for lack of space we cannot elaborate on them. An example might suffice: Sy remembered minute details about the Center, which the other children had completely repressed. These details were syncretically retained by his ego's pathological memory function (*SPI*:11).

Sy's behavior at times seemed a caricatured emulation of his mother, at other times he seemed a bizarre diminutive replica of his father. Instead of repression, the extensive splitting operations described by Kernberg resulted in a morbidly combined father-mother image. There was hardly any opportunity for his ego to identify selectively with desexualized and deaggressivized paternal or maternal traits. We observed an unusual confusion between the paternal images and dissociation and lack of neutralization of his erotic and aggressive impulses.

It is very difficult to conceptualize Sy's ego ideal or his identifications and self-representation. The unassimilated introjective identification of part images of mother and father was predominant at the expense of transmuting internalization.

We believe that the positive qualities that saved Sy from psychosis were his excellent endowment, for example, the way in which he made up for his slow locomotor development by becoming extremely proficient in gymnastics (his favorite activity was acrobatics). From material gained from him, his mother, and teacher, one can surmise that Sy liked to be away from home. He was the least homesick when the class went to camp. The mother also told of times when Sy did not come home from school but went to his teacher's house instead. He had obviously succeeded in creating an island for himself where his ego developed without constant intrusion and interference by his disorganized, disorganizing, and aggressive environment.

Sy's intrapsychic conflicts can be only guessed at, of course, and we would like to get Sy into analysis, but both parents are opposed to it.

Follow-up home and school interviews of Sy in his eleventh year described him as faring much better than we would have predicted. His academic achievement in an honors class in a local public school is excellent and he is fairly popular with his classmates. The teachers, however, could not suppress their irritation with Sy and his family. They described Sy as a fresh, sexually precocious child who bragged and engaged in disruptive, exhibitionistic, clowning and crudely inappropriate sex talk. Moreover, the teachers felt that the parents overestimated Sy's creative and intellectual potential, very often insisting that he be treated specially.

The psychological tests, which were administered without knowledge of the follow-up interviews or the early developmental history, revealed a diagnostic picture of borderline personality organization at the lower level of the borderline spectrum. When tested, Sy's characteristic posture was hunched over and limp, as though his body were totally devoid of muscle tone. He handled the examiner's test materials in a way that suggested that he was appropriating and possessing them—but without active intentionality. In his passivity there was a decided blurring of the boundaries between yours and mine.

Even though Sy's behavior betrayed no signal or social anxiety, he was apparently in a *state of overwhelming anxiety*. The palms of his hands would sweat profusely, leaving moisture on everything he touched. His hands would shake and he looked helpless and vulnerable. Alternately, Sy was often able to pull back and take an active, more rationally bound view of reality. At these times his body was firmly erect and alertly mobilized. His mental functioning also improved and toned up. He concentrated actively and sharpened his previously vague responses. He then smiled happily and even tried to show off.

Such unpredictable alternation in affect states, body posturing, and modes of responding typified Sy's Rorschach responses. Most often, Sy would be pulled into the cards—his loss of distancing was prominent. Repeatedly he would confuse his inner bodily feelings with external perceptions. He yawned, for example, and then said the wolf on the card was tired. Now and then he would project his impulses and then become inundated by the anxiety aroused by his own projections. He experienced the projected impulse simultaneously with the fear of the impulse. Primitive denial and externalization were prominent defenses. Notably absent during the testing were any indicators of shame or guilt and there was very little signal anxiety—only overwhelming primitive anxiety.

When Sy is able to extricate himself, put distance between himself and the stimuli of external reality, he is able to maintain fantasy-reality distinctions. Secondary-process thinking and logic were evident in many of Sy's responses, although it was abundantly clear that his mode of thought organization was subject to easy regression.

In his eleventh year, Sy's good basic endowment has allowed him to extricate himself and create distance, analogous to the way he actively pushed, crawled, and turned away from the engulfing mother-child symbiosis—and thereby to escape outright psychosis. Nevertheless, the prolonged symbiosis has cast its shadow over all future subphases of separation-individuation. It continues as a grossly erotic, overly aggressivized, out-of-phase oedipal constellation which has left an indelible stamp on Sy's body representations.

On the tests, the ego-inundating nature of Sy's castration anxiety was apparent in his body mutilation fantasies and the fragmented quality of his body representations. Moreover, in Sy's perceptions body parts merged with one another, were interchangeable with one another, and were in fact interchangeable with the inanimate objects of reality.

CATHY

By way of contrast, we will briefly describe the separation-individuation process of Cathy, a child whose development proceeded along more or less neurotic lines, but who at thirteen showed signs of a narcissistic disturbance.

Cathy joined our project at twelve months of age. She immediately conquered our mother-infant room with her spectacular self-assurance and verbal precocity, without the slightest "stranger" and "strangeness" reactions. Her mother—a somewhat colorless, depressive woman—seemed to enjoy Cathy greatly as the narcissistic, glamorous extension of "her self."

Cathy had mastered walking by eleven months. Her exuberance, however, did not include the usual abandon and daring observed in other children in the practicing subphase. Cathy's much praised and encouraged "independence" had been bought at the expense of bodily closeness, that is, libidinal supplies of her body self. Mrs. C., who stressed that Cathy was not a cuddly baby, never picked her up except for brief comforting followed by distraction tactics.

At around nineteen months Cathy's mood definitely deteriorated. Mrs. C. complained about Cathy's crying, temper tantrums, and often incomprehensible behavior. Her toilet training had been uneventful and she was practically trained by nineteen months without coercion. The mother, however, complained, "She doesn't want me to touch her, to dress her, to put her on the toilet, although she will let others do so." We felt that at this point a "bad" and dangerous maternal part representation was actively split off from the "good object representation." We may also assume that Cathy's moodiness indicated dissociation of aggressive and libidinally invested part-self representations.

We watched our radiant, narcissistic "queen-bee" of the nursery become—intermittently—a petulant, hard-to-understand, and for the moment very aggressive little girl. Not only were we faced with a full-fledged rapprochement crisis, but with a sudden and abrupt collapse of Cathy's omnipotent grandeur. Only many weeks later were we able to piece together the events that culminated in this intense and prolonged rapprochement crisis. Between her sixteenth and eighteenth month Cathy often visited a little boy from the nursery. One day this boy's mother bathed the two children together and Cathy came home declaring that the little boy had *two* belly buttons.

Six to seven weeks after Cathy's discovery of the anatomical sex difference she became extremely aggressive, pulling the hair of other children in our nursery. The mother recalled that when she took Cathy into the shower to facilitate washing her long, fine hair, Cathy pulled at her mother's pubic hair. *Cathy's desperate search for a penis was quite clear.* Disturbances of both sleep and toileting followed. We felt that Cathy's aggressive provocativeness represented a demand to her mother to make amends for her anatomical short-coming (even at twenty-seven months of age she asked for a penis for Christmas!).

At two and a half years Cathy briefly wanted mother, father, and herself all to be together. We thought this was to be the beginning of a true phallic-oedipal relation. Cathy, however, soon preferred ex-clusive dyadic relations, vacillating between selection of *either* father *or* mother. From then on and throughout her second to fifth year, Cathy alternated between weakly energized forays into a triadic relation which included both the mother and the father and frantic claims for exclusive dyadic relations.

Also at two and a half Cathy attempted to give up the bottle, but was unsuccessful. Her mother declared that "the bottle was the only thing that Cathy was really attached to." Her overestimation of her transitional object—the bottle—betrayed a certain pathology in Winnicott's (1953) terms. From her third year on, Cathy required a mirroring, exclusively dyadic relation in order to maintain her ideal state of self. The search for shifting dyadic relations became a major theme in Cathy's life.

When Cathy entered nursery school at three, she turned with her unspecific object hunger to the nursery-school teacher as a mother substitute—entwining her, seeking her exclusive attention. A crisis soon occurred involving child, mother, and teacher. Unable to cope with Cathy's intense need for exclusive attention, the teacher sent her home to her mother. Mrs. C.'s reaction was one of angry depression directed toward the teacher and also toward her own daughter.

Cathy, as never before, clung to her mother's body—clutching her thighs. Mother extricated herself by angrily pushing her off. Cathy responded to this dual rebuff by engaging in compulsive talking to an imaginary audience from whom she anticipated mirroring admiration. It was as though Cathy were trying to recapture the ideal state of self she experienced in her twelfth to nineteenth month when she was the omnipotent "queen bee" of the nursery. Even though Cathy's clinging behavior declined, we felt that Cathy had abandoned hope rather than resolved the rapprochement crisis. We believe that the ambivalently loved, needed and hated object, who regarded herself and Cathy as failures, was at this point split off and externalized, in favor of an internally retained, differentiated, negatively cathected self-representation.

Cathy's later school experiences continued to be disappointing. She hated school and at six declared that the children hated her and would not play with her. From her sixth year on Cathy blamed her mother for all the ills of her life, calling her "the worst mother in the world."

In Cathy's seventh year an interview with the father revealed a complex and ever-worsening sadomasochistic relation between his wife and Cathy. He said, "They are more like sisters than a mother and daughter." He also felt that Cathy often daydreamed. He thought it quite natural, however, that Cathy, like daughters in general, should be closer to her mother than to her father.

The outstanding impression conveyed by follow-up interviews, school and home visits when Cathy was thirteen was her sense of her personal inadequacy and low self-esteem. Although her full-scale IQ was 134, her school achievement was in the B minus to C range.

When Cathy was tested her voice was barely audible and she tried to keep her head positioned so that her hair would cover her face. The omnipotent, self-assured, exhibitionistic toddler had become an adolescent who seemed to want to disappear. Whereas the follow-up testing of Sy revealed some of the inner dynamics of borderline personality organization, in the personality picture of Cathy at thirteen we recognized what is typically called obsessive-compulsive personality organization. *Repression* was evident and the additional defenses of reaction-formation and isolation were well maintained without evidence of decompensation. Her excessively exalted ego ideal led to easy self-devaluation and to continuing prominence of anxiety and shame. Nevertheless, in contrast to Sy, the affect of guilt was the major regulator of instinct defense activity. Overwhelming panic and diffuse anxiety did not replace *signal anxiety*.

Cathy perceived bodies as hidden, blocked in action, slouched down, and trapped. These images represented her basically *masochistic* orientation. In hindsight we can now hypothesize that these hidden and trapped bodies echoed Cathy's ungratified longings for bodily libidinal supplies during practicing and rapprochement. In turn, the sudden shattering of her omnipotence—her desperate demands for the undoing of her anatomical shortcoming—added to Cathy's growing predisposition to disparage herself and her femininity.

Whereas Sy's body image was distorted, fragmented, and confused with the inanimate, Cathy's body image was intact and well-bounded. Nevertheless, Cathy's self-image, her dissatisfaction with herself and with her feminine gender identity was evident. She was disappointed in herself and expected disappointment and defeat in her relations with others.

In Sy we noted perilous regression and the disorganization of secondary-process thinking by condensations and contaminations. Cathy's reality testing was excellent. However, even temporary regressions were forbidden and when things were not "just so" she gave up rather than taking the chance that she might be wrong.

In Cathy's case, we believe that neither the overidealized and overidealizing, all-good, admiring mother-image nor the grandiose, omnipotent ego-ideal were gradually adjusted to reality. The infantile self-object image was never cut down to size so that the real mother would be able to match that image. Nor did the ego-ideal become reconciled with the realistic potential of Cathy's autonomous actual self-image.

The characteristic and unique feature of Cathy's struggle was her seeking substitutions in the outside world in order to approximate the highly overestimated, exceptional, and exclusive self-object representation unit. She sought these substitutions in dyadic relations that would match the idealized self-object image of her longed-for omnipotent past.

Cathy's mother's inability to provide a balance of libidinally satisfying, intermittent body closeness and to recognize Cathy's hunger for physical contact during practicing led to an intensification of the splitting mechanisms which characterized Cathy's rapprochement period. The narcissistic reserve, which might have enabled Cathy to overcome later narcissistic hurts, was depleted on two fronts during practicing. The excessively exalted ego ideal and the absence of practicing phase-specific libidinal refueling laid the groundwork for inflexible ego ideal and superego structures which would not allow for an adaptive tolerance for ambiguity and ambivalence. During rapprochement itself, Cathy's coercive wooing behavior was rebuffed by her mother. But, although Cathy was not prepared to experience a fully developed oedipal constellation, we know that some aspects of an advanced oedipal solution were achieved. This solution was characterized by a repression of the instinctual preoedipal and oedipal strivings. Cathy's narcissistic grandiosity was replaced by masochistic self-disparagement, but whole-object relations remained dominant, even though there seemed to be potential problems in gender-identity resolutions.

CONCLUSIONS

Our aim in this brief presentation was to adumbrate the explanatory power that full utilization of the symbiosis and the separation-individuation subphase theory contributes to the assessment of later personality organization, provided its complexities are taken into account. Rather than presenting a coordinated system of subphase-related failures in one subphase of the separation-individuation process with a corresponding specific form of narcissistic or borderline personality organization, we have tried to avoid over-simplification and closure.

In our assessments of the personality organization of narcissistic and borderline child and adult patients, the overriding dominance of one subphase distortion or fixation must not obscure the fact that there are always corrective or pathogenic influences from the other subphases to be considered. In Sy's case, for example, the luxuriation of the symbiosis prevented later subphases from making their specific *positive* contributions to personality development. In practicing, Sy was deprived of the internal source of narcissism derived from the autonomous ego sphere as well as the shaping influence of the normal aggression spurt. At the same time the age-appropriate separate self- and body awareness of rapprochement was inundated by castration anxiety and overstimulation of fantasy life. The distorted nature of Sy's oedipal constellation cannot be understood merely from the perspective of the symbiotic phase.

In Cathy's case the rapprochement theme of the search for exclusively dyadic relations to mirror her lost ideal state of self predominated. Yet the specific shape of Cathy's oedipal resolution cannot be adequately understood unless we include the dramatic imbalance in which Cathy's exalted omnipotence was not matched by the necessary body-libidinal supplies to her narcissism during the symbiotic, differentiation, and practicing subphases.

SOURCE NOTES

Chapter 1

Thoughts About Development and Individuation (1963). This paper is partly based on a research project originally sponsored by the Field Foundation, and at the time of original publication was sponsored by the National Association for Mental Health, Inc., The Psychoanalytic Research and Development Fund, Inc., and the Taconic Foundation.

Research was carried out at the Masters Childrens Center, New York, with the collaboration of Manuel Furer, M.D. and Mrs. Anni Bergman; and with the assistance of Mrs. Edith Atkin, Ann Haeberle, Ph.D., Mrs. Emmagene Kamaiko, David L. Mayer, M.D., Fred Pine, Ph.D., and Herman Roiphe, M.D.

This paper was given as the Abraham A. Brill Memorial Lecture at the New York Psychoanalytic Society, November 1962. REPRINTED FROM *Psychoanalytic Study of the Child* 18:307-324.

Chapter 2

Certain Aspects of the Separation-Individuation Phase (1963). In collaboration with Manuel Furer, M.D. This study was supported at original publication by a grant from the Psychoanalytic Research and Development Fund, and carried out at Masters Children's Cen-

ter, New York, in collaboration with David L. Mayer, M.D., Fred
Pine, Ph.D., and Herman Roiphe, M.D., and with the assistance of
Anni Bergman and Edith Atkin. REPRINTED FROM *Psychoanalytic
Quarterly* 32:1-14.

Chapter 3

Mother-Child Interaction During Separation-Individuation (1965).
In collaboration with Kitty La Perriere, Ph.D. This paper is based on
research supported by Grant MH08238 of the National Institute of
Mental Health, carried out at Masters Children's Center, New York.
    This paper was presented at the Symposium on Research in
Mother-Infant Interaction at the Annual Meeting of the American
Orthopsychiatric Association, March 1964, Chicago. REPRINTED
FROM *Psychoanalytic Quarterly* 34:483-498.

Chapter 4

On the Significance of the Normal Separation-Individuation Phase:
With Reference to Research in Symbiotic Child Psychosis (1965).
This paper is based on research which had been supported by the
Field Foundation, The Psychoanlytic Research and Development
Fund, the National Association of Mental Health, and the Taconic
Foundation; at original publication, sponsored by Grant MH08238
of the National Institute of Mental Health, USPHS, Bethesda, Md.
REPRINTED FROM *Drives, Affects, Behavior*, vol. 2, ed. M. Schur. New
York: International Universities Press.

Chapter 5

Notes on the Development of Basic Moods: The Depressive Affect
(1966). This paper is based on research supported by Grant MH08238
from the National Institute of Mental Health, USPHS, Bethesda,
Md. REPRINTED FROM *Psychoanalysis—A General Psychology: Essays in Honor of Heinz Hartmann*, eds. R. Loewenstein, L. M.
Newman, M. Schur, and A. J. Solnit. New York: International
Universities Press.

Chapter 6

On Human Symbiosis and the Vicissitudes of Individuation (1967). This paper is partly based on research supported by Grant MH08238 of the National Institute of Mental Health, USPHS, Bethesda, Md., and previously by Grant M3353; as well as by the Field Foundation, Taconic Foundation, National Association for Mental Health, Inc., and the Psychoanalytic Research and Development Fund, Inc.

The author wishes to express her gratitude, first of all to Dr. John McDevitt, and also to Emmagene Kamaiko, Anni Bergman, Laura Salchow, and Dr. Ernest Abelin, and many others.

This paper was presented at the Plenary Session of the Annual Meeting of the American Psychoanalytic Association, May 1967, Detroit. It was published in slightly different form as chapter 1 of *On Human Symbiosis and the Vicissitudes of Individuation: Volume 1, Infantile Psychosis*. New York: International Universities Press, 1968. REPRINTED FROM *Journal of the American Psychoanalytic Association* 25:740-763.

Chapter 7

Observations on Adaptation and Defense *In Statu Nascendi* (1968). In collaboration with John B. McDevitt, M.D. This paper is based in part on research supported by Grant MH08238 of the National Institute for Mental Health, USPHS, Bethesda, Md., carried out at the Masters Children's Center. Presented at the New York Psychoanalytic Society, March 1967; and the Philadelphia Psychoanalytic Society, May 1967. REPRINTED FROM *Psychoanalytic Quarterly* 37:1-21.

Chapter 8

On the First Three Subphases of the Separation-Individuation Process (1972). This paper was originally presented as the first introductory contribution to a series of three panels: The Experience of

Separation-Individuation in Infancy and Its Reverberation Through the Course of Life, jointly sponsored by the Association for Child Psychoanalysis and the American Psychoanalytic Association, December 1971.

This paper appeared in slightly different form in *Psychoanalysis and Contemporary Science*, vol 3. New York: International Universities Press, 1974. REPRINTED FROM *International Journal of Psycho-Analysis* 53:333-338.

Chapter 9

Rapprochement Subphase of the Separation-Individuation Process (1972). The work described in this paper was partially supported by the Foundations Fund for Research in Psychiatry, New Haven, Connecticut. Presented at a meeting of the Washington Psychoanalytic Society, April 1972, and at a meeting of the Philadelphia Psychoanalytic Society, May 1972. REPRINTED FROM *Psychoanalytic Quarterly* 41:487-506.

The follow-up study conducted by John B. McDevitt, M.D. with Anni Bergman, Emmagene Kamaiko, and Laura Salchow, and the author of this paper serving as consultant; sponsored by the Board of the Masters Children's Center.

Chapter 10

Symbiosis and Individuation: The Psychological Birth of the Human Infant (1974). This paper was read as the Fifteenth Sophia Mirviss Memorial Lecture to the San Francisco Psychoanalytic Institute, November 1973. REPRINTED FROM *Psychoanalytic Study of the Child* 29:89-106.

The systematic study of "The Natural History of Symbiotic Child Psychosis" referred to in this paper was conducted at the Masters Children's Center, with Dr. M. Furer. It was funded by Grant 3363 of the NIMH, 1959-1963. See further source notes appended to the first volume: Infantile Psychosis and Early Contributions.

Chapter 11

A Study of the Separation-Individuation Process: And Its Possible Application to Borderline Phenomena in the Psychoanalytic Situation (1971). This paper was partly based on research carried out at Masters Children's Center, New York, which was sponsored by Grant MH8238 of the National Institute of Mental Health, USPHS; by the Foundation for Research in Psychoanalysis, Los Angeles; the Strick Foundation, Philadelphia; and by the Foundations Fund for Research in Psychiatry, New Haven, Conn. In association with John B. McDevitt, M.D. and Mrs. Anni Bergman; with the assistance of Mrs. Emmagene Kamaiko, Laura Salchow, and Margaret Hawkins, and in consultation with Fred Pine, Ph.D.

Presented as the Twentieth Freud Anniversary Lecture, April 1970. REPRINTED FROM *Psychoanalytic Study of the Child* 26:403-424.

Chapter 12

On the Current Status of the Infantile Neurosis (1975). This paper was a discussion given as part of a panel on "The Current Status of the Infantile Neurosis" at the Annual Meeting of the Association for Child Psychoanalysis, July 1973, Paris. REPRINTED FROM *Journal of the American Psychoanalytic Association* 23:327-333.

Chapter 13

Developmental Aspects in the Assessment of Narcissistic and So-Called Borderline Personalities (1977). In collaboration with Louise Kaplan, Ph.D. REPRINTED FROM *Borderline Personality Disorders: The Concept, The Syndrome, The Patient,* ed. Peter Harticollis, pp. 71-85. New York: International Universities Press.

BIBLIOGRAPHICAL NOTE

SP: The Selected Papers of Margaret S. Mahler, M.D., two volumes. Volume I: *Infantile Psychosis and Early Contributions*. Volume II: *Separation/Individuation*. New York: Jason Aronson, 1979.

BIBLIOGRAPHY

Abelin, E.L. (1971). The role of the father in the separation-individuation process. In: *Separation-Individuation: Essays in Honor of Margaret S. Mahler*, ed. J.B. McDevitt and C.F. Settlage, pp. 229-253. New York: International Universities Press.

Abraham, K. (1921). Contribution to a discussion of the tic. In: *The Selected Papers of Karl Abraham*, pp. 323-325. New York: Basic Books, 1953.

——— (1924). A short study of the development of the libido, viewed in light of mental disorders. In: *Selected Papers of Karl Abraham*, pp. 418-501. New York: Basic Books, 1953.

Aichhorn, A. (1925). *Wayward Youth*. New York: Viking Press, 1935.

——— (1932). Erziehungsberatung [child guidance]. *Ztschr. f. psa. Pädagogik* 6:445-488.

——— (1933). Erziehungsberatung—Seminar [child guidance seminar]. *Ztschr. f. psa. Pädagogik* 7:153-159.

——— (1936). Zur Technik der Erziehungsberatung [The technique of educational guidance]. *Ztschr. f. psa. Pädagogik* 10:5-74.

Alexander, F. (1943). Fundamental concepts of psychosomatic research. *Psychosom. Med.* 5:205-210.

Alpert, A. (1959). Reversibility of pathological fixations associated with maternal deprivation in infancy. *Psychoanalytic Study of the Child* 14:169-185.

Alpert, A., Neubauer, P.B., and Weil, A.P. (1956). Unusual variations in drive endowment. *Psychoanalytic Study of the Child* 11:125-163.

Angel, K. (1967). On symbiosis and pseudosymbiosis. *J. Amer. Psychoanal. Assn.* 15:294-316.

Anthony, E.J. (1961). A study of "screen sensations." *Psychoanalytic Study of the Child* 16:211-246.

Bak, R. (1939). Regression of ego orientation and libido in schizophrenia. *Int. J. Psycho-Anal.* 20:64-71.

—— (1954). The schizophrenic defense against aggression. *Int. J. Psycho-Anal.* 35:129-134.

Bally, G. (1933). Die frühkindliche Motorik im Vergleich mit der Motorik der Tiere [The infant's motor activity compared with that of animals]. *Imago* 19:339-366.

Bender, L. (1942). Childhood schizophrenia. *Nerv. Child* 1:138-140.

—— (1947). Childhood schizophrenia: Clinical study of 100 schizophrenic children. *Amer. J. Orthopsychiat.* 17:40-56.

Bender, L., and Schilder, P. (1940). Impulsions: a specific disorder of the behavior of children. *Arch. Neur & Psychiat.* 44:990-1008.

Benedek, T. (1938). Adaptation to reality in early infancy. *Psychoanal. Quart.* 7:200-214.

—— (1949). The psychosomatic implications of the primary unit: mother-child. *Amer. J. Orthopsychiat.* 19:642-654.

—— (1959). Parenthood as a developmental phase: a contribution to the libido theory. *J. Amer. Psychoanal. Assn.* 7:389-417.

—— (1960). The organization of the reproductive drive. *Int. J. Psycho-Anal.* 41:1-15.

Benjamin, J.D. (1961). The innate and the experiential in child development. *Lectures on Experimental Psychiatry*, ed. H. Brosin, pp. 19-42. Pittsburgh: University of Pittsburgh Press.

Beres, D. (1960). Perception, imagination, and reality. *Int. J. Psycho-Anal.* 41:327-334.

Bergler, E. (1932). Zur Problematic der Pseudo-debilität [The problem of pseudodebility]. *Int. Ztschr. f. Psa.* 18:528-538.

Bergman, P., and Escalona, S.K. (1949). Unusual sensitivities in very young children. *Psychoanalytic Study of the Child* 3/4:333-352.

Bergmann, M. (1963). The place of Paul Ferdern's ego psychology in psychoanalytic metapsychology. *J. Amer. Psychoanal. Assn.* 11:97-116.

Bergmann, T. (1945). Observations of children's reactions to motor restraint. *Nerv. Child* 4:318-328.

Bettelheim, B. (1959). Joey, a "mechanical boy." *Sci. Amer.* 200(3):116-127.

Bibring, E. (1953). The mechanism of depression. In: *Affective Disorders*, ed. P. Greenacre. New York: International Universities Press, 1954.

Bibring, G.L., Dwyer, T.F., Huntington, D.S., and Valenstein, A.F. (1961). A study of the psychological processes in pregnancy and of the earliest mother-child relationship. *Psychoanalytic Study of the Child* 16:9-72.

Blatz, W.E., and Ringland, M.C. (1935). *The Study of Tics in Pre-School Children*. Toronto: University of Toronto Press.

Blos, P. (1967). The second individuation process of adolescence. *Psychoanalytic Study of the Child* 22:162-186.

Boenheim, C. (1930). Ueber den Tic im Kindesalter [On childhood tic]. *Klin. Wchschrift.* 9:2005-2011.

Bonnard, A. (1958). Pre-body-ego types of (pathological) mental functioning. *J. Amer. Psychoanal. Assn.* 6:581-611.

Bornstein, B. (1930). Zur Psychogenese der Pseudodebilität [Psychogenesis of pseudodebility]. *Int. Ztschr f. Psa.* 16:378-399.

——— (1935). Phobia in a two-and-a-half-year-old boy. *Psychoanal. Quart.* 4:93-119.

Bouvet, M. (1958). Technical variations and the concept of distance. *Int. J. Psycho-Anal.* 39:211-221.

Bowlby, J. (1951). *Maternal Care and Mental Health*. Geneva: World Health Organization, Monograph 2.

——— (1960). Grief and mourning in infancy and early childhood. *Psychoanalytic Study of the Child* 15:9-52.

Bowlby, J., Robertson, J., and Rosenbluth, D. (1952). A two-year-old goes to hospital. *Psychoanalytic Study of the Child* 7:82-94.

Bradley, C. (1945). Psychoses in children. In: *Modern Trends in Child Psychiatry*, ed. N.D.C. Lewis and B.L. Pacella. New York: International Universities Press, pp. 135-154.

Brody, S. (1956). *Patterns of Mothering*. New York: International Universities Press.

Brody, S., and Axelrad, S. (1966). Anxiety, socialization, and ego-formation in infancy. *Int. J. Psycho-Anal.* 47:218-229.

——— (1970). *Anxiety and Ego Formation in Infancy*. New York: International Universities Press.

Burlingham, D. (1932). Kinderanalyse und Mutter [Child analysis and the mother]. *Ztschr. f. Psa. Pädagogik* 6:269-289.

―――― (1934). Mitteilungsdrang und Geständniszwang [The urge to tell and the compulsion to confess]. *Imago* 20:129-143.

―――― (1936). Die Einfühlung des Kleinkindes in die Mutter [The empathy between infant and mother]. *Imago* 21:429-444.

Bychowski, G. (1956a). The ego and the introjects. *Psychoanal. Quart.* 25:11-36.

―――― (1956b). The release of internal images. *Int. J. Psycho-Anal.* 37:331-338.

Cocteau, J. (1930). *Les Enfants terribles.* (Tr. S. Putnam) Norwood, Mass.: Brewer and Warren.

Coleman, R.W., Kris, E., and Provence, S. (1953). The study of variations of early parental attitudes: A preliminary report. *Psychoanalytic Study of the Child* 8:20-47.

Despert, J.L. (1938). Schizophrenia in children. *Psychiat. Quart.* 12:366-371.

―――― (1941). Thinking and motility disorder in a schizophrenic child. *Psychiat. Quart.* 15:522-536.

―――― (1955). Differential Diagnosis between Obsessive Compulsive Neurosis and Schizophrenia in Children. In: *Psychopathology of Childhood*, ed. P.H. Hoch and J. Zubin. New York: Grune & Stratton, pp. 240-253.

Deutsch, F. (1947). Analysis of postural behavior. *Psychoanal. Quart.* 16:195-213.

Deutsch, H. (1919). A two-year-old's first love comes to grief. In: *Dynamic Psychopathology of Childhood*, ed. L. Jessner and E. Pavenstedt. New York: Grune & Stratton, 1959.

―――― (1945). *The Psychology of Women*, vol. 2: *Motherhood.* New York: Grune & Stratton.

Eissler, K.R. (1953). Notes upon the emotionality of a schizophrenic patient, and its relation to problems of technique. *Psychoanalytic Study of the Child*, 8:199-251.

Elkisch, P. (1947). Diagnostic and therapeutic values of projective techniques: A case of child tiqueur. *Amer. J. Psychother.* 1:270-312.

―――― (1952). Significant relationship between the human figure and the machine in the drawings of boys. *Amer. J. Orthopsychiat.* 22:379-385.

—— (1953). Simultaneous treatment of a child and his mother. *Amer. J. Psychother.* 7:105-130.

—— (1956). The struggle for ego boundaries in a psychotic child. *Amer. J. Psychother.* 10:578-602.

—— (1957). The psychological significance of the mirror. *J. Amer. Psychoanal. Assn.* 5:235-244.

Erikson, E. H. (1950). *Childhood and Society.* New York: Norton.

—— (1959). *Identity and the Life Cycle. Psychological Issues,* Monograph No. 1. New York: International Universities Press.

—— (1968). The life cycle: epigenesis of identity. In: *Identity, Youth and Crisis.* New York: Norton.

Escalona, S.K. (1968). *The Roots of Individuality: Normal Patterns of Development in Infancy.* Chicago: Aldine.

Escalona, S.K. and Heider, G.M. (1959). *Prediction and Outcome: A Study in Child Development.* New York: Basic Books.

Federn, P. (1952). *Ego Psychology and the Psychoses.* New York: Basic Books.

Fenichel, O. (1928). Ueber organlibidinoese Begleiterscheinungen der Triebabwehr. *Int. Ztschr. f. Psa.* 14:45-64. Reprinted as: Organ libidinization accompanying the defense against drives. In: *Collected Papers of Otto Fenichel,* vol. 1. New York: Norton, 1953.

—— (1936). Die symbolische Gleichung: Maedchen-Phallus. *Int. Ztschr. f. Psa.* 22:299-314. Reprinted as: The symbolic equation: girl=phallus. In: *Collected Papers of Otto Fenichel,* op. cit., vol. 2.

—— (1945a). *The Psychoanalytic Theory of Neurosis.* New York: Norton.

—— (1945b). The nature and classification of so-called psychosomatic phenomena. *Psychoanal. Quart.* 14:287-312.

Ferenczi, S. (1911). On obscene words. In: *Sex in Psychoanalysis,* pp. 132-153. New York: Basic Books, 1950.

—— (1913). Stages in the development of the sense of reality. In: *Sex in Psychoanalysis.* New York: Basic Books, 1950, pp. 213-239.

—— (1919). Thinking and muscle innervation. In: *Further Contributions to the Theory and Technique of Psychoanalysis,* pp. 230-232. New York: Basic Books, 1952.

———— (1921). Psycho-analytical observations on tics. In: *Further Contributions to the Theory and Technique of Psychoanalysis,* op. cit., pp. 142-174.

———— (1924). *Thalassa: A Theory of Genitality.* New York: Norton, 1968.

———— (1928). Gulliver phantasies. *Int. J. Psycho-Anal.* 9:283-300. Reprinted in: *Final Contributions to the Problems and Methods of Psychoanalysis.* New York: Basic Books, 1952.

Fischer, C. (1965). Psychoanalytic implications of recent research on sleep and dreaming. *J. Amer. Psychoanal. Assn.* 13:197-303.

Fliess, R. (1957). *Erogeneity and Libido: Addenda to the Theory of the Psychosexual Development of the Human.* New York: International Universities Press.

———— (1961). *Ego and Body Ego.* New York: Schulte Publishing.

Frank, A. (1969). The unrememberable and the unforgettable: passive primal repression. *Psychoanalytic Study of the Child* 24:48-77.

Frankl, L. (1963). Self-preservation and the development of accident proneness in children and adolescents. *Psychoanalytic Study of the Child* 18:464-483.

Freud, A. (1936). *The Ego and the Mechanisms of Defense.* New York: International Universities Press, 2nd ed., 1966.

———— (1949). Notes on aggression. *Bull. Menninger Clin.* 13:143-151. Reprinted in: *The Writings of Anna Freud,* vol. 4. New York: International Universities Press.

———— (1951a). A connection between the states of negativism and emotional surrender. Abstr. in: *Int. J. Psycho-Anal.* 33 (1952): 265.

———— (1951b). Observations on child development. *Psychoanalytic Study of the Child* 6:18-30. Reprinted in *The Writings of Anna Freud,* vol. 5. New York: International Universities Press, 1969.

———— (1952a). Studies in passivity, part 2: Notes on a connection between the states of negativism and of emotional surrender. In: *The Writings of Anna Freud,* vol. 4. New York: International Universities Press, 1968.

———— (1952b). The role of bodily illness in the mental life of children. *Psychoanalytic Study of the child* 7:69-81. Reprinted in: *The Writings of Anna Freud,* vol. 4, op. cit.

—— (1952c). Mutual influences in the development of ego and id. *Psychoanalytic Study of the Child* 7:42-50. Reprinted in: *The Writings of Anna Freud*, vol. 4, op. cit.

—— (1953). Some remarks on infant observation. *Psychoanalytic Study of the Child*. 8:9-19. Reprinted in: *The Writings of Anna Freud*, vol. 4, op. cit.

—— (1954). Problems of infantile neurosis: A discussion. *Psychoanalytic Study of the Child* 9:25-31; 40-43; 57-62; 68-71. Reprinted in: *The Writings of Anna Freud*, vol. 4, op. cit.

—— (1958). Child observation and prediction of development: A memorial lecture in honor of Ernst Kris. *Psychoanalytic Study of the Child* 13:92-116.

—— (1962). Assessment of childhood disturbances. *Psychoanalytic Study of the Child* 17:149-158.

—— (1963). The concept of developmental lines. *Psychoanalytic Study of the Child* 18:245-246. Reprinted in: *Normality and Pathology in Childhood*, infra.

—— (1965). *Normality and Pathology in Childhood: Assessments of Development*. New York: International Universities Press.

Freud, A., and Burlingham, D.T. (1943). *War and Children*. New York: International Universities Press, 1944.

Freud, A., and Dann, S. (1951). An experiment in group upbringing. *Psychoanalytic Study of the Child* 6:127-169. Reprinted in: *The Writings of Anna Freud*, vol. 4, op. cit.

Freud, S. (1905a). Three essays on the theory of sexuality. *Standard Edition* 7:130-245.

—— (1905b). Jokes and their relation to the unconscious. *Standard Edition* 8.

—— (1910a). Leonardo da Vinci and a memory of his childhood. *Standard Edition* 11:63-137.

—— (1910b). The psychoanalytic view of psychogenic disturbance of vision. *Standard Edition* 11:209-218.

—— (1911a). Formulations on the two principles of mental functioning. *Standard Edition* 12:213-226.

—— (1911b). Psycho-analytic notes on an autobiographical account of a case of paranoia (dementia paranoides). *Standard Edition* 12:3-82.

—— (1915). Repression. *Standard Edition* 14:141-158.

—— (1917 [1915]). Mourning and melancholia. *Standard Edition* 14:237-260.

—— (1923). The ego and the id. *Standard Edition* 19:3-66.

—— (1924a). The loss of reality in neurosis and psychosis. *Standard Edition* 19:183-187.

—— (1924b). The dissolution of the oedipus complex. *Standard Edition* 19:173-179.

—— (1926). Inhibitions, symptoms and anxiety. *Standard Edition* 20:77-175.

—— (1930). Civilization and its discontents, *Standard Edition* 21:59-145.

—— (1938). Splitting of the ego in the process of defence. *Standard Edition* 23:271-178.

—— (1940 [1938]). An outline of psycho-analysis. *Standard Edition* 23:141-207.

Friend, M.R. (1956). Report on panel: On sleep disturbances in children. *J. Amer. Psychoanal. Assn.* 4:514-525.

Fries. M.E., and Woolf, P.J. (1953). Some hypotheses on the role of congenital activity type in personality development. *Psychoanalytic Study of the Child* 8:48-62.

Frijling-Schreuder, E.C.M. (1969). Borderline states in children. *Psychoanalytic Study of the Child* 24:307-327.

Frosch, J.A. (1966). A note on reality constancy. In: *Psychoanalysis— A General Psychology,* ed. R.M. Lowenstein, L.M. Newman, M. Schur, and A.J. Solnit, pp. 349-376. New York: International Universities Press.

Frosch, W.A. (1970). Report on panel: Psychoanalytic evaluation of addiction and habituation. *J. Amer. Psychoanal. Assn.* 18:209-218.

Furer, M. (1964). The development of a preschool symbiotic boy. *Psychoanalytic Study of the Child* 19:448-469.

Galenson, E. (1971). A consideration of the nature of thought in childhood play. In: *Separation-Individuation: Essays in Honor of Margaret S. Mahler,* ed. J.B. McDevitt and C.F. Settlage, pp. 41-60. New York: International Universities Press.

Geleerd, E.R. (1945). Observations on temper tantrums in children. *Amer. J. Orthopsychiat.* 15:238-246.

Gerard, M.W. (1946). The psychogenic tic in ego development. *Psychoanalytic Study of the Child* 2:133-162.

Goldfarb, W. (1945). Psychological privation in infancy and subsequent adjustment. *Amer. J. Orthopsychiat.* 15:247-266.

Gouin-Décarie, T. (1965). *Intelligence and Affectivity in Early Childhood*. New York: International Universities Press.

Greenacre, P. (1944). Infant reactions to restraint: Problems in the fate of infantile aggression. *Amer. J. Orthopsychiat.* 14:204-218. Reprinted in: *Trauma, Growth and Personality*. New York: Norton, 1952.

——— (1945a). The biologic economy of birth. *Psychoanalytic Study of the Child* 1:31-51. Reprinted in: *Trauma, Growth and Personality*, op. cit.

——— (1945b). Conscience in the psychopath. *Amer. J. Orthopsychiat.* 15:459-509. Reprinted in: *Trauma, Growth and Personality*, op. cit.

——— (1947). Vision, headache and the halo. *Psychoanal. Quart.* 16:177-194. Reprinted in: *Trauma, Growth and Personality*, op. cit.

——— (1952a). Pregenital patterning. *Int. J. Psycho-Anal.* 33:410-415.

——— (1952b). Some factors producing different types of genital and pregenital organization. Reprinted in: *Trauma, Growth and Personality*, op. cit.

——— (1953). Certain relationships between fetishism and the faulty development of the body image. *Psychoanalytic Study of the Child* 8:79-98.

——— (1957). The childhood of the artist: Libidinal phase development and giftedness. *Psychoanalytic Study of the Child* 12:27-72. Reprinted in: *Emotional Growth*, vol. 2. New York: International Universities Press, 1971.

——— (1958). Early physical determinants in the development of the sense of identity. *J. Amer. Psychoanal. Assn.* 6:612-627. Reprinted in: *Emotional Growth* op. cit. vol. 1.

——— (1959). On focal symbiosis. In: *Dynamic Psychopathology in Childhood*, ed. L. Jessner & E. Pavenstedt. New York: Grune & Stratton, pp. 243-256.

———— (1960). Considerations regarding the parent-infant relationship. *Int. J. Psycho-Anal.* 41:571-584. Reprinted in: *Emotional Growth*, op. cit., vol. 1.

———— (1962). The theory of the parent-infant relationship. *Int. J. Psycho-Anal.* 43:235-237, 255-256.

———— (1966). Problems of overidealization of the analyst and of analysis: Their manifestations in the transference and countertransference relationships. *Psychoanalytic Study of the Child* 21:193-212.

———— (1969). The fetish and the transitional object. *Psychoanalytic Study of the Child* 24:144-164. Reprinted in: *Emotional Growth*, op. cit., vol. 1.

———— (1970). The transitional object and the fetish: with special reference to the role of illusion. *Int. J. Psycho-Anal.* 51:447-456. Reprinted in: *Emotional Growth*, op. cit., vol. 1.

Greene, W., Jr. (1958). Early object relations: Somatic, affective, and personal. *J. Nervous and Mental Disease* 126:225-252.

Greenson, R.R. (1954). The struggle against identification. *J. Amer. Psychoanal. Assn.* 2:200-217.

———— (1958). On screen defenses, screen hunger, and screen identity. *J. Amer. Psychoanal. Assn.* 6:242-262.

Gross, A. (1936). Zur Psychologie des Geheimnisses. *Imago* 22(2).

Harley, M. (1961). Masturbation conflicts. In: *Adolescents—Psychoanalytic Approach to Problems and Techniques,* ed. S. Lorand and H. Schneer. New York: Paul B. Hoeber Inc.

———— (1971a). Some reflections on identity problems in prepuberty. In: *Separation-Individuation: Essays in Honor of Margaret S. Mahler,* ed. J.B. McDevitt and C.F. Settlage. New York: International Universities Press.

———— (1971b). The current status of transference neurosis in children. *J. Amer. Psychoanal. Assn.* 19:26-40.

Hartmann, H. (1939). *Ego Psychology and the Problem of Adaptation.* New York: International Universities Press, 1958.

———— (1947). On rational and irrational action. In: *Psychoanalysis and the Social Sciences,* vol. 1, pp. 359-392. New York: International Universities Press.

———— (1950a). Psychoanalysis and developmental psychology. *Psychoanalytic Study of the Child* 5:7-17.

—— (1950b). Comments on the psychoanalytic theory of the ego. *Psychoanalytic Study of the Child* 5:74-96.

—— (1952). The mutual influences in the development of the ego and id. *Psychoanalytic Study of the Child* 7:9-30.

—— (1953). Contribution to the metapsychology of schizophrenia. *Psychoanalytic Study of the Child* 8:177-198.

—— (1964). *Essays on Ego Psychology: Selected Problems in Psychoanalytic Theory.* New York: International Universities Press.

Hartmann, H. and Kris, E. (1945). The genetic approach to psychoanalysis. *Psychoanalytic Study of the Child* 1:11-30.

Hartmann, H., Kris, E., and Loewenstein, R.M. (1946). Comments on the formation of psychic structure. *Psychoanalytic Study of the Child* 2:11-38.

——, (1949). Notes on the theory of aggression. *Psychoanalytic Study of the Child* 3/4:9-36.

Heimann, P. (1966). Comment on Dr. Kernberg's paper [Structural derivatives of object relationships]. *Int. J. Psycho-Anal.* 47:254-260.

Hendrick, I. (1942). Instinct and the ego during infancy. *Psychoanal. Quart.* 11:33-58.

—— (1951). Early development of the ego: identification in infancy. *Psychoanal. Quart.* 20:44-61.

Hermann, I. (1934). Vorlaufige Mitteilung: Urwahrnehmungen, insbesondere Augenleuchten und Lautwerden des Inneren. [Preliminary report: primitive perceptions, especially gleaming of the eyes, and inner noises]. *Int. Ztschr. f. Psa.* 20:553-555.

—— (1936). Sich-Anklammern, Auf-Suche-Gehen. [Hanging on, going in search]. *Int. Ztschr. f. Psa.* 22:349-370.

Hoffer, W. (1949). Mouth, hand and ego-integration. *Psychoanalytic Study of the Child* 3/4:49-56.

—— (1950a). Oral aggressiveness and ego development. *Int. J. Psycho-Anal.* 31:156-160.

—— (1950b). Development of the body ego. *Psychoanalytic Study of the Child* 5:18-24.

—— (1952). The mutual influences in the development of ego and id: earliest stages. *Psychoanalytic Study of the Child* 7:31-41.

—— (1955). *Psychoanalysis: Practical and Research Aspects.* Baltimore: Williams & Wilkins.

Homburger, A. (1922). Ueber die Entwicklung der menschlichen Motorik. *Zeit f. d. gesamte Neur. und Psychol.* 78.

—— (1923). Zur Gestaltung der normalen menschlichen Motorik und ihre Beurteilung [On the structure of normal human motor behavior and its judgment]. *Zeit. f. d. gesamte Neur. und Psychiat.* 75:274.

Jacobson, E. (1932). Lernstorungen beim Schulkinde durch masochistiche Mechanismen [Learning difficulties of the schoolchild through masochistic mechanisms]. *Int. Ztschr f. Psa.* 18:242-251.

—— (1946). A case of sterility. *Psychoanal. Quart.* 15:330-350.

—— (1947a). The child's laughter. *Psychoanalytic Study of the Child* 2:39-60. Reprinted in: *Depression.* New York: International Universities Press, 1971.

—— (1947b). The effect of disappointment on ego and super-ego formation in normal and depressive development. *Psychoanal. Rev.* 33:129-247.

—— (1953a). The affects and their pleasure-unpleasure qualities in relation to the psychic discharge processes. In: *Drives, Affects, Behavior,* vol. 1. ed. R.M. Loewenstein, pp. 38-66. New York: International Universities Press.

—— (1953b). Contribution to the metapsychology of cyclothymic depression. In: *Affective Disorders,* ed. P. Greenacre, pp. 49-83. New York: International Universities Press.

—— (1954). The self and the object world: vicissitudes of their infantile cathexes and their influence on ideational and affective development. *Psychoanalytic Study of the Child* 9:75-127.

—— (1957a). Denial and repression. *J. Amer. Psychoanal. Assn.* 5:61-92. Reprinted in: *Depression,* op. cit.

—— (1957b). Normal and pathological moods: their nature and function. *Psychoanalytic Study of the Child* 12:73-113.

—— (1961). Adolescent moods and the remodeling of psychic structures in adolescence. *Psychoanalytic Study of the Child* 16:164-183.

—— (1964). *The Self and the Object World.* New York: International Universities Press.

——— (1967). *Psychotic Conflict and Reality.* New York: International Universities Press.

James, M. (1960). Premature ego development: some observations on disturbances in the first three months of life. *Int. J. Psycho-Anal.* 41:288-294.

Joffe, W.G., and Sandler, J. (1965). Notes on pain, depression, and individuation. *Psychoanalytic Study of the Child* 20:394-424.

Kanner, L. (1942). Autistic disturbances of affective contact. *Nerv. Child.* 2:217-250.

——— (1944). Early infantile autism. *J. Pediat.* 25:211-217.

——— (1949). Problems of nosology and psychodynamics of early infantile autism. *Amer. J. Orthopsychiat.* 19:416-426.

Kanner, L., and Eisenberg, L. (1955). Notes on the follow-up studies of autistic children. In: *Psychopathology of Childhood,* ed. P.H. Hoch and J. Zubin. New York: Grune & Stratton, pp. 227-239.

Kaufman, I.C., and Rosenblum, L.A. (1968). The reaction to separation in infant monkeys: anaclitic depression and conservation-withdrawal. *Psychosom. Med.,* 29:648-675.

Kernberg, O. (1967). Borderline personality organization. *J. Amer. Psychoanal. Assn.* 15:641-685.

——— (1970). Factors in the psychoanalytic treatment of narcissistic personalities. *J. Amer. Psychoanal. Assn.* 18:51-85.

Kestenberg, J. (1941). Mother types encountered in child guidance clinics. *Amer. J. Orthopsychiat.* 11:475.

——— (1956). On the development of maternal feelings in early childhood. *Psychoanalytic Study of the Child* 11:257-291.

——— (1971). From organ-object imagery to self and object representations. In: *Separation-Individuation: Essays in Honor of Margaret S. Mahler,* ed. J.B. McDevitt and C.F. Settlage, pp. 75-99. New York: International Universities Press.

——— (1975). *Children and Parents.* New York: Jason Aronson.

Khan, M.M.R. (1964). Ego distortion, cumulative trauma, and the role of reconstruction in the analytic situation. *Int. J. Psycho-Anal.* 45:272-279.

Kleeman, J.A. (1967). The peek-a-boo game. Part I: its origins, meanings, related phenomena in the first year. *Psychonalytic Study of the Child* 22:239-273.

Klein, M. (1932). *The Psycho-Analysis of Children*. New York: Norton.

Klein, M., Heimann, P., Isaacs, S., and Riviere, J. (1952). *Developments in Psycho-Analysis*. London: Hogarth Press.

Kohut, H. (1966). Forms and transformations of narcissism. *J. Amer. Psychoanal. Assn.* 14:243-272.

——— (1968). The psychoanalytic treatment of narcissistic personality disorders: outline of a systematic approach. *Psychoanalytic Study of the Child* 23:86-113.

——— (1971). *The Analysis of the Self*. New York: International Universities Press.

Kris, E. (1933). A psychotic sculptor of the eighteenth century. In: *Psychoanalytic Explorations in Art*. New York: International Universities Press, 1952, pp. 128-150.

——— (1936). The psychology of caricature. *Int. J. Psycho-Anal.* 17:285-303.

——— (1938a) Das Lachen als mimischer Vorgang. *Int. Zeit. f. Psa. und Imago* 24:146.

——— (1938b). Ego development and the comic. *Int. J. Psycho-Anal.* 19:77-90.

——— (1940). Laughter as an expressive process. *Int. J. Psycho-Anal.* 21:314-341.

——— (1950). Notes on the development and on some current problems of psychoanalytic child psychology. *Psychoanalytic Study of the Child* 5:24-46.

——— (1955). Neutralization and sublimation: observations on young children. *Psychoanalytic Study of the Child* 10:30-46.

——— (1956a). The recovery of childhood memories. *Psychoanalytic Study of the Child* 11:54-88.

——— (1956b). On some vicissitudes of insight in psycho-analysis. *Int. J. Psycho-Anal.* 37:445-455.

Kris, E. et al. (1954). Problems of infantile neurosis: A discussion. *Psychoanalytic Study of the Child* 9:16-71.

Kris, M. (1957). The use of prediction in a longitudinal study. *Psychoanalytic Study of the Child* 12:175-189.

Kubie, L. (1941). The repetitive core of neurosis. *Psychoanal. Quart.* 10:23-43.

Kubie, L., and Israel, H.A. (1955). "Say You're Sorry." *The Psychoanalytic Study of the Child*, 10:289-299.

Lampl-de Groot, J. (1967). On obstacles standing in the way of psychoanalytic cure. *Psychoanalytic Study of the Child* 22:20-35.

—— (1973). Vicissitudes of narcissism and problems of civilization. *Freud Anniversary Lecture.* March 28, 1973. [Published in: *Psychoanalytic Study of the Child* 30:663-682.]

Landauer, K. (1926). Die kindliche Bewegungsunruhe; das Schicksal der den Stammganglien unterstehenden triebhaften Bewegungen [Infantile restlessness; the fate of impulsive movements controlled by the primitive ganglia].. *Int. Ztschr. f. Psa.* 12:379-390.

—— (1927). Automatismen, Zwangneurose und Paranoia [Automatisms, compulsion neuroses and paranoia]. *Int. Ztschr. f. Psa.* 13:10-19.

—— (1929). Zur Psychosexuellen Genese Der Dummheit [On the psychosexual genesis of stupidity]. *Ztschr. f. Sexual-wissenschaft u. Sexualpolitik* 16:12-22.

Lebovici, S. (1973). Current trends in infantile neurosis. Paper presented at the meeting of the Association for Child Psychoanalysis, Paris, July 22, 1973.

Levy, D.M. (1937). Primary affect hunger. *Amer. J. Psychiat.* 94:643-652.

—— (1938). Maternal overprotection. In: *Modern Trends in Child Psychiatry*, ed. N.D.C. Lewis and B.L. Pacella, pp. 27-34. New York: International Universities Press, 1945.

—— (1944). On the problem of movement restraint: Tics, sterotyped movements, hyperactivity. *Amer. J. Orthopsychiat.* 14:644-671.

Lewin, B.D. (1933). The body as phallus. *Psychoanal. Quart.* 2:24-47.

—— (1950). *The Psychoanalysis of Elation.* New York: Norton.

—— (1952). Phobic symptoms and dream interpretation. *Psychoanal. Quart.* 21:295-322.

Lichtenstein, H. (1961). Identity and sexuality: a study of their interrelationship in man. *Int. J. Psycho-Anal.* 45:49-56.

—— (1964). The role of narcissism in the emergence and maintenance of a primary identity. *Int. J. Psycho-Anal.*, 45:49-56.

Linn, L. (1955). Some developmental aspects of the body image. *Int. J. Psycho-Anal.* 36:36-42.

Loewald, H.W. (1951). Ego and reality. *Int. J. Psycho-Anal.* 32:10-18.

—— (1974). The current status of the concept of infantile neurosis: a discussion. *Psychoanalytic Study of the Child* 29:183-188.

Lourie, R.S. (1955). Experience with therapy of psychosomatic problems in infants. In: *Psychopathology of Childhood,* ed. P.H. Hoch and J. Zubin. New York: Grune & Stratton, pp. 254-266.

Maenchen, A. (1936). Denkhemmung und Aggression aus kastrationangst [Thought inhibition and aggression caused by castration anxiety]. *Ztschr. f. Psa. Pädagogik* 10:276-299.

Mahler [Schoenberger], M. (1941). Discussion of Dr. Silberpfennig's paper: Mother types encountered in child guidance clinics. *Amer. J. Orthopsychiat.* 11:484.

—— (1942). Pseudoimbecility: A magic cap of invisibility. *Psychoanal. Quart.,* 11:149-164. SPI:1

—— (1944). Tics and impulsions in children: A study of motility. *Psychoanal. Quart.* 13:430-444. SPI:4

—— (1945). Introductory remarks to: The symposium on tics in children. *Nerv. Child* 4:307.

—— (1946). Ego psychology applied to behavior problems. In: *Modern Trends in Child Psychiatry,* ed. N. Lewis and B. Pacella. New York: International Universities Press.

—— (1947). Various clinical pictures of psychosis in children (schizophrenia-like). Paper read at the Schilder Society, New York.

—— (1948). Contribution to round-table discussion on aggression. Annual Meeting of the American Psychiatric Association, Washington, D.C.

—— (1949a). A psychoanalytic evaluation of tic in psychopathology of children: Symptomatic tic and tic syndrome. *Psychoanalytic Study of the Child* 3/4:279-310. SPI:3

—— (1949b). Remarks on psychoanalysis with psychotic children. *Quart. J. Child Behav.* 1:18-21.

—— (1950). Discussion of papers by Anna Freud and Ernst Kris. Symposium on "Problems of Child Development," Stockbridge, Mass. (unpublished). (For the Symposium on "Problems of Child Development," see *Psychoanalytic Study of the Child* 6:9-60, 1951.)

—— (1952). On child psychosis and schizophrenia: autistic and symbiotic infantile psychoses. *Psychoanalytic Study of the Child* 7:286-305. *SPI*:7

—— (1953a). Notes on early ego disturbances. *Psychoanalytic Study of the Child*, 8:262-270.

—— (1953b). Some aspects in the development of childhood psychoses. Contribution to a seminar on child psychiatry, roundtable discussion: basic problems in early childhood, Los Angeles.

—— (1954a). Contribution to: Problems of infantile neurosis: a discussion. *Psychoanalytic Study of the Child* 9:65-66.

—— (1954b). On normal and pathological symbiosis: A contribution to the understanding of psychoses in children. Read at the Baltimore Psychoanalytic Society.

—— (1955). Discussion [of papers by Kanner and Eisenberg, Despert, Lourie]. In: *Psychopathology of Childhood*, ed. P. H. Hoch and J. Zubin. New York: Grune & Stratton, pp. 285-289.

—— (1958a). Autism and symbiosis: two extreme disturbances of identity. *Int. J. Psycho-Anal.*, 39:77-83. *SPI*:9

—— (1958b). On two crucial phases of integration of the sense of identity: separation-individuation and bisexual identity. *J. Amer. Psychoanal. Assn.* 6:136-139.

—— (1960). Symposium on psychotic object relationships: III. Perceptual de-differentiation and psychotic object relationship.' *Int. J. Psycho-Anal.* 41:548-553. *SPI*:10

—— (1961). On sadness and grief in infancy and childhood: Loss and restoration of the symbiotic love object. *Psychoanalytic Study of the Child* 16:332-351. *SPI*:14

—— (1963a). Thoughts about development and individuation. *Psychoanalytic Study of the Child* 18:307-324. *SPII*:1

—— (1963b). Subphases of the separation-individuation process. Paper and film presented at the Annual Meetings of the American Psychoanalytic Association, St. Louis.

—— (1965a). On early infantile psychosis: The symbiotic and autistic syndromes. *J. Amer. Acad. Child Psychiat.* 4:554-568. *SPI*:7

—— (1965b). On the significance of the normal separation-individuation phase: with reference to research in symbiotic child psychosis. In: *Drives Affects, Behavior,* vol. 2, ed. M. Schur, pp. 161-169. New York: International Universities Press. *SP*II:4

―――― (1966). Notes on the development of basic moods: the depressive affect. In: *Psychoanalysis—A General Psychology: Essays in Honor of Heinz Hartmann,* ed. R.M. Loewenstein, L.M. Newman, M. Schur, and A.J. Solnit, pp. 152-168. New York: International Universities Press. *SP*II:5

―――― (1967). Development of defense from biological and symbiotic precursors: Adaptive and maladaptive aspects. Contribution to panel on: Development and Metapsychology of the Defense Organization of the Ego, rep. R.S. Wallerstein. *J. Amer. Psychoanal. Assn.* 15:130-149.

―――― (1968). *On Human Symbiosis and the Vicissitudes of Individuation,* vol. 1, *Infantile Psychosis.* New York: International Universities Press.

―――― (1971). A study of the separation-individuation process and its possible application to borderline phenomena in the psychoanalytic situation. *Psychoanalytic Study of the Child* 26:403-424. *SP*II:11.

―――― (1972a). On the first three subphases of the separation-individuation process. *Int. J. Psycho-Anal.* 53:333-338. *SP*II:8.

―――― (1972b). Rapprochement subphase of the separation-individuation process. *Psychoanal. Quart.* 41:487-506. *SP*II:9.

―――― (1976). Longitudinal study of the treatment of a psychotic child with a tripartite design. J. Philadelphia Assn. for Psychoanal. 3:21-42. *SP*I:15

Mahler, M.S., and Elkisch, P. (1953). Some observations on disturbances of the ego in a case of infantile psychosis. *Psychoanalytic Study of the Child* 8:252-261. *SP*I:11

Mahler, M.S., and Furer, M. (1960). Observations on research regarding the "symbiotic syndrome" of infantile psychosis. *Psychoanal. Quart.* 29:317-327. *SP*I:13

―――― , (1963). Certain Aspects of the Separation-Individuation Phase. *Psychoanal. Quart.,* 32:1-14. *SP*II:2

―――― , (1966). Development of symbiosis, symbiotic psychosis, and the nature of separation anxiety: Remarks on Weiland's paper. *Int. J. Psycho-Anal.* 47:559-560.

Mahler, M.S., Furer, M., and Settlage, C.F. (1959). Severe emotional disturbances in childhood: Psychosis. In: *American Handbook of Psychiatry*, ed. S. Arieti. New York: Basic Books, 1:816-839.

Mahler, M.S., and Gosliner, B.J. (1955). On symbiotic child psychosis: Genetic, dynamic and restitutive aspects. *Psychoanalytic Study of the Child* 10:195-212. *SPI*:6

Mahler, M.S., and Gross, I.H. (1945). Psychotherapeutic study of a typical case with tic syndrome. *Nerv. Child* 4:358-373.

Mahler, M.S., and La Perriere, K. (1965). Mother-child interaction during separation-individuation. *Psychoanal. Quart.* 34:483-498. *SPII*:3.

Mahler, M.S., and Luke, J.A. (1946). Outcome of the tic syndrome. *J. Nerv. Ment. Dis.* 103:433-445.

Mahler, M.S., Luke, J.A., and Daltroff, W. (1945). Clinical and follow-up study of the tic syndrome in children. *Amer. J. Orthopsychiat.* 15:631-647.

Mahler, M.S., and McDevitt, J.B. (1968). Observations on adaptation and defense *in statu nascendi:* developmental precursors in the first two years of life. *Psychoanal. Quart.* 37:1-21. *SPII*:7.

Mahler, M.S., Pine, F., and Bergman, A. (1975). *The Psychological Birth of the Human Infant.* New York: Basic Books.

Mahler, M.S., and Rangell, L. (1943). A psychosomatic study of maladie des tics (Gilles de la Tourette's disease). *Psychiat. Quart.* 17:579-603.

Mahler, M.S., Ross, J.R., Jr., and De Fries, Z. (1949). Clinical studies in benign and malignant cases of childhood psychosis (Schizophrenia-like). *Amer. J. Orthopsychiat.* 19:295-305.

Mahler, M.S., and Silberpfennig, I. (1938). Der Rorschach'sche Formdeutversuch als Hilfsmittel zum Verstandnis der Psychologie Hirnkranker. [The Rorschach test as an auxiliary psychological method for understanding the organic brain-damaged patient]. *Schweiz. Arch. Neurol. Psychiat.* 40:302-327.

Meige, H., and Feindel, E. (1907). *Tics and Their Treatment.* (Tr. S. A. K. Wilson.) New York: William Wood.

Nagera, H. (1966). *Early Childhood Disturbances: The Neurosis and the Adult Disturbances.* Monograph Series of *The Psychoanalytic Study of the Child*, No. 2. New York: International Universities Press.

Nunberg, H. (1932). *Principles of Psychoanalysis*. New York: International Universities Press, 1955.

Oberndorf, C. (1939). The feeling of stupidity. *Int. J. Psycho-Anal.* 20:443-451.

Olden, C. (1947). Headline intelligence. *Psychoanalytic Study of the Child* 2:263-370.

Pacella, B.L. (1945). Physiologic and differential diagnostic considerations of tic manifestations in children. *Nerv. Child* 4:313-317.

Parens, H., and Saul, L.J. (1971). *Dependence in Man*. New York: International Universities Press.

Piaget, J. (1923). *The Language and Thought of the Child*. New York: Humanities Press, 1952.

——— (1936). *The Origins of Intelligence in Children*. New York: International Universities Press, 1952.

Piaget, J., and Inhelder, B. (1953). Contribution to symposium. In: *Discussions on Child Development*, vol. 1. [First meeting of the World Health Organization Study Group on Psychobiological Development of the Child, Geneva, 1953]. New York: International Universities Press.

Pine, F., and Furer, M. (1963). Studies of the separation-individuation phase: A methodological overview. *Psychoanalytic Study of the Child* 18:325-342.

Piotrowski, Z.A. (1945). Rorschach records of children with a tic syndrome. *Nerv. Child* 4:342.

Potter, H.W. (1933). Schizophrenia in children. *Amer. J. Psychiat.* 12:1253-1270.

Rado, S. (1919). Eine besondere Äusserungsform der Kastrationsangst [A specific manifestation of castration anxiety]. *Int. Ztschr. f. Psa.* 5:206.

Rangell, L. (1972). Aggression, Oedipus and historical perspective. *Int. J. Psycho-Anal.* 53:3-11.

Rank, B. (1949). Adaptation of the psychoanalytic technique for the treatment of young children with atypical development. *Amer. J. Orthopsychiat.* 19:130-139.

——— (1955). Intensive study and treatment of preschool children who show marked personality deviations, or "atypical development," and their parents. In: *Emotional Problems of Early Childhood*, ed. G. Caplan. New York: Basic Books, pp. 491-501.

Rank, B. and Macnaughton, D. (1950). A clinical contribution to early ego development. *Psychoanalytic Study of the Child* 5:53-65.

Rapaport, D. (1958). The theory of ego autonomy: A generalization. *Bull. Menninger Clin.* 22:13-25.

Reich, A. (1949). The structure of the grotesque-comic sublimation. *Bull. Menninger Clin.* 13:160-171. Reprinted in: *Psychoanalytic Contributions*. New York: International Universities Press, 1973.

Reich, W. (1924-1925). Der psychogene Tics als Onanie-äquivalent [The psychogenic tic as a substitute for masterbation]. *Ztschr. f. Sexualwissenschaft.* 11:302-313.

Ribble, M. (1941). Disorganizing factors of infant personality *Amer. J. Psychiat.* 98:459-463.

——— (1943). *The Rights of Infants: Early Psychological Needs and Their Satisfaction*. New York: Columbia University Press.

Ritvo, S. (1945). Review of recent literature on tics in children. *Nerv. Child* 4:308-312.

——— (1974). The current status of the concept of the infantile neurosis: implications for diagnosis and technique. *Psychoanalytic Study of the Child* 29:159-181.

Ritvo, S., and Solnit, A.J. (1958). Influences of early mother-child interaction on identification processes. *Psychoanalytic Study of the Child* 13:64-91.

Rochlin, G. (1953a). Loss and restitution. *Psychoanalytic Study of the Child* 8:288-309.

——— (1953b). The disorder of depression and elation. *J. Amer. Psychoanal. Assn.* 1:438-457.

——— (1959). The loss complex: A contribution to the etiology of depression. *J. Amer. Psychoanal. Assn.* 7:299-316.

Roffwarg, H.P., Muzio, J.N., and Dement, W.C. (1966). Ontogenetic development of the human sleep-dream cycle. *Science* 152:604-619.

Roiphe, H., and Galenson, E. (1972). Early genital activity and the castration complex. *Psychoanal. Quart.* 41:334-347.

Rollman-Branch, H.S. (1960). On the question of primary object need: Ethological and psychoanalytic considerations. *J. Amer. Psychoanal. Assn.* 8:686-702.

Rose, G.J. (1964). Creative imagination in terms of ego 'core' and boundaries, *Int. J. Psycho-Anal.* 45:75-84.

——— (1966). Body ego and reality. *Int. J. Psycho-Anal.* 47:502-509.

Ross, N. (1967). The "as if" concept. *J. Amer. Psychoanal. Assn.* 15:59-82.

Rotter-Kertész, L. (1936). Der tiefenpsychologische Hintergrund der inzestuösen Fixierung [The depth psychological background of incestuous fixation]. *Int. Ztschr. f. Psa.* 22:338-348.

Rubinfine, D.L. (1958). Report of panel: problems of identity. *J. Amer. Psychoanal. Assoc.* 6:131-142.

——— (1961). Perception, reality testing, and symbolism. *Psychoanalytic Study of the Child* 16:73-89.

Sachs, H. (1933). The delay of the machine age. *The Creative Unconscious.* Cambridge, Mass.: Sci-Art Publishers, 1951, pp. 100-131.

Sandler, J., Holder, A., and Meers, D. (1963). The ego ideal and the ideal self. *Psychoanalytic Study of the Child* 18:139-158.

Sandler, J., and Joffe, W.G. (1965). Notes on childhood depression. *Int. J. Psycho-Anal.* 46:88-96.

Schilder, P.F. (1935). *The Image and Appearance of the Human Body: Studies in the Constructive Energies of the Psyche.* New York: International Universities Press, 1951.

Schoenberger, M., *see* Mahler, M.S.

Schur, M. (1955). Comments on the metapsychology of somatization. *Psychoanalytic Study of the Child* 10:119-164.

——— (1960). Introductory remarks to panel on psycho-analysis and ethology, rep. M. Ostow. *J. Amer. Psychoanal. Assn.* 8:526.

——— (1966). *The Id and the Regulatory Principles of Mental Functioning.* New York: International Universities Press.

Searles, H.F. (1960). *The Nonhuman Environment.* New York: International Universities Press.

Sechehaye, M.A. (1947). *Symbolic Realization: A New Method of Psychotherapy Applied to a Case of Schizophrenia.* New York: International Universities Press.

———, (1950). *Reality Lost and Regained: Autobiography of a Schizophrenic Girl.* New York: Grune & Stratton, 1951.

——— (1956). The transference in symbolic realization. *Int. J. Psycho-Anal.* 37:270-277.

Sperling, M. (1946). Psychoanalysis of ulcerative colitis in children. *Psychoanal. Quart.* 15:302-329.

——— (1951). The neurotic child and his mother: A psychoanalytic study. *Amer. J. Orthopsychiat.* 21:351-364.

Spiegel, L.A. (1959). The self, the sense of self, and perception. *Psychoanalytic Study of the Child* 14:81-109.

Spitz, R.A. (1937). Wiederholung, Rhythmus, Langeweile [Repetition, rhythm, and boredom]. *Imago* 23:171-196.

——— (1945). Diacritic and coenesthetic organizations: the psychiatric significance of a functional division of the nervous system into a sensory and emotive part. *Psychoanal. Rev.,* 32:146-162.

——— (1946a). The smiling response: a contribution to the ontogenesis of social relations. (With the assistance of K.M. Wolf). *Genet. Psych. Monogr.* 34:57-125.

——— (1946b). Anaclitic depression. *Psychoanalytic Study of the Child* 2:313-342.

——— (1948). Somatic concomitants of emotional vicissitudes in infancy. Paper read at the Annual Meeting of the Association for Psychosomatic Research, Atlantic City, May 1948.

——— (1950a). Relevancy of direct infant observations. *Psychoanalytic Study of the Child* 10:215-240.

——— (1950b). Anxiety in infancy. *Int. J. Psycho-Anal.* 31:138-143.

——— (1951). The psychogenic diseases in infancy. *Psychoanalytic Study of the Child* 6:255-275.

——— (1953). Contribution to a symposium on "Basic Problems in Early Childhood." Annual meeting of the American Psychoanalytic Association, Los Angeles.

——— (1955). The primal cavity: A contribution to the genesis of perception and its role for psychoanalytic theory. *Psychoanalytic Study of the Child* 10:215-240.

——— (1957). *No and Yes: On the Genesis of Human Communication.* New York: International Universities Press.

——— (1963). Life and the dialogue. In: *Counterpoint,* ed. H.S. Gaskill, pp. 154-176. New York: International Universities Press.

——— (1965). *The First Year of Life: A Psychoanalytic Study of Normal and Deviant Development of Object Relations.* New York: International Universities Press.

Spock, B. (1963). The striving for autonomy and regressive objective-relationships. *Psychoanalytic Study of the Child* 18:361-364.

Spruiell, V. (1974). Theories of the treatment of narcissistic personalities. *J. Amer. Psychoanal. Assn.* 22:268-278.

———— (1975). Three strands of narcissism. *Psychoanal. Quart.* 44:577-595.

Starr, P.H. (1954). Psychoses in children: Their origin and structure. *Psychoanal. Quart.* 23:544-565.

Stein, M. (1956). The marriage bond. *Psychoanal. Quart.* 25:238-259.

Stirnimann, F. (1947). Das Kind und seine früheste Umwelt [The child and his early environment]. *Psychologische Praxis* 6. Basel: Karger.

Stone, L. (1961). *The Psychoanalytic Situation.* New York: International Universities Press.

Sylvester, E. (1947). Pathogenic influences of maternal attitudes in the neonatal period. In: *Problems of Infancy and Early Childhood,* ed. M.J.E. Senn. New York: Josiah Macy, Jr. Foundation.

———— (1953). Developmental truisms and their fate in child-rearing: Clinical observations. In: *Problems of Infancy and Early Childhood,* op. cit.

Szasz, T. (1957). *Pain and Pleasure: A Study of Bodily Feelings.* New York: Basic Books.

Tartakoff, H.H. (1966). The normal personality in our culture and the Nobel Prize complex. In: *Psychoanalysis—A General Psychology,* ed. R.M. Loewenstein, L.M. Newman, M. Schur, and A.J. Solnit, pp. 222-252. New York: International Universities Press.

Tausk, V. (1919). On the origin of the "influencing machine" in schizophrenia. In: *The Psychoanalytic Reader,* ed. R. Fliess. New York: International Universities Press, 1948, pp. 52-85.

Waelder, R. (1930). The principle of multiple function. *Psychoanal. Quart.* 5:45-62.

———— (1937). The problem of the genesis of psychical conflict in earliest infancy. *Int. J. Psycho-Anal.* 18:406-473.

———— (1963). Psychic determinism and the possibility of predictions. *Psychoanal. Quart.* 32:15-42.

Weil, A.P. (1953). Clinical data and dynamic considerations in certain cases of childhood schizophrenia. *Amer. J. Orthop-sychiat.* 23:518-529.

—— (1956). Some evidences of deviational development in infancy and early childhood. *Psychoanalytic Study of the Child* 11:292-299.

—— (1970). The basic core. *Psychoanalytic Study of the Child* 25:442-460.

Weiland, I.H. (1966). Considerations on the development of symbiosis, symbiotic psychosis, and the nature of separation anxiety. *Int. J. Psycho-Anal.* 47:1-5.

Weinberger, J.L. (1964). A triad of silence. *Int. J. Psycho-Anal.* 45:304-309.

Werner, H. (1948). *Comparative Psychology of Mental Development.* New York: International Universities Press, 1957.

Whitehorn, J. (1932). Concerning emotion as impulsion and instinct as orientation. *Amer. J. Psychiat.* 11:1093-1118.

Wilder, J., and Silbermann, I. (1927). *Abhandl. a. d. ges. Neurologie,* Heft 43. Berlin, Karger.

Winnicott, D. W. (1953a). Psychoses and child care. *Brit. J. Med. Psychol.* 26:68-74.

—— (1953b). Transitional objects and transitional phenomena: a study of the first not-me possession. *Int. J. Psycho-Anal.* 34:89-97.

—— (1956a). Primary maternal preoccupation. In: *Collected Papers,* pp. 300-305. New York: Basic Books, 1958.

—— (1956b). On transference. *Int. J. Psycho-Anal.* 37:386-388.

—— (1957). *The Child and the Outside World.* New York: Basic Books.

—— (1958). *Collected Papers.* New York: Basic Books.

—— (1960). The theory of the parent-infant relationship. *Int. J. Psychoanal.* 41:585-595.

—— (1962a). *The Maturational Processes and the Facilitating Environment.* New York: International Universities Press, 1965.

—— (1962b). The theory of the parent-infant relationship: Further remarks. *Int. J. Psycho-Anal.* 43:238-239.

—— (1969). The use of an object. *Int. J. Psycho-Anal.* 50:711-716.

Wolff, P.H. (1959). Observations on newborn infants. *Psychosom. Med.* 21:110-118.

Yazmajian, R.V. (1967). Biological aspects of infantile sexuality and the latency period. *Psychoanal. Quart.* 36:203-229.

Zazzo, R. (1953). In: *Discussions on Child Development,* vol. I. [First meeting of the World Health Organization Study Group on Psychobiological Development of the Child, Geneva, 1953], ed. J.M. Tanner & B. Inhelder. New York: International Universities Press.

Zetzel, E.R. (1953). The depressive position. In: *Affective Disorders,* ed. P. Greenacre. New York: International Universities Press.

Zetzel, E.R. (1960). Symposium on depressive illness. *Int. J. Psycho-Anal.* 41:476-480.

NAME INDEX

SUBJECT INDEX